The Garden Ran Down to the Nile

Copyright © 2012 by Christina Harris

All rights reserved. No part of this book may be reproduced in any form without permission in writing from the author.

Cover photo by the author.

The Garden Ran Down to the Nile

The Garden Ran Down to the Nile

The Garden Ran Down
To the Nile

Christina Harris

Red Kestrel Small Press 2012

The Garden Ran Down to the Nile

The Garden Ran Down to the Nile

To Ian

To Egypt

To things remembered

The Garden Ran Down to the Nile

The Garden Ran Down to the Nile

Contents

Prologue	Eastern Promise	
Chapter 1	Cairo—A City of Paradox	1
Chapter 2	The Residence	24
Chapter 3	An Elite Society	46
Chapter 4	The Pyramids of Ghiza	73
Chapter 5	The Sphinx—Father of Terror	89
Chapter 6	Sakkarah	100
Chapter 7	Khan el Khalili	120
Chapter 8	Port Said	128
Chapter 9	Helouan	136
Chapter 10	Thebes	144
Chapter 11	Assouan	161
Chapter 12	Abou Simbel	174
Chapter 13	Alexandria	181
Chapter 14	The Overland Route	189
Chapter 15	Dahabeyahs, Effendis, & Dragomen	206
Chapter 16	Dividing the Spoils	240
Chapter 17	Living Among the Egyptians	258
Chapter 18	Snippets	283
Epilogue		306
Glossary		309
Bibliography & Sources		313
Acknowledgements		320

The Garden Ran Down to the Nile

Prologue

Eastern Promise

'To travel hopefully is a better thing than to arrive'
                                        Robert Louis Stevenson

Not all people feel at home in their own country, with some there is a sense of restlessness, a thirst for travel, a fascination for all things foreign.

For as long as I can remember Egypt has held a fascination for me. In childish dreams I surrendered to my imagination, envisioning myself as an elusive Egyptian queen seated on dais, crook and flail held in crossed repose as my reed boat glided gently up the Nile through a carpet of lotus blossoms, or clad in khaki-drill and pith helmet crawling expectantly through dusty tombs in search of undiscovered treasure, lit only by my flickering candle. But somewhere between adolescence and maturity my dreams took a back seat while the reality of my life became the focus until I visited a cousin who was working at the American Embassy in Cairo.

The Garden Ran Down to the Nile

My first impression of Egypt was the Cairo Airport in 1976, where I found myself breathing in the dust of centuries when greeted with the unmistakable whiff of the Orient, that repugnant smell of dust, dung and burning rubbish that would grow acceptable with familiarity.

At the arrivals gate I was met with a confusion of shouting and anxious looking men holding placards with the names of disembarking passengers. Amongst them was Azziz, a driver of the American Embassy, who whisked me through the turmoil of customs, flung my luggage in the boot of a black Mercedes, and kamikazed me through aggressive Cairean traffic as I braced my knees against the back of the seat and crouched down in pretence safety.

The evening was turning swiftly into night. I could just make out the shadows of minarets soaring against a cobalt sky. Azziz drove with a lead foot in a series of lunges and swerves never once losing his composure as we shot past palaces and paupers, hurdled over potholes, and flew passed competing cars in a stream of never ending traffic.

Bolting through the Marine guarded gates of the American Embassy, Azziz jerked to a halt as I removed my embedded fingers from the seat and thanked him, not knowing for what.

I was awakened the next morning by the distant call of a Muezzin, his voice distorted by loud speakers. The streets outside were beginning to come alive with traffic and an escalating cacophony of seething humanity. It was not yet eight o'clock and already the heat was apparent, the atmosphere heavy with the sense of a day promising to be hot and placid.

From the fifth floor window of my cousin's flat I looked out over the Corniche Road lined with acacia and flame trees. On the far side of the Nile were ramshackle houseboats and lean-to shanties belonging to the people who made their living from the river. Washing hung from the windows and young children played on the banks where pampas-grass danced and swayed like gossamer next to stalwart bulrushes.

The Nile, brown and tranquil, was animated with the first of the day's fishermen and awakening to feluccas pushed by billowing sails and barges laden to capacity with limestone cut from nearby quarries. The river resembled a twisting serpent with scales glistening in the morning sun, a stark contrast to the surrounding pace of life.

Hazy with dust, buildings and tower-blocks loomed in the distance, reminiscent of any over populated ghetto. Scaffolding of newly erected apartment blocks fought for attention with sleek modern hotels and the glimmering domes and minarets that were peppered throughout the city.

Across the el Tarir Bridge in the center of the square, rose the imposing statue of the nationalist, Sa'ad Zahgloul standing under a tarboosh—one arm outstretched in salutation. His black silhouette framed against the pastel dawn gave an eerie Frankenstein appearance. To the left I could see where the city stopped and the desert began as the faint outline of the arcane Pyramids of Ghiza and Meidum wavered like a mirage. Beyond the pyramids the vast expanse of ochre coloured Libyan Desert disappeared into the horizon.

In 1978, I flew once again to Egypt where for four years my English husband and I lived within the realms of the British Embassy. It was like an endless holiday, stimulating and all encompassing. Inspired by the timeless history and the continual energy of Cairo, I found the remnants of the belle époque still in evidence, frozen in time, and I wanted to find it—the oriental Cairo of my imagination—that which I thought was Cairo, and in searching for it realized that past Cairo cannot be disengaged from present Cairo. And yet a remote, mysterious resonance seemed to connect me to a past epoch I infinitely felt a part of, but had not personally experienced, and realizing I had probably come to Egypt a century too late left me longing for a period of time that was impossible to recapture.

When we left Egypt in 1981, I did not return until 2005, and seeing just how much the country had changed, I realized how fortunate I had been to have had that last glimpse, that brief encounter with a country whose ambiance has taken its place in the archives of history.

The Garden Ran Down to the Nile

Within these pages, a researched history of the British in Egypt and the anthological perspectives of past travellers, are combined with my own reminiscences and recollections of the cultural contrasts of Egypt's grandeur and decadence in a first-hand encounter of the country before the onslaught of tourism.

Now, nearly three decades on, the race for modernization has moved all too quickly, obliterating that oriental quality that had set the country apart from the democratic west. In the pursuit of technology and commerce, the old city has been trampled under by a new generation of Caireans who have embraced the modern world with open arms creating yet another layer on the plates of Egypt's glorious history.

Cairo today is as cosmopolitan as any big city around the world. Ring roads and flyovers are everywhere trying to cope with the bursting expansion of traffic, and a subway system now connects Cairo to outlying suburbs as far away as Helwan. The Cairo Airport had no traffic control tower in the 1970s; now it has four terminals and there are plans for a monorail in the city by the year 2020.

There were six five-star hotels lining the banks of the Nile at the beginning of the 1980s in Cairo. Today dozens of elaborate hotels, including the enormous and opulent Five Seasons Hotel, dominate the skyline simulating downtown Las Vegas and leaving the older hotels dated and fatigued. Walking around the streets I once knew was disorienting. The city seemed detached, an image of its former self—everything so familiar, yet different, less substantial, less real. I tried to imagine the old shops and haunts, but it was difficult to fix the surroundings in my memory, and I found myself in a world that had changed to the extent of being barely recognisable; and a little distorted through the passage of time. Being surrounded by mementos of a vanished society produces vivid and enormous impressions in the imagination. The sensation of time slips from one dimension to another, and memories seen through older eyes seem contorted. Yet the nostalgia was still there and with it that inexplicable impulse to breathe it all in: the aroma of hot Turkish coffee, apple scented shishas, night blooming jasmine, and smoke-filled alleyways.

Remembering the city I once knew generated emotions of sadness, frustration, and even anger at whoever was responsible for the urban neglect of the architecturally magnificent buildings that were now twenty-five years worse off. The present, unable to live with the past, has difficulty grasping the diversity of its cultural heritage and disregards it as reprehensible and uneconomical, part of the enemy property before the British and other foreigners were ousted in 1956.

Egypt is now run by a government that sees its economic value in black and white. Tourism is the country's main commodity. The exploitation of history by a conquering people has brought mindless commercialization and shifting boundaries around historical monuments. Hordes of Europeans and Americans armed with digital cameras and guidebooks intermingle with Japanese tourists hidden under parasols, cotton gloves and breathing apparatus as they swarm the entrance to the Great Pyramid.

Hawkers of postcards and cheap souvenirs replicating an imagined past, deface the once peaceful and picturesque areas of historical monuments for the business of extracting currency from gullible travellers. Even as far out as the red-pyramid, where once no tourists would venture, there are reminders of the exploitation of modern society in the accumulated debris from fast-food restaurants by uncaring people.

Radical changes have also found their way to Upper Egypt where the race for modernization has brought the on-going building of hotels, roads, bridges, parking lots, and a residential housing project in Aswan. The beauty and solitude of the East Bank and the untouched West Bank of Luxor have been obliterated. Today the Nile is lined with three-level tourist ships that rest side-by-side five deep in the stagnating, permanent sludge of oil and garbage. Yet the country's history has survived, and evokes as much interest throughout the length of the Nile today, as it has in the past. Unfortunately, the thousands of tourists who come to Egypt every year only touch the surface of the country. They are herded in groups from modern hotel to historical sites by story-worn guides whose credentials are sometimes suspect, and hurried through temples and tombs with impassive indifference.

Travel today has become too easy as the world is being reduced in size by time zones and air travel. Once countries were separated by vast expanses of sea that would take weeks or even months to traverse, now it's a matter of hours, and somewhere along the way the romance of travel has been lost as planes land in continual succession releasing hordes of holiday-makers and vacationers who are 'seeing Cairo' in two days or 'doing the Nile' in one week.

The anticipation of adventure has been obliterated by travel agents offering packaged-tours and tailor-made holidays complete with day excursions, special features, and unique sightseeing opportunities; the museum in the morning, the pyramids in the afternoon. People are shown much more than they can possibly hope to remember, only to fly out as quickly as they flew in, with a camera full of hastily taken snapshots and an opinion of Egypt being too hot, too crowded, too noisy, and too dirty. Egypt cannot be seen in a few days, weeks, or months. Even the four years I was there offered only a brief encounter with a country that I came to love.

The Garden Ran Down to the Nile

The Garden Ran Down to the Nile

One

Cairo – A City of Paradox

▲▲▲

'He who hath not seen Cairo, hath not seen the world'
One Thousand and One Nights

The very name Cairo suggests a romantic, seductive city enticing you with promises of intrigue and adventure, conjuring up images of the Kasbah and smoke filled places seasoned with incense and espionage. But present day reality soon destroys the illusion, slapping you hard in the face with the 21st Century and leaving you wondering where Cairo went.

The mother of the world has faded into an old woman. Her sands have lost their glitter, her river has been restrained and her city has been polluted by modern technology and a quarter of a million inhabitants spread over eight square kilometres. Still, Cairo has the power to fascinate and hypnotise with an all-encompassing awareness of time and history where you can lose yourself in its atmosphere.

The Garden Ran Down to the Nile

Cairo offers no gradual adjustment into Egypt, no comfortable cultural transition. It drops you straight in at the deep end where confusion seems an essential part of everyday life. Modern Cairo is overpowering when taken in all at once. The city is a systematic multi-layering of cultures and epochs: Oriental, Moorish, Rococo, Art Deco, Classical French, and Italian Renaissance.

Everything is tinged with a burnished dun-colour from years of smoke, humanity, and dust blown in from the desert. Domineering billboards loom overhead where larger than life cinema stars in overly made-up faces frozen in grotesque expressions, are portrayed in exaggerated melodrama. The ever-present pungent smell of cooking fat, dust and dung, merge with Kentucky Fried Chicken and Wimpey burgers to offend your sense of smell.

Polyglot Cairo is the largest city in Africa and the most densely populated urban sprawl in the world, 17 million people, and walking through the city you become acutely aware of them. With all the right combinations to create an atmosphere of stress and frustration, the Egyptian people take it in their stride; they seem to revel in the chaos exhibiting a spirit of friendliness and accommodation.

Bulak is one of the oldest quarters in the city, the nucleus of the trading industry. A sprawling circus of humanity engulfing you with every kind of activity, noise, and smell associated with daily life. Shop goods spill onto the pavements in gaudy disarray blocking the footpaths. Fruit and vegetable sellers bargain their wares in the street markets. Vendors of sticky pink candyfloss hawk their wares from brightly painted push-carts. Sherbulis dispense lemonade in long streams from brass kirbehs strapped to their backs.

The Garden Ran Down to the Nile

Between the buildings, women shout the day's gossip, their washing dripping overhead motionless in the dust and smoke. Thin gaunt men on bicycles laden with sheep's heads and flying entrails, dart and dodge the chaos of the streets; competing with cyclists balancing enormous trays of baladi bread on their heads with competence and agility. Families on motorbikes roar passed kiosks selling Cleopatra cigarettes, bottled water, and Sport Cola; a flat sweet imitation of Coke. Buta Gaz sellers push huge carts of butane cylinders, banging out their presence with heavy metal rods.

A perpetual rhythm of noise and traffic intertwine with the clamour of workshops where gold painted, reproduction furniture is made. The garish French style that became popular with the bourgeoisie during the reign of King Farouk is fondly referred to as 'Louis Farouk'.

Automotive garages invade the sidewalks where over the pandemonium of the traffic, young mechanics hammer bent fenders back to the original plane. Old jalopies and vintage cars are still in operation all over Egypt—some improvised with fly screens where windshields once existed. On the streets, there is an unending procession of people: women in black ma'alayahs, young girls in brightly coloured western dress, sun dried old men on donkeys, and children with amazingly beautiful faces.

At night when the heat of day subsides, whole families of Caireans emerge to promenade through the once cosmopolitan shopping district of Kasir el Nil and Talaat Harb; an area of unlimited shoe shops and clothing stores. Gaudy window displays are illuminated by brilliant neon signs in Arabic script. Michael Jackson, Amr Diab, and the latest Arab pop group's boom out over the cacophony of the city.

The Garden Ran Down to the Nile

Disjointed fragments of once beautiful pink tiled pavements peek through the increasing filth of a dozen decades of neglect and pedestrians. Broken curb-stones protrude and recede in ruinous disarray with no hope of repair, and parked cars make crossing junctions a lesson in navigation.

Overhead, dilapidated air-conditioning units continually drip water, and plant-pots perch precariously on window sills, making it safer to walk in the streets. Everywhere you look the elegance of the city is hidden by the accumulated debris of generations. Yet, it is this ambivalence of old and new, of affluence and decadence, of grandeur and squalor, that attracts with magnetic appeal.

The once magnificent commercial and residential buildings: the Baehler Mansion's, the Khedival Buildings, the Claridge Hotel, the Continental, and the once famous department stores: Sednaoui, Cucurel, Ade's, Tiring, Omar Effendi, and the Davies-Bryant building, have been left to their own fate—tolerated, but not cherished. Yet the city hangs on grimly to the vestige of respectability both rich in architectural heritage and visual reminders of an historical past that cannot be recaptured.

Remnants of beaux-art opulence loom from the buildings over the traffic jammed streets where Khedive Ismail, under the spell of Paris, built his new city in about two years. He employed Italian architects who were involved in creating many of the major buildings: Abdin Palace, the Opera House, the Cities' Squares, and the Egyptian Museum.

During the belle époque, buildings sprang up in grandiosity combining ostentatious styles with pediments, cantilevers, and balconies. Flamboyant stone columns, marble staircases, twisting balustrades, and scrollwork were everywhere whilst wrought-iron dragons guarded private gates. The extravagant architectural designs varied from Gothic, French Baroque, Italian Renaissance, drab Neo-Arabic, and Art Nouveau. The Metro and Miami cinemas in Suleiman Pasha Street are fine examples of the latter.

With the innovation of plaster-of-Paris, ornamentation ran rampant. Windows were embellished with flora-garlands and mouldings. Faces of lions, angels, and sphinxes looked down from doorways, and domes dominated the rooftops. For years the warm climate of Cairo was sympathetic to the plaster, now after decades of neglect, the deterioration is sadly evident.

Speeding over the Mousky flyover towards the Khan el Khalili, the 1912 Tiring Department Store on Attaba Square is perceptible. Amid the high-rise buildings its massive glass-globe dome held high by four herculean figures, looms over the chaos and confusion of the street below. Once a celebrated four-floor emporium, it offered all manner of goods from Austrian textiles to the latest haute-couture from Paris. It now houses hundreds of squatters and dilapidated workshops with broken windows. Copper leeched from the alloy of the building runs down the façade in verdigrise trails. Today it's recognized by young Cairene's as the al-Tofaha building, as it was called when it was used in a 1990s film 'Ataba Square'.

Everything looks incongruous. Everything is in a state of change, and with this change and the ever-increasing population, most of the splendid mansions, some dating around 1870, have been torn down to make way for more high-rise tenements of ugly grey concrete. It seems it is more economical to let these beautiful old buildings decay and collapse than to preserve them. The Kasr Sherif Pasha Sabry villa, belonging to the statesman, Adly Yeken

Pasha and his wealthy wife, was razed to the ground without compassion in 1978. The grace and elegance of Renaissance architecture obliterated into dust and rubble within a moment. It stood on a sought after plot of land on the Corniche in Garden City—where the five star Four Seasons Hotel now stands.

The villa of the beloved Egyptian singer, Umm Kulthum, was demolished shortly after her death in 1975, just before Parliament was to place a conservation order on it. So piece-by-piece Ismail's city vanishes, leaving only a handful of reminders of its exotic past. But despite the decadence and cosmopolitan jumble, you can still breathe in the enormous impact made by Khedive Ismail.

Inside the old buildings many details have withstood the ravages of time. The cracked marble floors, the yellowing ceilings ornately decorated with friezes and rosettes, the cool marble staircases, the burnished-brass hanging-lamps, rows of brass post-boxes, elaborate wrought-iron caged elevators, and timeworn panelled doors, all echoing a glorious past, and still aesthetically pleasing.

In 1997 a national campaign to stop the destruction of Cairo's architectural heritage was initiated by the Mubarak Library, the al-Ahram weekly newspaper, and the Fulbright Commission; supported by the Preservation of the Architectural Heritage of Cairo. Only time and money will tell if this layer of Egypt's history can be preserved. But with rising land prices, many of the old remaining buildings are still being crowded out by hideous monolithic tenements. Extended ever upwards, more and more floors are being added to compensate for the increasing population of the city. The law states that these buildings are not to be over six stories high, yet property developers add as many as fourteen. Roofs are never added as another floor might be needed. They are built without planning permission and sustained with bribes. Occasionally a building will collapse—with devastating consequences. But still the building goes on, the tower blocks competing with minarets to reach the Heavens.

Beyond the tenements, disintegrating dwellings fill the narrow alleyways. They house uncharted communities of the poor people of Cairo. Doomed to stagnation, and without proper sanitation, they accept their lot with quiet dignity. Thousands of rooftop dwellers live with their chickens, rabbits, and goats, where once rooftop gardens and courtyards existed.

Other communities live amongst the tombs in the City of the Dead surrounded by the medieval aqueduct and the walls of one of the oldest cities in the world.

The Zabayeen, a Coptic sect, work the rubbish heaps in the City of the Dead. The government provides them with water, electricity, and schools, consolidating the needs of the people with the environmental needs of the city.

Most of the remaining buildings of the belle époque are in Garden City, Zamalek, Heliopolis, Maadi, and downtown Cairo. The Ezbekiyeh Gardens still exist. Festooned with fairy lights, it's a pleasant retreat in the center of a frantic city. The famous Groppi's ice cream parlour; now café and patisserie, occupies a corner in Midan Talaat Harb. You can sit in the cool of its high ceiling room, sip mint tea or Néscafe, and indulge in the sticky confectionery known as baklava.

The Manial Palace was built by Mohammed Ali on the Island of Rhoda. In the late 1970s, the hotel comprised a series of bungalows and was frequented mainly by French tourists.

The Garden Ran Down to the Nile

Bougainvillea, fern, and overgrown palm trees surrounded the hotel bungalows, giving a feeling of Hollywood. The swimming pool was the only one in the city where topless sunbathers lounged, and needless to say the service they received from the poolside waiters was five-star.

Within the palace a small hunting museum contains the trophies of King Farouk. Hanging from the walls trophy heads of deer stare down through sightless glass eyes. Cases of dishevelled stuffed animals and birds are displayed in unrealistic scenes. Rows of animal hooves give a macabre impression in the dim light, and there is a collection of butterflies, moths, insects, and beetles, buried under layers of accumulated dust. Farouk had a reputation for extravagance, but one wonders if all these unfortunate creatures were actually killed by him, as reputed.

Overlooking the Nile from Gezira Island, and occupying one of Cairo's most spectacular and prestigious waterfront locations, stands the city's most hideous hotel, the El Borg. It has been labelled 'Godless architecture', and not unjustified. The El Borg is positively exempt of any redeeming or inspiring feature, and one can only wonder why this box shaped monstrosity of mud-coloured concrete, was ever allowed to be built. It looks out across the river to the Semiramis Intercontinental, the Shepheard's Hotel, and the Nile Hilton.

To the right of the El Borg stands another blot on the landscape, the Cairo Tower. Built in 1957 amid the lush green of the Andalusian Gardens, this sand coloured observation column rises to a height of 187 metres. The outer shaft is punched out in a fretwork of diamond shapes. Hundreds of mosaic lozenges ascend to the top of the tower creating the illusion of upward movement. At least that was the theory.

The concrete tower represents a lotus flower, and one does get a sense of Pharaonic influence. Lollipop shaped trees form an avenue to the entrance, where over the door looms the national emblem of Egypt—the Eagle. Under the shade of the trees is a small café where you can relax in wicker chairs and enjoy coffee or ice cream.

Once inside the building there is a small lift that takes you to the top—when it's working. In the 1970s, there was a young man who operated it. He wore white gloves and a brown uniform with a pill box hat reminiscent of the Philip Morris cigarette boy. He peered out through thick framed government-issue glasses with lens like the bottoms of coke bottles, giving him the appearance of a Cheshire Cat.

At the top of the Tower there is a revolving restaurant, the Belvédère, though I never it saw revolve. The 360° view from the Belvédère is spectacular and usually occupied by young Cairean lovers. On a clear day you can see up and down the Nile for miles: the Mokattam Hills to the east, and to the west, the pyramids of Ghiza and Meidum, wavering in the heat of the desert.

The Gezira Sporting Club is one of the last remaining vestiges of Ismail's perfect city. A former playground of the British, it was presented to the British High Command in the early 1880s by Khedive Tewfik. The land was carved out of the surrounding Botanical Gardens, which was laid out by French horticulturist, Délchevalérie in the 1860s. The 150-acre membership club covers the entire southern end of Gezira Island; a popular retreat for wealthy Egyptians and Europeans alike.

The Garden Ran Down to the Nile

Penthouse apartments overlook the tennis courts and the clubhouse known as the Lido. In its heyday the club boasted: a racetrack, thirteen tennis courts, an eighteen-hole golf course, four polo grounds, a cricket pitch, squash courts, hockey and football grounds, a pergola, a clubhouse, croquet greens, an Olympic-sized swimming pool, and a children's paddling pool. Though not as grandiose as it once was, the racetrack is still very much in operation, as are the swimming pools. The tennis courts are always full and lovely to play on in the shade of the acacia and jacaranda trees that line the adjacent road.

In the 1890s Mabel Caillard spent several winters in Cairo where she first realized the spell of Egypt and even then that it was changing: "When you came to Cairo it was as if you had entered upon another world. You were in the East-nay, more than this: Cairo was the East, its substance and its essence. Cairo was luring you to your everlasting enchantment by her beauty and her strangeness, her spirit and her fascination. The sky is pure cobalt. The sunshine is pure gold. The shadows that lie across your path are of the purest violet and as clear-cut as the facets of a gem."

Cairo in the nineties was still picturesque. Its three hundred minarets towered above the flat roofs of the city. Its gardens still had space to flourish. Its Nile still caught the reflections of the pink and mauve Mokattam hills; reflections now blurred by superimposed outlines of ugly grey tower blocks along the river bank.

Florence Nightingale, while staying at the Hotel de l'Europe, wrote home recounting the beauty of Cairo: "I thought it was a place to buy stores at and pass through on one's way to India, instead of its being the rose of cities, the garden of the desert, the pearl of earth below. Oh, could I but describe those Moorish streets, in red and white stripes of marble; the latticed balconies, with little octagonal shrines . . . the innumerable mosques and minarets . . . But there are no words to describe an Arabian city, no European words at least."

R. Talbot-Kelly remembers the "sniff" of Cairo: "Wherein the smell originates it is hard to say, but there is a peculiar odour, common to all Eastern towns, whose quiet intensity pervades everything, and it is a literal fact that I have smelt Cairo three miles away! Wandering about the streets is tiring, but it is the only way in which the real Cairo can be understood. Never mind books; walk about by yourself and see what you can discover for yourself, and enjoy that. In doing so you will find many quaint bits, and see much of a life whose every incident is worth your attention."

In 1898 Eustace Reynolds-Ball found Cairo a society with innumerable gaieties and entertainments: "Bicycling is now a particularly popular amusement in the City of the Caliphs; and the sight of an American or English girl bicycling down the Mooski, preceded by a running footman (syce) to clear the way, may perhaps provoke a smile from her compatriots at the startling incongruity. This is only one instance, however, of the strange contrasts between the latest development of European civilisation and fashionable culture and the old-world Orientalism so constantly seen in Cairo of to-day."

Bicycling was not the only form of entertainment to be had on the streets of European Cairo. The British and Europeans could enjoy themselves on all levels. The notorious Fish Market behind the Gezira Palace was described as depraved and being inhabited by the lowest of the low. The city overflowed with the patronage of male travellers who indulged in the sexual delights and hashish dens of the red light district, during the late 1800s. The infamous brothel known as 'Madame Fatima's', was extremely alluring with gyrating dancing girls who performed in little more than gold bangles and tattoos.

In 1893 Améedé Baillot de Guerville alludes to the: "Infamous gambling-hells which are one of the most abominable plagues of the town. Places of debauchery, ruin and perdition."

He once made an arrangement with a donkey boy to take him to one of the houses in the Fish Market where he was "completely overcome" by a trio of young scantily clad dancing girls, but emphasized: "as to the houses where one can witness indescribable orgies, I pass them by in silence, simply remarking that they would not exist a day if it were not for the tourists who support them." One wonders how he knew of such places.

Gustave Flaubert held quite a different opinion. He was a great supporter of brothels, and a lover of prostitutes. He frequented the brothels around Cairo and enjoyed various forms of erotic entertainment—with a great deal of enthusiasm. The letters to his friends are a detailed account of his liaisons with various "blue-stocking whores." The letters to his mother, however, read quite differently.

The Garden Ran Down to the Nile

Egypt was never part of the Commonwealth, but under the Veiled Protectorate, Egypt was as British as the Raj in India. It was Ismail's love of French architecture and Europe's way of life that influenced him so greatly. Ismail received the greater part of his education in France where he acquired a strong preference for European institutions. He opened schools, hospitals, and training colleges, while trying to bring a modern structure to the country.

During Ismail's time, a writer remarked on the Pasha: "The reign of Ismail promises to be the beginning of a new era for Egypt. A man of undoubted ability, possessed of unusual energy in administration, fully appreciative of the importance of western civilization, fired with the ambition proper to a grandson of Mehemet Ali, the Khedive is a ruler such as Egypt has scarcely seen since the Arab conquest."

To perpetuate the lure of Europeans to Egypt and make them feel less alienated, Ismail introduced a system, under an Ottoman treaty—known as the Capitulations. Foreigners paid no taxes and were not subject to Egyptian jurisdiction. When Ismail died, his son, Prince Tewfik took over. Tewfik, like his father was pro-European.

But Ismail's egotism to impress Europe, rather than concern for his own people, plunged the country into hopeless debt—the main underlying reason for the establishment of the Protectorate. When in time his debts overwhelmed him, it was not repentance he suffered, rather, a sense of injustice that progress, which he had welcomed so handsomely, should have rewarded him as a defaulter in the eyes of the law. Still his legacy remains in the bits and pieces of his glorious and extravagant epoch. By the time Ismail was overthrown in 1879, most of the elaborate houses had already been converted into flats and office blocks.

When his son, Tewfik came to power, he plunged the country into a hotbed of Oriental corruption and intrigue. As a ruler, Tewfik proved too weak to control the Nationalist Movement headed by rebel leader, Ahmet Arabi, who in 1881 was chosen to take control of the government ministries.

King Farouk was crowned in 1936, and became even more idealistic than his great uncle Ismail. Farouk was forced to abdicate in 1952 by Aboul Nasser, as a result of his excessively materialistic and irresponsible flamboyant lifestyle; thus ending a century and a half of the Mohammet Ali dynasty.

Around the same time, General Muhammad Neguib, who would become the first president of Egypt, abolished the titles of Bey and Pasha that had been given to high-ranking persons of respect—along with the wearing of the fez (tarboosh) worn by the *Effendis*.

Farouk's vision of a European city had allowed the British elite the privilege of enjoying an aristocratic existence amongst the fashionable society cafés and private clubs throughout the city. Today a vanished class of cosmopolitan Egyptians, of whom few are left, sit alone in the cool of their comfortable apartments sipping gin fizz and remembering with affection, a time of official balls, receptions, gymkhanas, polo matches, lawn tennis, parties, and concerts. Yet the majority of the population cannot remember, and could care less about a part of their history which they consider a European intrusion into the culture of their country. Few have time to grieve the loss of an era that they did not share and which they now suffer from.

The year 1952 saw the start of the decline of Cairo's Golden Age, when on Black Saturday, Egyptian demonstrations took place in a bid to oust the British and take back the country. Many of the famous hotels and landmarks associated with foreign powers met their demise as the new order of Gamal Abdel Nasser raged through Cairo, initiating the change in the country.

Today, with three million people living in the City of the Dead, and tens of thousands of rooftop dwellers, places to live are harder to find than jobs. Cairo is now six times larger than the medieval city and spreading farther out each day into the green land that is steadily being lost to urbanization. Even the ancient Egyptians did not build on green land. Warnings have been discovered—inscribed on papyrus and carved in stone. There is not one ancient monument, temple, or city that was built on green land. Yet, with one thousand people a day needing housing, the government turns a blind eye to a problematic situation too big to control.

There have been attempts by the government to entice people from the city by offering better housing in the developments of Tenth of Ramada and Sadat City; located in the desert fifty miles from Cairo. The developments have their own mosques, shops, and schools, but the unfinished apartment blocks, and more importantly, the lack of work, means the problem goes on.

Outside downtown Cairo, the old medieval city is in a state of dilapidation and urban decay. Yet, many of the ancient buildings with Turkish facades and jutting upper windows have survived. Their beautiful supporting corbels are richly carved in arabesque latticework, known as meshrabeya, which shuts out much of the light, but allows air to flow through and the inhabitants to see out.

The Garden Ran Down to the Nile

In 1882 an official committee for the preservation of Arab monuments was formed to protect the remaining great monuments of Islamic art in Cairo including the mosques, madrasahs, the Citadel and Gates, the walls of Salah Al-Din surrounding the Fatimid City of the Dead, and the Museum of Islamic Art in the Bab el Khalq Square, which is one of the most beautiful buildings in the city. The arched doorways and windows are surrounded by alternate pink and grey stonework suggesting a Pharaonic persona. The museum houses a collection of Koranic manuscripts, including a parchment that dates back to the 8th century. There are hundreds of books, gold-leafed and hand-painted in rich colours of artistic and intricate calligraphy, a collection of meshrabeya, hand-woven prayer-mats, rugs, tapestries, textiles, and a treasure-trove of medieval artefacts and military objects found in the debris of the old Fatimid city.

One of the first things people noticed when they come to Cairo is the traffic. The large red and white buses seen in 1976 in the city were given to Egypt by the American Aid Program. A popular mode of transportation for the locals, they were in a state of dilapidation through over use and sheer neglect. Most of the seats had been removed, along with the windows and doors to allow for more passengers. The cost was three piasters for a seat, one piaster to stand, and free to the people who hung on the outside grasping sheer surface. Sprinters would leap at the moving buses to be caught by unknown hands, while the over-loaded vehicles roared lopsidedly down the road, belching thick black exhaust fumes into the already heavily polluted air.

The Garden Ran Down to the Nile

Taxis, as in London and New York, were as plentiful as they are today. Very few had meters and if they did, the drivers would conveniently forget to turn them on. It was advisable to bargain the price before getting in, and it was not uncommon for the driver to pick up other passengers *en route*. I once found myself jostled through town next to two women in black ma'alayahs, a basket of vegetables, and a dirty-faced child with dark staring eyes. The springs of the well-worn car seat were non-existent and proved extremely painful every time the driver slammed into a pothole. Arabic music screamed from the portable radio that was lashed to the orange, fur-lined dashboard. The driver peered out through the fringed windshield that was adorned with plastic fruit, rubber dolls, and countless good-luck charms—which I hoped worked. The back windshield was also fur-lined and sported a string of coloured fairy-lights and a waving 'Hand of Fatima,' another object to dispel the evil-eye.

At that time it had been the rage with Egyptian drivers to implant a bird-call device up the tail of the exhaust pipe. Every time the brake was applied an incessant chirping noise was emitted. You would hear them all over town. The novelty finally wore off, no doubt when the bird-call devices wore out.

Lord Edward Cecil recalls his adventure in a taxi in the early 1900s: "Driving in a native-driven taxi on a dark night is a very fair test of nerve. The streets in our suburbs are lighted on strictly economical [sic] principles. You can just see one street lamp from the next. They no doubt give one a line as to the way the road runs, and prevent one's entering some one's garden, or, worse still, a canal, in a hurried and undignified manner, but except in their immediate vicinity, they show no part of the road itself. This would not matter so much if the taxis carried good headlights, but they don't. The one I have to-night has two things like policemen's bull's-eye lanterns tied on to it in front. Even these modest illuminations are bent by previous collisions, and only show about two yards of road in front of us. A trifle like lack of illumination, however, does not disturb the driver, who as long as he goes fast enough and keeps his horn sounding the whole time, has every confidence that all will be well. We spin across the bridge and plunge into the darkness beyond . . . we miss an elderly peasant by the fraction of an inch, swerving as we do so very nearly into a cart laden with passengers on the other side of the road. We continue our wild career, swerving from side to side, catching glimpses of terrified faces and flying limbs as we pass."

Fortunately in the early 1980s the roads in town were a little better illuminated and no one would ever drive outside the city at night. Driving in daylight was a lesson in negotiation. The steady stream of traffic aggressively crawled through the city, as a battle of nerves, determination, and fenders was waged. Drivers competing for space leaned on their horns, most of which had been blown to exhaustion, and Cairo became a city without patience.

The Egyptian driver regards safety with astonishing gay abandon and wins hands down as some of the world's worst drivers, with the possible exception of India. Traffic regulations were loosely abided by and the few traffic signals that existed, more an option then a rule. Lane markings on the wider roads were only a suggestion and nearly always ignored by drivers that would divert to the opposite side of the road when their side was gridlocked.

The Garden Ran Down to the Nile

The constant overflow of cars, taxis, buses, and motorbikes jockeyed for position on the ever increasing roads and flyovers that were being built daily. Thick black exhaust fumes choked the air, and countless pedestrians darted or strolled complacently amid oncoming traffic that simply would not stop. With the windows opened you were polluted with diesel fumes, dust, and noise. Rolled up, you suffocated from the heat.

Traffic police in white uniforms, gloves, and French style caps, directed traffic at main intersections within the city. They stood on raised dais' waving their arms and blowing whistles that could barely be heard above the noise and continual honking of the traffic. One of the most dangerous and foolhardy jobs a person could do—standing in the middle of aggressive Cairean traffic was like playing a game of Russian roulette.

These traffic police carried note pads and recorded the license number of cars they saw committing traffic offences. When it came time for the driver to renew his license, which was once a year, they were made to pay for all offences that had been written down, real or alleged.

A friend and I were involved in a small accident on the Pyramids Road one morning when a battered old pick-up truck in the right-hand lane, decided to cross over in front of us to turn left. As we were in the left-hand lane, he hit the side of the car with great impact dragging it up the division of the road. A crowd immediately gathered to the shouts of two hysterical women, and an astonished Egyptian truck driver. Out of the commotion a policeman appeared and we ended up at the Ghiza police station. We were detained for nearly two hours. The room had tiled floors and was vacant of any furniture other than several hard rickety chairs and a desk with a telephone. Over the desk hung a dim incandescent light-bulb covered with a red plastic bowl, which served as a lampshade. A portrait of Nassar decorated the wall. The driver of the pick-up was indignant, demanding that we should pay him compensation for being in his way when he wanted to turn. This defied belief, let alone logic, and I believe the only reason we were allowed to leave without having to pay, was the diplomatic license plate on our car.

Although it was commonplace to complain about the traffic, I quite enjoyed driving in the city. The more I drove the more well-tuned I became to the rules and pecking order of the ebb and flow, and once I knew my way around I found that keeping the car moving, and a friendly smile, would more often than not ease me into the correct lane of the funnelling system that snaked throughout the city.

In 1930 Mildred Alice Oliver must have had a much easier time driving in what she called the heart of Cairo traffic: "I am getting on with the little Ford car and drove right into the heart of Cairo yesterday all among the traffic and the straggling natives and the trams. Tomorrow I am to drive over to Gezira across a lot of bridges and so on."

A year later her confidence had grown as she ventured into the desert: "I am driving the car in all sorts of traffic again and find no difficulty. The Ford car has already taken us several good trips . . . and if we can get hold of another car full of friends we go on more adventurous trips up the big wadis or ravines; but one must have two or three cars in case of trouble. Sticking in the sand or losing one's way is very frequent."

By this time there were around 24,000 motor vehicles in Cairo. In 1980 only one quarter of the population owned their own cars, and although the roads were quite crowded, you could still drive and park with comparable ease. Today there are 2,000,000 and increasing every day.

Two

The Residence

▲▲▲

'In the end it may well be that Britain will be honoured by the historians more for the way she disposed of an empire than for the way in which she acquired it'
David Ormsby Gore

Sir Evelyn Baring (Lord Cromer) came to power as British Consul-General in 1882 and ruled Egypt with tenacity and absolute authority until 1907. He was a clever diplomat and an astute financier from an influential banking family. During his time in office, Lord Cromer brought order out of chaos re-organizing and establishing honesty within the government and Egypt's debt was paid off and money invested. He knew that the resources of Egypt lay almost entirely in agriculture that depended on the labour of the fellaheen (farmers). Lord Cromer abolished taxation levied on the fellaheen by the Pasha and rich land owners, thus giving them back their dignity. He invested money in projects that earned a quick return, but while the Egyptian people respected Lord Cromer, they had no love for him. Cromer looked on them as children to be tolerated; a 'nanny knows best' attitude. He held the opinion that education was not necessary to a third-world country, so no money went towards health or education for the poor, thus the Veiled Protectorate was born.

The Protectorate was an administration in which the Khedive, reduced to a figurehead, ruled through a parliamentary government with Egyptian minister. But behind each minister was a British civil servant. It worked well, and Egypt was well off under the British, or at least better off than they would have been under the Turks, but they were resentful. The British Administration had produced a system that educated the effendi Egyptian to civil servant and government status, and then left him frustrated in menial jobs as the British held every post in the government. The expression 'wogs' came about during this time referring to members of the effendi, 'Working on Government Service.' Some thought the meaning: Worthy Oriental Gentleman, while others quickly transcribed the word to meaning anything Egyptian, or more negatively, a term of abuse.

In the early years the Consul-General's chief offices were located in an affluent area of Alexandria. During the winter they resided in Cairo, having a branch office across from the Ezbekiyeh Gardens. The house in Alexandria was a large British establishment enclosed by a high wall. The dining room over-looked a tranquil garden with herbaceous boarders in the English country garden style. Later it became the home of the Vice-Consul.

In 1885 the Consul-General's offices in Cairo, moved from the Ezbekiyeh to the quiet Rue Maghreby, where Lord Cromer governed from a modest rambling house that subsequently became the Turf Club. It stood next to Sephardi Synagogue, and in 1906 the

The Garden Ran Down to the Nile

Oriental Secretary, Ronald Storrs, saw it as the "fenced city of refuge of the higher British community."

When Harry Boyle was made Oriental Secretary in 1890 under Lord Cromer, he was asked by Cromer if he spoke Arabic—to which he replied: "Hardly at all, Sir." Whereon Cromer, turning away, said to one of the Chancery: "What the devil does White mean by sending that boy here? He'll be worse than useless!" Upon which Boyle replied that he could learn Arabic in a month. Cromer gave him six weeks. Boyle learned it in five.

In 1899 Boyle was promoted to Consul, with the title of Counsellor of Legation. He would visit the native quarters at night disguised as a Turk and accompanied by his Montenegrin servant, Guiro. He learned the ways and habits of the local people, which came in very useful in his job. Boyle dined at the Agency on numerous occasions and remembers walking the extensive lawns that were reseeded annually. He spent long moonlit evenings in conversation with Lord and Lady Cromer and other guests, or just standing on the private dock where after an evening of socializing it was rumoured empty whisky bottles were flung into the Nile.

In 1889 Boyle accompanied the Prince of Wales (Edward VII) and Prince George (later George V) to the Khan el Khalili, where the Princes' went disguised in shabby clothing. The Prince of Wales did not want his identity known as he wanted to purchase rugs at a reasonable price. Boyle played the part well, explaining to the carpet dealer that: "this poor gentleman can't afford luxuries, moreover, he is a miser, and it would therefore be quite useless to ask for their usual inflated prices."

The Princes got their quality carpets at very moderate prices, but later their identities were discovered and Boyle was told that he would never again be allowed back in the bazaar, nor would any deals be made with him.

That same year the old palace grounds of Kasr al-Doubara that ran between Kasr al-Ali and the east bank of the Nile, were divided into streets and plots, and the palaces torn down. Lord Cromer had persuaded Whitehall to purchase one of the properties, and the following year a plot was secured on the riverfront and a new house commissioned. The house became the new British Agency, as this was how the old Agency on Adly Street (formerly Magrabi) had been known.

Mohammed Ali, in his bid to reclaim swampland had the entire area of Kasr al-Doubara refurbished during his reign—as he had done in the Ezbekiyeh. Known as Scorpion's Hill, the Doubara swamps and sand hills were transformed into orchards and bean fields before Ibraham Pasha built his palatial palaces. To the north of the new British Agency was Kasr al-Shoobra, surrounded by lofty walls where the Pasha's brother, Sultan Hussien Kamal had lived. Now it was occupied by the newly built Semiramis Hotel.

A second saraya (palace) sat amidst a large garden. To the south was the spacious Kasr al-Walda, the palace of the Khedive's mother (Ismail's grandmother), and on the bank of the Nile, Kasr al'Doubbara, the grandiose residence of Ibrahim Pasha.

The agricultural engineer, José Lamba, designed Garden City in 1905 where the crème de la crème took up residence. Lamba's creation was a whimsical, Art Nouveau district set in a maze of narrow winding roads that criss-crossed and intersected in a fantasy of curves and rectangles. At that time the population of Cairo was

The Garden Ran Down to the Nile

655,500. After Garden City was created and the palace of Kasr al Ali demolished, the Agency expanded its gardens southward, purchasing land from Charles Bacos, one of the owners of the Nile Land and Agricultural Company. The Agency was often referred to as Bayt Al Kurd (the Lord's House) in reference to Lord Cromer. The crescent-shaped Chancery came much later, about the same time as the new Shepheard's Hotel a block away. Six high-rise buildings were also built in the space occupying the demolished Doubara palace. When the British Agency became known as the British Embassy in 1936, the daily business of Her Majesty's government was dealt with at the new crescent-shaped building joined by the garden of the Residence and entered through guarded gates by way of the tree lined Ahmed Ragheb Street.

The new colonial style Agency was designed by British architect, R.H. Boyce, and built at a cost of £E39, 984 in 1892. It was said that Cromer, being preoccupied with foreign affairs, had the building set in the wrong direction to the prevailing winds. At that time the garden ran down to the Nile where beyond the wall, Thomas Cook's boats were moored.

It was from the Agency's veranda and behind its large wooden doors that policy affecting the destinies of Egypt and the Middle East was conducted in typical imperial fashion by empire-builders, Allenby, MacMahon, and Lord Lloyd. In 1942 Sir Miles Lampson offered King Farouk two choices; appoint a pro-British cabinet, or abdicate. He chose the former option, keeping his throne for a few more years.

The Agency was not only the living quarters of the Consul-General and the seventy strong staff; it housed the offices. Lord Cromer's desk still stands in what is now the study. Lord Kitchener made many reforms. He changed the servants' liveries from the chocolate brown and yellow (the colour Sir Eldon Gorst had introduced) to scarlet and gold.

Kitchener was a tall good-looking man with style, authority, and a strong, yet sensitive face. He developed a passion for Egyptian antiquities, as well as porcelain and Byzantine icons (that some regarded as hideous) with which he decorated the middle drawing room. Once in his new position, he coerced the Swiss hotelier, Charles Baehler, into removing two marble lions from the newly renovated Gezira Palace Hotel, and had them placed at either side of the front entrance of the Agency, where they remain today.

Lord Allenby had an experience with lions of a different sort. When he was in residence he spent much of his time in the garden, which he enjoyed showing to visitors, and where he kept a pet marabou stork. The stork followed him everywhere and had a jealous dislike for any ladies or children that happened to be with him at the time. Allenby was a frequent visitor to the Cairo Zoo, where he would indulge his extensive knowledge of animals and birds. On one occasion two young lions on their way to the zoo had been brought to visit him and proceeded to chase the stork around the garden.

In Lord Lloyd's time the ceilings in the Agency's entrance hall were dark green and gold, with squares of mustard coloured carpet and velvet curtains edged with worsted balls.

In 1942 Sir Miles Lampson embellished the rooms with silk damask and Persian carpets to display the antique furniture he had brought back from China. The magnificent Heriz garden carpet graces the main reception room today. Four original watercolours by Edward Lear hang in the small sitting room, and a portrait of Lord

Cromer hangs over the fireplace in the study with one of Lord Kitchener on the opposite wall.

State dinner parties were regularly given at the Residence, where Hock and Burgundy flowed freely and guests would arrive in formal attire wearing as many medals as could be supported.

In 1912-13 Lord Kitchener added an enormous ballroom to the Agency's north wing and once a year a grand ball was held where gentlemen in white tie, danced with ladies in taffeta and lace well into the night on the first sprung dance floor in Africa. The Indian staff wore white turbans and gold embroidered breastplates. They served a piéce de résistance that was legendary—especially the prawn curry of which Queen Victoria's son, Prince George, had several helpings.

Seating protocol always seemed to be a problem and could take hours to adjudicate as Major C.S. Jarvis recalls: "At every dinner party, at least fifty per cent of the guests are under the impression that they have been deliberately affronted."

Joseph 'Bimbashi' McPherson attended many official receptions at the Agency while Lord Kitchener was British Consul General, but having little interest in 'big bugs,' as he called them, rarely mentioned them. Yet, for the most part, official balls and receptions held at the Agency demanded more than an incidental notice. One grand ball was given once a year during the fashionable season that lasted from January until April. Some members of the British community would feel offended if they had not been invited, as being British, they felt it was their right.

The Garden Ran Down to the Nile

Over the years there have been many dignified and illustrious guests who have graced the rooms of the Agency—now the Residence. In 1942, Prime Minister Winston Churchill stayed for a week while he assessed the war in the Middle East and held talks with his generals: Alexander, Smuts, Spears, Auchinleck, Montgomery, and Wavell.

Howard Carter stayed overnight in 1927, at the invitation of the new High Commissioner, Sir George Lloyd, later to be Lord. Other visitors have been: King Farouk, General Charles de Gaulle, Sir Anthony Eden, Noel Coward, Freya Stark, Cecil Beaton, and Evelyn Waugh.

Mildred Alice Oliver visited the Agency in 1930 when Sir Percy Loraine was High Commissioner and the gardens still ran down to the Nile. She describes it with favour: "On Friday Frank and I went for a tea party at the Residency, which turned out to be quite a pleasant informal affair, and I was glad to see the beautiful house and garden which is actually on the banks of the Nile. The room we had tea in was very beautiful and full of sweet peas in great bowls and very sweet smelling, and masses of deep yellow roses. The furniture which no doubt goes with the Residency was mostly old marquetry and sort of Louis XV. There is a full-length portrait of Queen Alexandra as a young woman over the mantelpiece and an immense fire was burning, though the day had been quite hot: it's apt to be cold at sunset."

In September 1954, Gamal Abdel Nasser, in his bid to liberate Cairo from the Ismailian reign, renamed fifteen streets and squares, and Midan Ismailia became Midan al Tahrir (Liberation Square). In October of the same year, when Sir Ralph Stevenson was Ambassador, the Egyptian government extended the Corniche Road from Helwan to Boulak, widening the Helwan-Cairo road and building a new road between Maadi and al-Madabegh Station straight through the bottom of the Residency's garden and the Residence lost a large chunk of its grounds: the WWII bomb shelter, the swimming pool, and five thousand square metres of lower garden running down to the dockside.

In the progress of Cairo's liberation, some beautiful historical buildings were destroyed, including All Saints Cathedral in Bulaq, the Palace of Suleiman Pasha, and part of the Kasr al-Aini Hospital.

Today the Residence remains a stately, two storied colonial style house set in a spacious area of manicured lawns, sparsely dotted with well-established trees and tidily trimmed hedges. Wrought iron railings and enormous gates, with the emblem of Queen Victoria, open to a sweeping drive that curves its way to the entrance of the Residence—flanked by Kitchener's lions. To the right of the building the original oak tree planted by Lord Cromer's second wife, Kathryn, shades the lawn. Above the windows and doorway are the floral emblems of the British Isles and those of Upper and Lower Egypt, recently replaced in a Millennium project.

The large reception hall is enhanced by parquet flooring in herringbone pattern part protected by enormous oriental carpets. The high ceilings are corniced, and each room is entered under an archivolt portal with pillar reliefs of the Doric order. Two ebony caryatids stand sentry on either side of the portal leading to the back doors that open to a lovely columned veranda.

Twenty enormous windows—ten on either side of the two floors, flank the veranda. Most of the furniture, including the mirrors, was made in the nineteenth and early twentieth centuries.

The Garden Ran Down to the Nile

The rooms have been painted in pale colours, and modern British fabrics have been used in the furnishings. The formal dining-room echoes the past historical and illustrious guests, where crystal chandeliers hang from rosettes over a long and highly polished mahogany table on which stand two silver candelabras.

The table is surrounded by thirty-two black leather chairs enhanced with the gold monogram of Queen Victoria. A French marble topped chiffonier stood against one wall with four magnificent Twenty-Sixth Dynasty canopic jars hewn out of alabaster by some long deceased stonecutter. The lids resemble the heads of ancient Egyptian gods: Anubis the jackal, Qebhsenuf the falcon, Hapi the baboon, and Imsety the son of Horus. Centuries later, presumably in the late 1940s or '50s, the Canopic jars were left for safe keeping by a departing Jewish merchant from Alexandria; where they were to remain in the Residence, until they were given to the British Museum—which never happened.

The canopic jars once held the viscera: lungs, liver, stomach, and intestines of some unknown king or dignitary, and had been relegated to the degradation of enclosing electric light-bulbs that shone through the transparency of the alabaster with diaphanous illumination. Since re-visiting the Residence I found they are no longer defaced with electrical wires and light-bulbs, and now stand pride of place on the fireplace mantle in the main drawing-room.

The Residence is full of the trappings from a former era adorned with decorative *objet de'art* and an overpowering ambiance of renowned visitors and inhabitants long since vanished—like Jones the Butler, who was employed from 1913-14. Jones was a very proper individual who held a strong opinion about women drinking wine, especially unmarried women. Ladies being entertained at the

Residence were astonished when offered wine by their host to find their glasses filled with barley water by the reserved Jones whose solemn expression was such that they dare not complain.

In Lord Cromer's time the staff ate together each day in the large dining-room. Now, behind the vast and gloomy kitchen, suffragi (kitchen staff) waste away their time in the butler's pantry.

The house has gone through many changes since 1883. The magnificent grand ball-room built by Lord Kitchener, has been re-instated, the Chancery is a billiards room, and the Registry a storeroom for papers kept locked behind the same steel door and barred windows. There are now only seven bedrooms, as some have been converted to bathrooms, a dressing room, a maid's flat, and an upstairs dining-room.

In 1980 the Ambassador, Sir Michael Weir, gave a fancy dress New Year's Eve party. We danced to a small orchestra in one of the drawing rooms. The ambience of the surroundings conjured images of formal parties given in years gone by as the room swelled with the ghosts of legendary figures immortalized in time and deed.

Diplomatic life could be very pleasant, especially for those who lived in Maadi, the suburban paradise about twelve miles south of the Cairo. Maadi was the product of careful and detailed planning—a green artificial creation laid out like a Raj hill station where beautiful grandiose villas with manicured lawns and herbaceous borders hinted of chocolate box elegance and Gertrude Jekyll. Acacia and jacaranda trees lined the streets and shaded the courtyards from the soaring afternoon heat; that always imposed a curfew. It was home away from home, and one of the few places that remained almost entirely European—stoically clinging on to an irretrievable era.

Northwest of Cairo is Heliopolis, the City of the Sun, created in 1906-7 by entrepreneur, Baron Edouard Empain, the prodigal son of a Belgian school teacher. Baron Empain connected his city to central Cairo by a tramway. He built a microcosm of Neo-Arabic structures, palatial hotels, a basilica church, and fairy tale structures set on roads with names like Lotus Street and Pyramids Avenue. Still standing in 1979, was the 1920s Luna Park with its rickety wooden roller coaster silhouetted against the skyline. Baron Empain was the creator of a palace widely known as the Barons Folly—a fantasy structure in the style of a Cambodian temple. It still stands on the Airport Road—formerly the Avenue des Palais.

In 1863 on the Island of Gezira, Khedive Ismail had a palace built to accommodate the visit of the Empress Eugénie of France, wife of Napoleon III, on the occasion of the inauguration of the Suez Canal in 1869. The palace sat on the banks of the Nile and was surrounded by an immense park.

Ismail had Eugénie's suite of rooms fitted out in an exact copy of her own apartments in Tuileries. Unfortunately, the Empress only stayed three days. The architecture was a simple Italian style with high windows, flat roofs, and cast-iron columns.

During the royal tour of the Prince and Princess of Wales in 1869, Mrs. Grey, the Princess's personal companion, wrote of the great state dinner given at the Palace by Khedive Ismail: "Driving up through the garden was really like something in fairy-land. It was all lit up with immensely high lamps, with large mat glass-shades, which threw the light down on the brilliant flower-beds. Standing in the outer marble court, with its beautiful Moorish arches and its pillars of a rich brown colour, their bases and capitals profusely and brilliantly decorated. The effect produced was indeed most splendid, and carried one at once back in imagination to one of the scenes you read of in the Arabian Nights."

Many of the rooms retained their original splendour amid the immense oriental gardens. In 1963 the Palace was sequestered by the state under Abdul Nasser, and became the Omar Khayam Hotel. When the hotel went bankrupt, it was hidden behind high shabby fencing. Twenty years later the rot infested Omar Khayam was refurbished, and around the former Palace a new luxury hotel, the Cairo Marriott, was built. The elegant cocktail bar, 'Eugenie's Lounge', is located in the former rooms of the Empress.

Around the palace were vast landscaped gardens abundant with tropical plants, a casino, and an ornamental lake that graced the setting by meandering throughout the garden and past a menagerie of animals and an aviary of rare birds. The old harem building, previously built by Ismail's grandfather, Mohammed Ali, sat at the north of the garden with a lavish fountain between the harem and the newly erected Palace.

Until 1872 there was no bridge to access the Island from mainland Cairo, so the Qasr al-Nil (castle on the Nile) bridge was built. The bridge is recognizable by the two enormous bronze lions that sit either side of the east entrance. In 1892 the Gezira Land Company was formed and the Gezira Palace grounds, now owned by the Land Company, divided the grounds, of which a large part would become the Gezira Sporting Club and the new prestigious residential district known today as Zamalek.

The Palace was then leased and became the Gezira Palace Hotel. In 1896, the hotel was placed under the stewardship of Charles Baehler who immediately upgraded the hotel and opened up the harem—increasing the guestrooms to nearly 400. The harem section of the hotel would eventually become the Baehler Mansions. In 1919 the Hotel had become a liability and was sold off to Habib Lotfallah, a wealthy Syrian, who bought it as a family home only to have it sequestered by President Nasser's regime and returned to a hotel—now called the Omar Khayyam. The casino was destroyed by fire in 1955 and the site is now occupied by All Saint's Cathedral, where my husband and I were married. Next to the cathedral was the small British International School (now gone) that our children attended. The site of the Omar Khayyam Hotel was behind high walls the whole time I was in Cairo as the hotel was again being refurbished and would open in 1983, two years after I left Egypt, as the Cairo Marriott.

In 1906-7, nineteen prestigious villas were built in Zamalek for the occupancy of high ranking British diplomats and Anglo-Egyptian administrators working under the auspices of Britain's most powerful proconsuls, Lord Cromer and Lord Kitchener. Other original tenants were three irrigation engineers who built the first Aswan Dam, and had streets in the area named after them (now renamed). They were: Sir William Wilcocks, Sir Scott Moncrieff, and Sir William Garstin.

These beautiful whitewashed villas, enclosed by high walls, and surrounded by extensive gardens, were built by the architect, Ernest Tatham Richmond, in the late Victorian style—embellished with colonial columns, architrave doorways, and moulded window surrounds. Generous in space and rooms, these grand and stately manors are a visual reminder of Cairo's beaux-arts influence and architectural legacy. With the opening of the Boulak Bridge in July 1912, Zamalek, known then as Gezira, continued to grow as a strictly residential posh community. But, with the rebellion in 1956, real estate prices soared, making it uneconomical for the British government to keep on the enormous villas with their extensive gardens. Various high-ranking Egyptians from the diplomatic realm acquired most of the villas, but the British managed to retain six. Four have now been sold, two of which were razed to the ground to make way for more building-block flats. From the garden of one of the British owned villas, 19 Ibn Zanki Street, I watched a concrete monstrosity being constructed over the historical remains of one of the villas—another layer of Cairo's archaeological past obliterated.

The two villas then remaining were 19 and 20 Ibn Zanki Street. In 1936 the Oriental Secretary, Sir Walter A. Smart, lived at number 19, and the British Consul, David Victor Kelly, lived at number 20. During my residence in Egypt, the First Secretary of the Commercial Department, and the Deputy Head of Mission, occupied Nos. 19 and 20 respectively. Receptions, diplomatic functions, and garden parties were held regularly at both villas.

In 2005 I visited No. 20 and found it exactly as I had remembered—although the trees were distinctly larger. Unfortunately, No. 19 had met its demise in the historical graveyard of Zamalek's belle époque.

The street that ran through Zamalek had lost all recognition as well. The 26th July Street was the main shopping area of the community shaded under lebbek trees where you could find a vast

The Garden Ran Down to the Nile

assortment of shops: butcher, fruit and vegetables, plastic kitchenware, electricians, music and videos. But in 2005 the scene had changed dramatically. Shop fronts had changed to full glass-fronted establishment where high-priced furniture, washing machines and refrigerators were now displayed. Saudi bank buildings with gold Arabic numerals and web-sites crowd the area where a huge ugly fly-over in grey concrete now sores over the once peaceful avenue; an extension of the newly erected bridge. In 1998 the old iron Bulak Bridge was torn down in spite of the conservationists appeals. Officials were accused of corruption and siding with a powerful group of property developers, most of whom were known to be Islamic fundamentalist using their Gulf acquired wealth at the detriment of Cairo's national heritage. From the fly-over you can just see the tops of Baehler Mansions. Charles Baehler would surely turn in his grave if he looked out of the window today.

Formal receptions were a regular occurrence in Cairo, sometimes two a day. There was always an amalgamate of diplomats and their wives, ministers of this and that, dignitaries of various British and Egyptian companies, forgotten names, half-remembered faces and an ample smattering of embassy representatives giving an animated aura to the gatherings.

Nowadays, the uniform of the Foreign Office: black frock coat, stripped trousers, and the old Etonian tie may not exist, but an archaic ambience still flavours the mood derived from a time when Great Britain ruled nearly a third of the world.

The hierarchy within the British Embassy was a complex pattern of aspiring career diplomats. Some were interesting people like one bright young Arabist who worked in the higher echelon of the embassy. He looked as if he had walked out of an F. Scott

Fitzgerald novel. He was a friend of Wilfred Thesinger, had raised and flown falcons in Arabia, and wrote *Falconry in Arabia*. He went on to become an MI6 agent in the counter-terrorism unit and was often referred to as the modern day Lawrence of Arabia.

His dossier reads like a John le Carré espionage novel with names like Megrahi and Gaddafi frequently popping out. Now retired, he was given a Knighthood in 2005.

Some of the wives of the Embassy employees did not always measure up to the genteel opinion of themselves. Within the small circle of expatriates you could always find one or two ladies who assumed a superior air when finding themselves part of the *nouveau élite*.

They had maids to do the housework; bowabs to tend the grounds and gardens, safragis to do the cooking, makwagis to do the washing and ironing, *au pairs* to look after the children and drivers to take them to and from their daily luncheons and mah-jong gatherings. Some of these ladies never ventured outside the realms of the embassy compound and sadly left Egypt never really having seen it.

The amount of gossip and unfounded rumours that were circulated around the ex-pat community was astounding; delicious scandals of infidelity and clandestine liaisons. So-and-so was seen at the Sheraton cocktail lounge with his secretary. Mrs. Jones was having a fling with her tennis instructor. Around the embassy's swimming pool women would discuss the latest hearsay as reputations fell like nine-pins. One must wonder what Lord Cromer's view would have been.

The Garden Ran Down to the Nile

Comer was a very moral man and kept well informed of the conduct of the British community. He was intensely displeased when he heard of a scandal that would threaten to put a slur on the British good name. A straight-laced, dictatorial Victorian gentleman, with a reputation for being blunt, he even objected to the young diplomats of the Agency spending their nights out in what was termed the 'fleshpots of Cairo', and instructed that the iron gates surrounding the Consulate be chained and locked after nightfall.

But scandal was nothing new to the British in Egypt, as even before the turn of the century tittle-tattle could be heard all over town. In the salons of the celebrated hotels or on the terraces of the fashionable clubs—the latest gossip was rife.

When the American, David Garrick Longworth came to Egypt on holiday, he was quick to spot a potentially good business. He stayed on and founded the illustrated social magazine called *The Sphinx*, a combination of the British *Tattler*, and the American *Private Eye*. Longworth reported the social events within the European society, and was never short of a snippet of gossip or hearsay that was picked up in Shepheard's Long Bar, the Turf Club, or the Sphinx Bar—which he himself originated.

Lord Edward Cecil described the Turf Club as a 'pot house' and 'bar': "It is the custom that before dinner every one should have a drink and talk with his friends. I really don't know which is the worse habit of the two. The first injures your nerves and stomach, but the second the reputation and well-being of your friends. I believe that more harm is done in the hall of the Turf Club than in all the other rooms occupied by Englishmen in Cairo."

The Turf Club still exists having survived the riots and fire of Black Saturday. Lord Cromer became a patron of the Turf Club on the condition that there should be no gambling on the premises. However, that condition seems to have been forgotten as card games soon became the vogue. Now the profile is less conventional and the dress code less formal. The attitude is still provincial—although women are allowed as guests of a member for lunch or a drink at the small bar.

European Cairo was not the only place one could find entertainment. The British could enjoy themselves on all levels. Parts of Bulaq in 1905 were seen as evil, with widespread prostitution, and widely available hashish.

Richard Tangye travelled to Egypt in 1884. His appreciation of the Orient was in the antiquities found in the National Museum, also situated in Bulaq at the time. He seems to have held a higher standard of decorum than the Frenchman, Gustave Flaubert, and did not elaborate on the evening's entertainment encountered by his travelling companions: "In the evening some of our party took donkeys and a guide and returned to Bulak to see some of the shows, but the first they visited was of so extraordinary a character they decided to see no more until their taste was educated up or down to the present Egyptian standard."

Three

An Elite Society
▲▲▲

*'All the world passed through Cairo
and the Shepheard's Hotel'*
Anonymous

The famous and celebrated establishment known as Shepheard's Hotel can trace its foundations back to the 9th century when the elaborate estate of Ibn Toulon, the builder of the big mosque, stretched over and beyond the site known today as Ezbekiyeh Gardens.

Toulon's son, Homarowiah, spent his life embellishing the extensive gardens with ornamental trees and flowers. He had pathways paved with mosaic tiles. He built ornamental fountains and rest areas around which rare date palms were cultivated so the fruit could be picked from a sitting position. In time the magnificent gardens disappeared. Then in 1771, the Mameluke ruler, Ali Bey, built a palace for his harem that was later destroyed during the fighting with the Turks. Once again another palace rose from the ashes built by another Mameluke ruler, Elfi Bey. But much was lost during the inundation—when the Nile waters spilled over the land from the Lake of Ez, which formed the Ezbekiyeh.

The Garden Ran Down to the Nile

After the Battle of the Pyramids in 1798, Napoleon Bonaparte commandeered the palace as the Headquarters for his Commander-in-Chief, General Kleber. On 14th June 1800, Kleber met a violent death when he was attacked under a sycamore tree while walking in his garden. The sycamore tree stood next to his headquarters, and from then on it became known as Kleber's Tree. The tree is still standing today.

Ultimately, the palace fell into the hands of Mohamet Ali, who, being concerned with public health, had the lake drained and a new square planted with flowers and numerous shade trees. He refurbished the building and turned it into a school of languages. Mohamet Ali was also responsible for the beginnings of a new road system that would allow the use of wheeled vehicles.

One of Ali's daughters, the infamous Princess Zeinab, eventually became heir and changed the school into a religious institute. It was around 1835, under a Turkish deed—or charitable bequest of the Princess and her family, that Mr. Hill, of Messrs Hill and Raven, agents for the East Indian Overland Route, converted the religious institute to a hotel to accommodate transit passengers to India. In 1841 Mr. Hill employed Samuel Shepheard as manager of his new British Hotel.

The son of a Yeoman Farmer, Samuel Shepheard was born on 21st January 1816 in Preston Capes, Northamptonshire. He had run away to sea at an early age and consequently knew little of running a hotel. But his insight and ability in organising the modest facilities soon became apparent, and it wasn't long before Hill relinquished all his interests in the hotel to Shepheard. The establishment stood in the Frank Quarter of Cairo surrounded by two mosques that gave a very Eastern ambience, amid a homely British sanctuary. The name Shepheard's soon became synonymous with travellers as the only place to stay when in Cairo.

Edwin de Leon, the American Consul in Cairo from 1854 to 1860, remembers Samuel Shepheard as: "A short sturdy, strong-built John Bull of the old type, both in looks and manner, independent and brusque to the very verge of rudeness and often beyond, no respecter of position or of persons, yet geniality and generous impulses, concealing a heart of gold under a rough husk. Ever following the footsteps of mine host was a genuine British Bulldog – dirty white in colour, built on the same model as his master."

John Gadsby stayed at Shepheard's on several occasions and found the hotel equal to any in England and remembered the bulldog: "Good food, good terms and no 'bugs'. . . . The landlord of the hotel had a dog of the bull breed, which used to watch on the steps and keep the donkey boys in check—and he did his work more effectually than half-a-dozen men could have done; for as soon as he was seen trotting down the hall, both donkeys and drivers would scamper away. His name was Toby.
"On my last visit to Egypt I took with me a tolerably thick walking stick, with the form of a bulldog's head, with glass eyes, at the top. This I took because I knew it would amuse the Arabs; and I was not disappointed. In every part of the country the people would press round me to examine it, and pass their remarks, in approving terms, on every part, - mouth, ears, eyes, nose, etc. Many of the boys would run away as soon as they saw it, until they found it was really not alive, though even then they approached it very carefully and timidly; and my donkey boy made dozens of them run away, by

merely holding it up to them and running after them. The donkey boys in Cairo called it Toby."

In 1850 Samuel Shepheard moved the British Hotel from the Tewfikieh Quarter to the site overlooking the Ezbekiyeh Square—where it became Shepheard's Hotel. The hotel became more like a barracks during the Crimean and Boar Wars. British officers of all rank stopped at the hotel on their way to or returning from India as Shepheard held a contract for supplying the regiments with food and drink.

As the number of tourists coming to Egypt increased each year, so did Shepheard's reputation for comfort and luxury. The hotel was well known to cosmopolitan travellers as the starting point for the desert, the Nile, and Palestine.

At the height of its prosperity in 1857, a correspondent of the Illustrated London News described the hotel: "Shepheard's Hotel has been long known as the fashionable resort of the Egyptian tourist as well as the great halting place for the Indian passenger *en route* for our great Eastern possessions. Perhaps in no hotel in the world do you find such an assembly of the people of rank and fashion from all countries as are found daily setting down to the *table d'hotel* in the great salon of this establishment."

At the turn of the century, Shepheard's boasted a balcony where fashionable clientèle could take afternoon tea, listen to a brass band, and watch the panorama of Oriental life pass by. It was within walking distance of the British Agency, Thomas Cook Tours, All Saints English Church, and the Opera House. There were gardens where pelicans roamed freely about the palms, fancy dress balls were held at the height of the season, and evening dress was required at late night dinner. Galabehya clad attendants stood on watch in the passageways ready to see to the comforts of the guests.

From the famous balcony there could be seen a unique and colourful flow of Circassian in brightly coloured costumes, Bedouin Arabs leading long trains of camels, Pashas in bejewelled turbans, merchants on small donkeys, and tattooed Negro's. African slaves merged with mysterious veiled figures in sedan chairs. Turks rode by on Arabian horses with richly clad saddlecloths of gold embroidery. Jugglers and snake charmers intermixed with Europeans in pith helmets and ladies with small corseted waistlines.

Formal balls were regularly given at all the best hotels around the city. Lord Edward Cecil notes that the smartest balls were held at the: "Savoy and Semiramis, followed by the Ghezira, Shepheard's and Heliopolis, and last of all, the Continental," which was frequented by the Pasha's entourage. During the five-month season, the Semiramis held regular daily concerts—and a military band could be enjoyed on the terrace of Shepheard's every Saturday afternoon. There were rumours of young ladies dressed in evening attire shooting down the wide staircase of one of the hotels—seated on large silver serving trays.

Eustace Reynolds-Ball writes of the opinions at the time: "The official balls and receptions at the Khedivial Palace or the British Agency are functions which demand more than an incidental notice. The British Agent gives at least a couple of large balls during the season, and the same hospitality is offered by the Khedive. In addition to these official entertainments, several important semi-official dances are given by the British officers quartered at Cairo.

The invitations to the Khedive's ball are invariably sent to the foreign visitors through their Ministers or Consuls; and as everybody in Cairo seems to regard a ticket almost as a right, there is occasionally a certain amount of friction between the accredited representatives of the different Powers and the Khedive's officers."

Young unmarried ladies accompanied by their mothers, flocked to the city during the season to the delight of the unattached officers. These romantically inclined young ladies came with marriage on their minds, and were known locally as 'the fishing fleet'.

Mabel Caillard would come down to Cairo from Alexandria during the party season and remembers one handsome officer: "The regimental dances, that were a feature of the Cairo season . . . I remember being told at a dance given by the Connaught Rangers at Kasr-el-Nil that the floor on which we were disporting ourselves was hardly expected to last out the evening! . . . a prancing energetic officer of the Seaforth Highlanders always entailed repairs in the cloakroom, where one would meet a train of fellow victims, with innumerable yards of flounces between them, waiting their turn to have their damaged furbelows sewn on by the patient attendant. All were agreed that the young man in question was far too handsome to forgo a dance with him on that account."

Activities available to the European community were numerous. The Mena House gave small dances from time to time, and there were gymkhanas held on the racecourse at the Gezira Sporting Club. At the Residence there were always dances, fêtes, charity balls, and tea parties. Today: buffets, cocktail parties, luncheons, and dinners for up to 500 are given—as well as television interviews, lectures, and concerts. The garden can accommodate 2000 people for fêtes, although now it tends to be charity bazaars that are held once a year.

When Britain became a member of the League of Nations in 1922, relinquishing her hold on diplomatic affairs, the Capitulations were abolished, and in 1936 the Agency became an Embassy. The High Commissioner, Sir Miles Lampson became Ambassador—the pro-eminence of Britain's diplomatic representation. He headed the only Embassy in Egypt at that time—as all other countries had legations or consulates headed by diplomatic ministers or consuls, respectively.

In 1849 Samuel Shepheard had the foresight to record the names of the hotel's guests in a large leather bound Visitor's Book. The visitors left their signatures, nationalities, and if applicable, the name of the ship they were sailing on. Some of the guests recorded compliments and humorous remarks. Accompanying this was another, more luxuriously bound book embossed in gold leaf with gilt edges and tiny padlock in which Royalty signed their names. The two books were referred to as the *'Golden Books'* and were to become one of the most famous records in the history of hotel keeping— until they were destroyed by fire in the uprisings of 1952.

The books were kept in a massive Chubb safe and remained intact as the hotel burnt to the ground around it. But the disaster came after the fire was put out—when the order was given that under no circumstance was the safe to be opened until it had cooled down. Unfortunately, the order was either misunderstood, or the guests were anxious to maintain their possessions. The safe was opened when still red hot letting in a swift rush of air which ignited the books and instantly turned them into a pile of ashes.

Among the numerous famous personage of Europe recorded in the books were: Florence Nightingale, Amelia B. Edwards, Winston Churchill, General Gordon, the Aga Khan, Edward VIII, Rudyard Kipling, Lord Kitchener, the Empress Eugenie, Theophile Gautier, H.M. Stanley, Mark Twain, Theodore Roosevelt, Gertrude Bell, Bernard Shaw, Sir Richard Burton, Frederick Peake, King Farouk, Mary Pickford, Douglas Fairbanks, and Noel Coward—to name but a few.

In 1861 Samuel Shepheard retired at the early age of forty. He had amassed a small fortune and wanted a quiet life with his family back in England. The hotel was sold to a Bavarian, M. Philip Zech for £10,000 and shortly after, in 1863, Ezbekiyeh Square was renamed Ezbekiyeh Gardens by Said Pasha, who had the gardens replanted and improved with grottoes, fountains, and cafes.

When the hotel was partially destroyed by fire in 1869, it was once again rebuilt with various improvements. Another storey was added, and two small sphinxes taken from the Temple of Seraphis at Memphis, now flanked the front doorway. A year later the chief gardener to the city of Paris, Monsieur Barilet, laid out the newly planned Ezbekiyeh Gardens. Two thousand five hundred jets of gas, in tulip-shaped glasses, lighted the gardens that were opened every evening, where music and plays were performed in a small theatre.

Amelia B. Edwards sang the praises of Shepheard's Hotel in the first line of her famous book, *A Thousand Miles Up The Nile*: "It

The Garden Ran Down to the Nile

is the traveller's lot to dine at many table-d' hotels in the course of many wanderings, but seldom befalls him to make one of a more miscellaneous gatherings than that which overfills the great dining room at Shepheard's Hotel in Cairo during the beginning and height of the regular season. Here assemble daily some two to three hundred persons of all ranks, nationalities, and pursuits; half of whom are Anglo-Indians homeward or outward bound, European residents, or visitors established in Cairo for the winter. The other half, it may be taken for granted, are going up the Nile."

Shepheard's was indeed the rendezvous of the famous. Before the First World War the hotel was known as the playground of international aristocracy. Charles Dudley Warner described it as: ". . . a caravansary through which the world flows. . . .one would be more Orientally surrounded and better cared for at the Hotel du Nil; and the Khedive, who tries his hand at everything, has set up a New Hotel on the public square; but, somehow one enters Shepheard's as easy as he goes into a city gate."

By 1876 the hotel had been surrounded by unfinished houses and a conspicuous foreground of patient donkeys—the cabs of Cairo, that were permanently stabled amidst the promenading passers-by awaiting enthusiastic tourists. On one side of the hotel was the house belonging to the Khedive's mother, where ambling ostriches roamed unrestricted and shutters were always closed to obscure the harem. To the back of the hotel there was a dusty palm grove where a creaking sakieh was rotated by a lethargic cow—a complete contrast to the pelicans that strolled freely in the tropical gardens of the adjacent hotel.

The Garden Ran Down to the Nile

The hotel was completely rebuilt again in 1891 by Philip Zech, who enlarged it to accommodate many more guests. It was all done in the record time of five months. A private generating plant was installed and Shepheard's became the first hotel in the Middle East to have electric lights. Luxury and refinement in the form of lifts, telephones, and a tennis court were added, and it was often compared to the Cecil or the Savoy in London.

The electric bell was now preferred to the old method of summoning attendants by the clapping of hands. Elegantly appointed private apartments made Shepheard's a first-class residential hotel that was patronised by Americans, British, and Anglo-Indians. With 180 bathrooms—the sanitation was beyond reproach. There was an elegant garden where one could sit protected from the noise of the streets, a telegraph office, a restaurant, a grand ballroom, and the famous Long Bar where in 1913-14 stories of espionage were the order of the day.

The managing director's office now stood on the site next to the sycamore tree, where General Kléber had been assassinated. The hotel was open all year round, but now the terrace looked down upon a rather different procession of pushing and shouting guides and porters, donkey boys, and dragomen. Loud, uncouth Australian soldiers had replaced the Victorian gentlemen. Yet the charm remained and the hotel ranked as one of the most splendid of the day.

In 1908 Lance Thackeray enjoyed sitting on the balcony taking in the spectacle of the street below: "No one could desire a more delightful way of spending an hour than to sit on the balcony of Shepheard's Hotel and watch the curious crowd of natives who decorate the front in every imaginable costume of Egypt. It is unique, and gives a character to this 'old-established and polished hotel' which you might search for in vain elsewhere. Millions of piasters must have passed through its balcony railings in exchange for the various articles which the natives hawk in the street below. Shawls, beads, scarabs, fly-whisks, stuffed snakes and crocodiles, and many other charms and horrors, are here bargained for and bought to decorate or disfigure our Western homes. The juggler who is allowed to go through his old-fashioned tricks on the balcony, the boy with the monkey who is pushed on by the 'comic' policeman, the quiet calm-faced Hindoo who will tell your fortune and take some of it, the prosperous looking Dragomans, the picturesque Bedouin Arab, and the scarlet-skirted syrup-seller represent but a few of the types who make up this interesting crowd."

Harry Boyle, Oriental Secretary to the British Agency in Cairo, was sitting on the veranda of Shepheard's Hotel one day when he noticed at another table, Sir Thomas Lipton, of Lipton Tea fame. Lipton had been bothering him for weeks about a post for his nephew. At that precise moment, an American tourist who had been watching Boyle for some time, and taking him to be the hotel 'pimp', advanced to ask whether he would introduce him to a 'personable young man' and pressing 2/6d into his hand. Boyle immediately saw the chance for revenge and pointing to Sir Thomas, said: "I am off duty at the moment, but that gentleman over there is now carrying on my work; you had better address yourself to him. Remember, even we pimps have our pride."

While the American approached Sir Thomas, Boyle quietly disappeared to watch the proceedings a little ways away: "With a growl this extremely virile Englishman flung himself upon his unfortunate victim, knocked him down, and pummelled him to pulp, until the *Maitre d'Hotel* himself came to the rescue. Both the American and Sir Thomas were equally bewildered and the tourist had no chance to explain matters."

Eustace Reynolds-Ball remembers Shepheard's after Philip Zech had refurbished it: "The historical Shepheard's has a world-wide reputation. It must, however, be remembered that not a stone remains of the old Shepheard's with its world-renowned balcony, its lofty rooms, and terraces. The new Shepheard's, completely rebuilt in 1891, lacks there historical adjuncts; but the high reputation for comfort remains, and certainly, in point of luxury and refinements of civilisation, in the form of electric lights, lifts, telephones, etc., there can be no comparison."

In 1885 Elizabeth Butler found the terrace of Shepheard's Hotel an impressive glimpse of the vanishing past: "It takes two or three days to rid oneself of the idea that the streets are parading their colours and movement and their endless variety of Oriental types and costumes for your diversion only, on an open-air stage. To sit on the low shady terrace of the old Shepheard's hotel under the acacias and watch the pageant of the street below was to me an endless delight. The very incongruity of the drama unrolling itself before one's eyes had a charm of its own.

"About 5:30 p.m. weird music and flaring torches brings us out again on the terrace, and we see a tumultuous crowd of pilgrims just arrived from Mecca by the five o'clock Suez train. They gather the crowd by their unearthly din and sweep it along with them.

The Garden Ran Down to the Nile

Beggars, flower-sellers, snake-charmers, tourists, and touts are all rolling along in a continuous buzz of various noises. Perhaps the full escort of cavalry jingles past our point of observation and the native crowd salutes the Khedive. Not so the British officers on the terrace, who keep their seats."

Charles Baehler, an accountant from Thoune, Switzerland, now replaced Philip Zech as manager; although the hotel would pass into the ownership of the International Sleeping Car Company on the death of Zech. Baehler brought more fame and fortune to Shepheard's and he was soon to be known as the Hotel King and undisputed Hospitality Czar. The Golden Age of Egypt had begun.

Baehler was a handsome man, six foot 6 inches tall, innovative and ambitious. Born in Switzerland, he had worked as a greengrocer's assistant, and later as an apprentice in the Commercial Bank at Basle. His hotel career began in 1889 and lasted fifty years.

In 1897 he acquired the controlling interest of the Egyptian Hotels Limited, which included: the Semiramis, the Shepheard's (both of which he enlarged), and the Gezira Palace (enlarged twice in his lifetime). In 1904 he founded the Upper Egyptian Hotels Limited, built the Winter Palace and the Karnak in Luxor and the Grand, the Savoy, and the Cataract Hotel in Aswan.

Amongst Baehler's many other accomplishments, was the King David Hotel in Jerusalem, and the Baehler Buildings overlooking Talaat Harb Square, which replaced the once famous Savoy Hotel in the heart of downtown Cairo. He used the land on Gezira Island in Zamalek, that had once been the harem of the Omar Khayam, where he built a large block of flats known as the Baehler Apartments. In 1907 he formed the Electric Light and

Power Supply Company to feed electricity to the Gezira Island and the outlying districts of Cairo. He enlarged Shepheard's Hotel twice during his lifetime.

Another remarkable hotelier just as renowned as Charles Baehler, and probably his greatest competitor, was George Nungovich, a Greek Cypriot who in 1883 had started work as a porter for the Cairo railway. He joined the British Army in its first Sudanese campaign, as a caterer, and returned to Cairo after saving enough money to purchase a building situated in the Ismailia Quarter of the city, which he called D'Angleterre. He turned the D'Angleterre into a first-class hotel boasting, 'approved sanitary principles', and combining every modern comfort—electric lights, hydraulic lifts, and saloons.

His hotel was so successful with British officers that he soon found himself branching out. He established the George Nungovich Hotels Company in 1897, and converted some palatial buildings that had belonged to the Turkish Princess, Toussoun, into the resplendent Savoy Hotel—which opened on St. Andrews Day, 28th November 1897.

The Savoy was reputedly patronised by crowned heads, Royals, and other distinguished personages. It boasted to be the finest and most luxurious hotel in Egypt with fireplaces in every room. The hotel was located on Sharia Kasr el Nil shaded by lebbek trees and surrounded by the villas of officials and diplomats. He built the Grand Hotel, and the Hotel Des Baines in the health resort of Helouan, the Victoria Hotel in Ismailia on the Suez Canal, and the Grand Continental in the Ismailia Quarter of Cairo—that was also patronized by Royals and the elite of British society.

The Continental offered every modern comfort; two large verandas, winter gardens, drawing rooms, lady's salon, reading, smoking, and billiards rooms. There were twenty-four private suites, each having a separate staircase, and a French restaurant and grillroom with excellent cuisine. The hotel had one of the first hydraulic lifts, and arrangements could be made for electric lights.

A popular saying of the day, which was generated by the manager of the Savoy, Auguste Wild, described the four top hotels in Cairo as: 'Propriety, Society, Sobriety, Notoriety,' referring to the Continental, D'Angleterre, the Savoy, and Shepheard's, respectively. Egyptologists and scholars who preferred seclusion in oriental surroundings, rather than the gay society life, stayed at the Hotel de Nil. Around 1898 Egypt was a formidable rival to the Riviera with its affable climate, social amenities, and commodities of every kind. The country was at the height of popularity as a winter resort, rich and prosperous, having a large assemblage of English, French, and European residents. It was a time when men were courteous, ladies were gracious, and protocol was observed.

In 1908, while residing at his hotel, the San Stefano in Alexandria, George Nungovich suffered a stroke and died at the early age of fifty-two. Hundreds of mourners gathered outside the Hotel D'Angleterre in Cairo to pay their last respects. At the gravesite the pall-bearers were Landaur, the manager of the Grand Continental, Herrling, manager of the D'Angleterre, Klingler, of the

Mena House, and Auguste Wild, of the Savoy—who would become manager of the Nungovich Hotels Company

In 1925, under the Egyptian Hotels Ltd., Charles Baehler agreed to manage the George Nungovich Group; the Continental, the Mena House, and the Helwan de Bains. Charles Baehler now owned, or controlled, most of the hotels in Egypt at the time.

In 1969 James Aldridge had difficulty in reliving the Golden Age of Protocol: "The society hotels then were the British colonial hotels like Shepheard's and the Continental-Savoy. Old Shepheard's is a grave, but anyone who remembers the pre-war Continental-Savoy might weep now to see its famous terraces built over with arcades of tourist shops. The dusty old courtyard behind it, and its pleasant garden, have been filled in with a cheap shopping centre, and you can no longer enjoy tea in the wicker chairs of the wide salons because there aren't any salons. If you want tea in the Continental-Savoy now you have to sit somewhere behind the entrance hall and survive the non-stop TV."

The new Shepheard's Hotel evokes the same kind of feeling. Standing a block away from the British Residence, the new Shepheard's is a mundane grey building, unimaginative in design and lacking in everything but the name—including the apostrophe. There are no big stone baths, no Renaissance-style dining room, and no famous Long Bar. Mansour's elegant jewellery shop is a faded memory, and the pelicans have long since disappeared from the garden that no longer exists. Probably the most lamentable—there is no terrace overlooking the heartbeat of Cairo—no parade of local humanity to entertain. Now in the cool interior of the dining room you look through large archivolt windows onto the noise and dust of the traffic of the Corniche and into a phlegmatic reality.

"Shepheard's left behind him a name that is identified with Egypt and with Cairo as closely as it would have been had its owner built a pyramid." Edwin de Leon.

In 2005, and again in 2007, I stayed at the Winsor Hotel at 3 Alfi Bey Street across from where the old Shepheard's Hotel once stood. The Windsor is one of the few original hotels in the city that was spared from the fires of 1952 as they raged throughout Cairo.

The hotel was purchased by Mr. William Doss in 1962, after his family's cotton industry was confiscated by the government following the Revolution in the 1950s. The hotel remains trapped in an unchanged environment of eclectic furniture and paraphernalia from a past era. Vintage Swiss posters of Alpine skiing holidays decorate the walls surrounding the wooden staircase that creaks and wraps itself around an original iron gated Schindler lift that jumps and groans its way up. It was a press to get in more than two people in at a time, including the young boy who manually operated it, and his attempts at stopping at the precise level was a gamble, but usually managed within a few inches either side of the attempted floor. The luggage came up separately. In the breakfast room hung a large framed canvas of an undeterminable subject, burnt black from the fires of black Saturday when it had originally hung in Shepheard's Hotel; as the brass plaque below it testified.

The Art Nouveau glass canopy that was once the entrance to the Parisiana Café, now graces the entrance to the hotel and the front desk retains the illusion with its Bakelite switchboard, outdated maps, and wooden pigeon-holed key-holder. The Barrel

The Garden Ran Down to the Nile

Lounge and the bedroom furnishings have not changed since William Doss bought the hotel and for me, it was a joy to lose myself in a past era.

One of the finest and loveliest hotels in Cairo is the Mena House. It sits at the foot of the Great Pyramid and at one time was surrounded by desert. The Mena House started life as a hunting lodge and rest house for Khedive Ismail. When arriving in Cairo his guests would traverse the Nile by ferry, to be transported on donkeys—sometimes for many miles, as canals and flooded areas of land had to be avoided. When the canals were shallow enough for crossing, the guests would be born upon the shoulders of the guides and then back on the donkeys to the hunting lodge.

In the early 1880s the lodge was sold to a wealthy young couple, Mr. and Mrs. Frederick Head, who had moved to Egypt for the dry and sunny climate because of Frederick Head's delicate health, and used it as a residence. The Heads built a second floor to their new residence, and entertaining their guests on their dahabeyah while the work was in progress. It was one of their guests, Professor A.H. Saya, who suggested the name Mena House—after the first King of Egypt.

Mrs Head started a kindergarten for young Arab children, teaching them basic subjects, and playing the piano for them. Five years later, on a visit to London, Frederick Head died, and Mena House was sold to Hugh Fortescue Locke-King, a fabulously wealthy land owner in England whose land stretched from Weybridge to Portsmouth. He was thirty-eight years of age when he married Ethel, just eighteen. Her father had been Governor of New

The Garden Ran Down to the Nile

South Wales, and later of New Zealand, where she grew up at Government House.

Hugh Locke-King was also of delicate health, and had been advised to winter in Egypt. Ethel loved Egypt and decided to transform the house into a luxury hotel, and the house was enlarged for the second time. Ethel, sympathetic in her refurbishment, retained the Oriental design in the architecture and kept the existing fittings of the Khedive, and of the Heads. She added great wood burning fireplaces and purchased original balconies of exquisite meshrabeya latticework; which still remain today, covering most of the hotel's facade.

The Locke-Kings purchased furniture inlaid with ivory and mother-of-pearl, Islamic brass lamps, which they hung from the domed ceilings, arabesque screens, beautiful blue tiles, mosaics, and heavily carved-wooden doors. In each bedroom there were French doors leading to a balcony where guests could enjoy breakfast in the open air—with a view of the Great Pyramid. Money was no object to the extravagant Locke-Kings, yet despite all the wealthy guests, Mena House was run at a loss. When time came to pay the bill, the visitors were usually told that they had been invited as their guests.

A.B. DeGuerville romanticizes on the Mena House: "At the tea-hour its terraces are crowded with a gay and brilliant throng. The large and comfortable salons, the delicious Moorish dining-room, the excellent food, the open-air swimming bath, the golf course, the tennis-courts, the croquet lawns, all go to make a stay at Mena House one of the most pleasant incidents of a trip to Egypt. The stables are excellent, and the charges reasonable. Carriages, hacks, donkeys, camels, and sand-carts . . . means many a pleasant excursion can be make into the Desert. There are often at Mena House sporting meetings, which are very popular. The camel races are particularly amusing.

"It is by moonlight that a stroll in the Desert is so charming when the Sphinx and Pyramids rise mysteriously from out the Desert."

To give themselves more freedom, the Locke-Kings engaged Baron de Rodakowski, a Polish friend, 'to see to things'. The Baron was quite a character. He used to drive to Cairo from Mena House in a dogcart pulled by a grey Arab pony that would make the eight-mile journey in less than a record forty minutes. Rodakowski, along with Swiss architect, Mr. Brugger, built stables, a villa, a stand for gymkhana's, and the famous marble swimming pool.

After the First World War, and the death of Hugh Locke-King, Ethel continued to hold the controlling interest in Mena House during the seven years that Baron Rodakowsky was there. When the Baron left, his responsibility was passed on to Mr. Schick and Mr. Weckel, before Ethel Locke-King finally sold the hotel to George Nungovich.

Evelyn Waugh and his wife stayed at Mena House in 1928 as part of a convalescent Grand Tour. His wife confesses that during her husband's recovery, she spent much of her time in the pool admiring the antics of a "splendid Negro swimming instructor."

In 1900 the *'Egyptian Gazette'* published an amusing snippet about a duel that had ostensibly taken place at the Mena House: "A duel, was lately fought between Alexander Shott and John S. Nott. Nott was shot and Shott was not. In this case it is better to be Shott than Nott. There was a rumour that Nott was not shot, and Shott avows that he shot Nott, which proves either that the shot Shott shot at Nott was not shot, or that Nott was shot. Notwithstanding, circumstantial evidence is not always good.

"It may be made to appear on trial that the shot Shott shot, shot Nott, or, as accidents with firearms are frequent, it may be possible that the shot Shott shot, shot Shott himself, when the affair would resolve itself into its original elements, and Shott would be shot, and Nott would not. We think, however, that the shot Shott shot, shot not Shott but Nott. Anyway, it's hard to tell who was shot and who was not."

During the First World War, Mena House, like Shepheard's Hotel, was filled with servicemen. Mena House became the Allied army headquarters with the Australian Light Horse regiment established in camps behind the hotel, and the hotel itself became a hospital. After the Great War a new wing was added, and the hotel saw many interesting guests, like Charlie Chaplin—who wrote one of his film scripts while staying there.

The Second World War also saw the hotel filled with servicemen and nurses. Unlike Shepheard's, Mena House was not restricted to officers, so the Australians came back, and gradually the hotel became so overcrowded, that more staff had to be engaged. In Cairo, the streets, bazaars, and cinemas were filled with soldiers, and it was virtually impossible to get a room anywhere.

The year 1943 saw the plans for 'Overlord,' the invasion of Europe. Churchill, Roosevelt, and Stalin held 'The Big Three' conference at the Mena House. Everything was heavily guarded. There was even an R.A.F. observation post on top of the Great Pyramid. The guests were given a three day notice to vacate the hotel; with only one elderly couple being allowed to stay on because of the man's ill health. Bedrooms were turned into offices and precious antiques and furniture had to be wrapped and put away—yet not one single item or piece of furniture was damaged.

In 1978, Mena House once again hosted negotiations when Presidents Anwar Sadat, Jimmy Carter, and Menachen Begin, held 'Peace Talks'.

Mena House is not only one of the most luxurious and famous hotels in Egypt, but also one of a very few original hotels that survived the fires of Black Saturday—when the camel drivers and peddlers begged the rioting gangs not to ruin their livelihood.

The hotel is now owned by the Indian Oberoi Hotels, and several million dollars have been spent on expansion and renovations to bring the hotel up to international standards. The original building has been preserved—though much of it was gutted. The kitchens have been totally redesigned with the most up to date equipment. The famous front terrace now comprises two floors; the foyer below and the coffee shop above. There's a new nightclub in addition to the old one, the walls of the public rooms have been faced with white marble, and a bust of Khedive Ismail sits pride of place in the foyer.

The Arabesque surroundings and Moorish vaulted ceiling still remain, and the antique lamps, meshrabeya screens, and wooden doors are still there. The staircase has been re-carpeted, and the mother-of-pearl inlaid furniture restored. The exquisite Louis XVI carved mahogany mantle-piece—supported on the heads of two beautiful caryatids, now stands in one of the private dining rooms. Many of these pieces had survived the nightclub fire of 1964.

Outside—the old marble swimming pool has been replaced with a large oval shaped pool where you can lay on your back and look up at the Great Pyramid. Beside the poolside lounge surrounded by bougainvillea, there is a large grassed area for sunbathing and an outdoor bar and barbecue area where you can relax under palm trees by day and fairy lights by night.

Unfortunately, the beautiful meshrabeya wood panels and doors throughout the hotel have been painted gold—giving a cheap, garish Saudi Arabian feel.

During the 17th century, Sheik Es Sinhaimi, interconnected two antiquated buildings of the sixteenth and seventeenth centuries, known as the Beit El Kritlia (House of the Cretans). The buildings have survived from the late Mameluke period and have direct access to the east entrance of the Ibn Tulon Mosque. They were rescued by the Committee for the Preservation of Arab Monuments and restored by an Englishman, Major Gayer-Anderson, who had lived in Cairo since 1907, first on secondment to the Egyptian army and later as British Oriental Secretary.

The Committee allowed Gayer-Anderson to live in the houses, which were restored by him in 1935. Gayer-Anderson was a fervent collector of Ottoman period antiques and filled the houses, known as the Gayer-Anderson Houses—with authentic Oriental furniture and acquisitions representing various other periods. The windows are meshrabeya—as are the screens that surround the galleries. In the main reception room a sunken fountain bubbles over mosaic tiles. There are Turkish rugs, brass lamps and a tiny staircase that twists itself up to the roof-garden with more meshrabeya and an ancient birthing-chair. The houses and roof-garden were used in the 1977 James Bond film, 'The Spy Who Loved Me'.

When Gayer-Anderson died in 1942, he left the bulk of his collection to the Egyptian government, with the exception of a statue—a black basalt cat with a gold ring through its nose. The cat now lives in the Egyptian Hall in the British Museum.

Four

The Pyramids of Ghiza

'All things dread time; but time itself dreads the Pyramids'
Abdel Latif

Thousands of people throughout history have written and romanticized about the Pyramids of Ghiza—their size, their beauty, the reason for them, and how and who built them. To say they are impressive is an understatement. But you cannot look at the Pyramids without a preconception of all the knowledge they are associated with and it is difficult to grasp their history and their enormity, and only with repeated visits can you fully start to appreciate them. Recognized as the first of the Seven Wonders of the Ancient World, the Pyramids are the last remaining.

Khufu, Khafre, and Menkura—more widely known by their Greek names—Cheops, Chephren, and Mycerinos were built 4,500 years ago in the fourth Dynasty. The precision that went into the building of them has not been matched to this day. It took 100,000 men twenty years to build Khufu, the Great Pyramid—and ten years to build the causeway for the conveyance of the stones which, according to Herodotus, was half a mile in length, sixty feet wide, and forty-eight feet at its highest point. Originally 481 feet high (before having lost its 30 foot top), Khufu could claim to be the tallest building in the world until the 19th century—a 4,500 year record.

Regarding them it becomes evident that they were not built by starving slave gangs whipped along by tyrannical masters, as some would have us believe. Egypt was not a slave society. The Ancient Egyptians did not believe in damnation. Herodotus wrote that the pyramids were built not by slaves, but men with purpose and a desire to fulfil what they believed would bring them favour with their Pharaoh, and thus, life ever after.

The government of that time used a huge work force of state employed fellahin that worked three months at a time during the inundation—when the God Osiris flooded the land. Herodotus recounts that 1,600 talents of silver—just over £5 million at today's scrap silver price, was expended on feeding, clothing, tools, and the housing of the labourers.

Recorded in hieroglyphics on the outer casing of the Great Pyramid were the number of onions, garlics and radishes that were provided for the workers. Unfortunately, in 1179 the limestone casing was stripped away by Saladin in order to build the Citadel—thus making the claim impossible to verify the account.

In the twelfth century, an Arab physician, Abd-el-Atif, described the casing stones: "Their adjustment is so precise that not even a needle or a hair can be inserted between any two of them. They are lined by a cement laid on to the thickness of a sheet of paper. These stones are covered with writing in that secret character whose import is at this day wholly unknown. These inscriptions are

The Garden Ran Down to the Nile

so multitudinous, that if only those which are seen on the surface of these two Pyramids were copied upon paper, more than ten thousand books would be filled with them."

Khafre, Khufu's son, built his pyramid on higher ground, giving the illusion that it is larger than Khufu's. In fact it is only 447½ feet high. To me, Khafre's is the most beautiful of the pyramids as the apex is still partially faced with Tura limestone—leaving one to imagine how these great monuments must have blazed in the radiance of the sun, and shown like snow-capped mountains under the illumination of moonlight.

Menkura was the son of Khafre, grandson of Khufu, and the builder of the third pyramid. Menkura rises just 204 feet high, less than half the height of the Great Pyramid. There are three smaller subsidiary pyramids at the foot of Menkura—presumed for his wives.

In the early 1840s, Sophia Poole was struck with the sheer size of the pyramids having approached them with an unobstructed view for over six miles: "The illusion so general in the East with regard to distance, occasioned by the extraordinary clearness of the atmosphere, is strikingly demonstrated in approaching the pyramids; it is very remarkable that the nearer we approached the objects of our destination, the less grand and imposing did they appear. From their aspect, as I first drew near to them, I should have formed a very inadequate idea of their dimensions. As soon as we had crossed the river they appeared within a mile of us. At this season it occupies three hours to reach the pyramids from Cairo, and this month, on account of its coolness, is particularly agreeable for such an excursion.

"As soon as possible after our arrival, we mounted the rock on which the pyramids are built. The general view from the rocky eminence on which they are built is the most imposing that can be conceived."

In 1847 Cairo still did not have the convenience of roads or bridges spanning the Nile, so when John Gadsby made his visit to the pyramids he had to hire a boat as well as a donkey: "The distance from Cairo to the pyramids, is about 8 miles. Passing through Old Cairo, we reached the Nile, nearly opposite Rhoda Island. Here we hire a boat, into which our donkeys were lifted by the legs, and we followed.

"Again we were on our donkeys, the pyramids being about 6 miles farther on. Passing several lots of pigsties, miscalled villages, enriched, however, by groves of palm trees, we came to what appeared to be a lake. While wondering how to cross it, 2 or 3 six-foot Arabs came up, and, taking us on their shoulders, quickly carried us over. Our donkeys made a regular bath of it. This lake was caused by the overflowing of the river, the water not having yet evaporated. At some seasons of the year, boats have to be used, while at others the waters are quite dried up.

"At last I began to be unmistakably conscious that I was approaching the objects of our visit. But we were yet nearly three miles off. They can indeed be seen at a distance of 30 miles. Another hour, and we stood at their base, when, casting my eyes to the right, to the left, and above, I was dumb with wonder. My companions and I were soon surrounded by clamorous Arabs, anxious to conduct us to the top. The behaviour of these men is, indeed, a great drawback to the pleasure of the trip, as neither money nor threats will induce them to let you alone. No sooner had I made known my resolve than two Arabs seized hold of me as though I had been a felon. One grappled my right wrist, and another my left, holding me as firmly as if I had been in a vice. The Arabs skipped up the steps like goats. In about ten minutes we reached a resting place, and glad enough I was, for the perspiration poured off me. Here the Arabs began to call out, 'Halff way! Bucksheesh, bucksheesh'; for that disease of the country is sure to manifest itself; but as I had been particularly cautioned about this, that the more I gave the more they would demand, I positively refused to give them a single farthing, until again on terra firma. In an instant they again took hold of me, and, without a word, bounding like rubber balls, conducted me to the top. They knew that if I told the sheikh how they had annoyed me, they would everyone have been bastinadoed. I therefore promised not to tell, when they skipped about the top of the pyramids like kids, and said no more about bucksheesh."

By 1888 a trip to the pyramids was getting easier. Murray's Handbook says that: "The excursion to the Pyramids is no longer what it used to be. Carriages, a bridge over the Nile, and a macadamised road, have superseded donkeys, the ferry at Geezeh, and the tortuous dusty footpath."

When Khedive Ismail built the Shari al-Ahram, the Pyramids Road, it was no longer necessary to go miles out of the way to avoid the canals and fields submerged under water by the inundation. The excursion to the pyramids would start about eight-thirty in the morning from the Ezbekiyeh, where a carriage could be hired for about sixteen shillings. The newly constructed road was built so the Empress Eugene could ride in comfort to the pyramids. It crossed the principle canals over stone bridges and continued along in a straight line, flanked by acacia trees. Flocks of ibis and waterfowl would alight on the broad sheets of water that covered the cultivated land on either side. Arriving at the base of the Great Pyramid in about one and-a-half hours, would leave enough time to ascend to the summit and visit the interior before lunching at the recently opened Mena House Hotel. The afternoon would be spent visiting the other two pyramids, the Sphinx, and the tombs. There was a regular tariff of two shillings that was paid to the sheikh of the nearby village, Kafr al-Ahram, whose men served as guides to the tourists.

By 1914 one could ride on the electric tramway (number 14, the Red Pyramids Line) from Boulak to the Mena House. The tram crossed the Boulak Bridge, a 300 yard long iron hydraulically lifted bridge, built during 1909-1912 by the son of Gustave Eiffel, of French tower fame. Folklore tells that on the bridge's completion it failed to open and Eiffel was so distraught that he threw himself from the railings into the Nile and was drowned. If in fact this is a true story, Eiffel took his life in vain, for each day between 12:00 a.m. to 12:45 a.m., and 3:00 p.m. to 3:45 p.m., the bridge was lifted to let passing ships through. After the nationalization of the Suez Canal in 1956 the bridge was renamed 26th July Bridge after the nationalization of Suez.

At one time porters from the Mena House would procure donkeys and camels for five piasters per hour. Mohammed Ali had

The Garden Ran Down to the Nile

previously appointed a sheikh to keep the Bedouin in some degree of order, and travellers were told to threaten the harassing offenders with discipline from the sheikh. But when the tariff was no longer paid to the sheikh for the privilege of seeing the pyramids, the police often had to be called to repel the insistence of un-official guides who pressed their services on the travellers. This precipitated tickets to be sold from a small office beside the Khedival Kiosk near the Great Pyramid. The cost for the ascent was ten piasters and a visit to the interior, the same.

Bedouin guides were, however, still procured through the sheikh at a fixed price of twenty piasters. Two Bedouin, one holding each of the climbers' hands, and one, if desired, pushing from behind, made the ascent of the pyramid safe—and in about ten to fifteen minutes or longer if stopping to rest.

Baedeker suggests that when visiting the complex, it should be done on a fine and calm day, as in windy weather the driving sand could be very unpleasant: "Sun Umbrellas and Smoked Spectacles are advisable precautions against the glare of the sun. Ladies who intend to ascend the pyramids should dress as they would for mountain-climbing." And remarking on the view from the apex: "There is perhaps no other prospect in the world in which life and death, fertility and desolation, are seen in so close juxtaposition and in such marked contrast."

Améedé Baillor DeGuerville found the Pyramids Road and the Mena House magnificent: "There is, to my mind, no more delicious road in the world than the large and lovely avenue which leads from Cairo to the Pyramids of Ghizeh, constructed at the entrance to the Desert. Along its length of seven miles are superb and lofty trees. At all hours of the day it is full of life: in the morning, ladies and gentlemen out for a canter; mules, donkeys and strings of camels, going and coming from the market. In the afternoon, fashionable Cairo, walking, driving or motoring, and on the left the electric tramway with its note of modernity."

In 1976 the Pyramids Road, that was built over the old macadamised road, was a modern dual carriageway lined with nightclubs, shops, modern villas, and high-rise blocks of flats. The central reservation was well maintained with grass, flowers, and every twenty-meters or so, three dense box shrubs trimmed in the shape of the three Ghiza Pyramids.

You can no longer see the Great Pyramid from a distance of thirty miles, or even eight miles as the metropolis and smoke from the city have rendered it impossible. But five or six miles outside central Cairo, on the approach to the pyramids, the apex of Khufu can still be seen. Ever increasing in size, its shadow engulfs everything around it, and its presence looms majestically above the high plateau it sits upon.

On the right, stands the celebrated Mena House Hotel. The road circles up to the Ghiza complex where below, in 1978, was a compound where camels were kept. We could drive onto the complex and park our car by the side of the Great Pyramid and then climb up onto the massive blocks and eat a picnic lunch. On Fridays local people had their picnics up the side of Khufu. One small kiosk sold Coca-Cola, post cards, and cigarettes, and only a few hawkers were pushing camel rides.

There was a village, Kafr al-Ahram, between the Great Pyramid and the Pyramids Road that held a market once a week.

The Garden Ran Down to the Nile

Flat-bed wagons overflowed with blood-red tomatoes and paint-box green vegetation. Woman in brightly coloured dresses sat cross-legged selling eggs or lemons from their laps, pigeons were cramped in small wooden cages, and chickens hung by their legs. Young boys in dirty galabehyas and bare feet curiously followed the non-Egyptian interlopers. The tops of the mud-brick houses had open flat roofs covered in straw and berseem, and women hung clothing in the dust that swirled up from the markets' activity.

Walking around to the northeast side of the Great Pyramid the noise of the city was absorbed by the enormity of the structure. The only sound was the silence of the desert.

Scaling the Great Pyramid was greatly discouraged, but still possible if you were really determined—and generous with the baksheesh. Nowadays it is no longer possible to climb the Great Pyramid. The government has put a stop to the practice as a number of people have fallen to their deaths.

A hundred years ago it was quite different. People were almost expected to climb to the top and experience the view. Guides would push and pull you up the granite blocks making the climb almost effortless. I attempted the climb once and made it two-thirds of the way up before I was beseeched to come down. Climbing alone is arduous and the stones are no small achievement, especially coming down, but I was torn between reaching the apex and the shouting demands of the Egyptian official. With hind sight, I should have ignored him. I compensated my thwarted climb to the summit, however, by numerous visits to the interior of both Khufu and Khafre, sometimes being completely alone in the burial chamber—which is impossible to do today.

The Garden Ran Down to the Nile

In 1848 at the age of forty-four, Harriet Martineau, who was suffering from heart disease and lack of hearing, defied convention when she scaled the Great Pyramid. She wore long skirts and took her ear trumpet and a stool: "On looking up, it was not the magnitude of the Pyramid which made me think it scarcely possible to achieve the ascent; but the unrelieved succession, almost infinite, of bright yellow steps; a most fatiguing image! Three strong and respectable looking Arabs now took me in charge. One of them, seeing me pinning up my gown in front, that I might not stumble over it, gave me his services as lady's maid. He turned up my gown all around, and tied it in a most squeezing knot, which lasted all through the enterprise.

"One of my Arabs carried a substantial camp stool, which had been given me in London with a view to this very adventure, that it might divide the higher steps, some of which, being four feet high, seem impracticable enough beforehand. But I found it better to trust to the strong and steady lifting of the Arabs in such places, and, above everything, not to stop at all, if possible; or, if one must stop for breath, to stand with ones face to the Pyramid. I am sure the guides are right in taking people quickly.

"It is trying to some heads to sit on a narrow ledge, and see a dazzling succession of such ledges for two or three hundred feet below; and there, a crowd of diminutive people looking up, to see whether one is coming bobbing down all that vast staircase. I stopped for a few seconds two or three times, at good broad corners or ledges. When I left the angle, and found myself ascending the side, the chief difficulty was over; and I cannot say that the fatigue was at all formidable. The greater part of one's weight is lifted by the Arabs at each arm; and when one comes to a four feet step, or a broken ledge, there is a third Arab behind.

"I was agreeably surprised to find at the top, besides blocks standing up which gave us some shade, a roomy and even platform, where we might sit and write, and gaze abroad, and enjoy ourselves, without even seeing over the edge, unless we wished it. There was only the lightest possible breeze, just enough to fan our faces, without disturbing us."

About twenty years later, Amelia B. Edwards described her impressions of the pyramids in her very discerning way: "The first glimpse that most travellers now get of the pyramids is from the window of the railway carriage as they come from Alexandria; and it is not impressive. It does not take one's breath away, for instance, like the Alps. It is only in approaching them, and observing how they grow with every foot of the road, that one begins to feel they are not so familiar after all.

"But when at last the edge of the desert is reached, and the long sand-slope climbed, and the rocky platform gained, and the great pyramid in all its unexpected bulk and majesty towers close above one's head, the effect is as sudden as it is overwhelming. It shuts out everything but the sense of awe and wonder.

"The colour again is a surprise. Few persons can be aware beforehand of the rich tawny hue that Egyptian limestone assumes after ages of exposure to the blaze of an Egyptian sky. Seen in certain lights, the pyramids look like piles of massy gold."

Women, when scaling the pyramid unaccompanied by a gentleman, and being hauled to the top by several Arabs, would be warned beforehand, according to A.B. DeGuerville, that the: ". . . greatest prudence should be exercised, as it seems sometimes happens, a disgusting experience. Two Bedouins are as a rule sufficient to hoist up a man, but three at least are required where a lady is concerned. Whilst one of these miscreants takes her by the hands, the other two push from behind, and it is then that they find an opportunity for playing their tricks."

Like myself, Annie Quibell though she had come to Egypt too late, even though the year was only 1925: "I suppose it must have been much more impressive to see the Pyramids thirty or forty years ago, when there was no road and no Nile bridge, and one crossed in a ferry boat to Giza and rode out the six miles from there on donkeys or camels. The electric tramway stops beside the big hotel at the foot of the slope, motors hoot up it and deposit their burdens at the very base of the Great Pyramid; a regular Bank-holiday crowd of Levantines pours out from Cairo every Sunday, and yet, hardly do we pass round the corner of the pyramid than the silence of the desert gets hold of us. It is very good to get away from the guides and the dragomans and think about it quietly. Perhaps the best thing of all is to stay out at Mena House or to camp near by and so be able to go about and see the morning lights, the sunset and the moon, and grow familiar with the mighty cemetery in all its aspects, but one can make excellent expeditions from Cairo by taxi or tram, and there is nothing more rewarding.

"The drive out is interesting . . . the road runs westwards through the cultivation. There is still a line of flooded basins near the desert edge, and the traveller is lucky who comes early enough to see the reflected in the water below."

The Garden Ran Down to the Nile

Charles Dudley Warner experienced the two-hour drive to the pyramids in a carriage over a very good road: "We drive through the wide and dusty streets of the new quarter. The fellaheen are coming in to market, trudging along behind donkeys and camel loaded with vegetables or freshly cut grass and beans for fodder. Squads of soldiers in white uniforms pass. We cross the river on a fine bridge of iron, and drive over the level plain, opposite, on a raised and winding embankment. We pass by the new summer palace of Geezeh. Other large ones are in process of construction. Through the trees we see green fields, intersected with ditches, wheat, barley, and beans. There are lines of palms, clumps of acacias; peasants are at work or asleep in the shade; there are trains of camels, and men plowing with cows or buffaloes. Leaving the squalid huts that are the remains of once beautiful Geezeh, the embankment strides straight across the level country.

"And there before us, on a rocky platform a hundred feet higher than the meadows, are the pyramids, cutting the stainless blue of the sky with their sharp lines."

At the southern side of the Great Pyramid stands a long glass walled museum that houses, what archaeologists and historians believe to be the oldest boat in the world. It was discovered by Egyptologist, Kamal el Mallakh in 1954, when a large stone sealed pit was uncovered beneath piles of rubble. Forty-one limestone blocks (the largest weighing just less than sixteen tons) concealed the pit in which the completely dismantled boat was found. It took years of painstaking work to reassemble it. The Solar Boat, as it is called, is believed to have been Khufu's funerary barge that floated down the Nile from Memphis to Ghiza. Khufu was the second ruler of the Forth Dynasty of the Old Kingdom, which dates the boat as being 4,500 years old. At forty-five meters long from stem to stern, and built completely from Lebanese cedar wood, the Solar Boat is the largest and best-preserved ancient boat known to archaeology.

The boat was crafted with such precision that only wooden pegs and hemp rope were used to hold it together—a testimony to the technical skills and abilities of the ancient Egyptian shipbuilders.

It closely resembles the vessels depicted in so many papyri and tomb paintings where the elaborate ceremony of the King's divine Ka (spirit) makes the solar journey to the after world where he is guaranteed survival and well-being in the eternal afterlife.

A marvel of ingenuity, the boat is so perfectly preserved that the wood has a lustrous patina. You can almost imagine the boat in Pharaonic times—its oars dipping and rising in unison to the perpetual rhythm of the beater—the sunlight streaming across the deck and glistening off the upturned prow. Along the banks where the bulrushes and papyrus merge into the green land, farmers would gather to pay homage to the passing pageantry.

Sadly, the splendid royal ship of Pharaoh Khufu is now threatened with deterioration caused by exposure to the elements and changes in humidity and temperature. The boat will eventually be moved to the new Grand Cairo Museum on its completion. A second boat belonging to Khufu was discovered in 1957, but left un-earthed due to finances and problems with insect infestation. Now work has now started to exhume, restore, and reassembly the smaller sister boat.

Five

The Sphinx – 'Father of Terror'

▲ ▲ ▲

'You dare not mock at the Sphinx'
Alexander Kinglake

Little is known about the Sphinx except as Guardian of the Pyramids and that it was associated with the Sun God Re, and with Horus of the Horizon. Even its age is a mystery. The Sphinx was generally believed to have been built in the image of the Pharaoh Khafre, during the reign of King Harmachis. Legend says that while on a hunting trip, Prince Thutmosis IV, took refuge in the shade of the Sphinx—then almost entirely covered by sand except for its head. The prince fell asleep and King Harmachis appeared to him in a dream and asked him to clear away the accumulated sand that had gathered around the Sphinx's body. He promised him that if he did this, he would bestow upon him the crown of Egypt. The sand was cleared and the promise was kept—but the sands of time once again accumulated around the divine guardian until 1817 when Giovanni Caviglia undertook excavations and found several stone tablets left by succeeding kings.

The Garden Ran Down to the Nile

After Caviglia's death, Agustus Mariette carried on the excavations followed in 1886 by Gustave Maspero, then Director-in-Chief of the Boulak Museum (now the Cairo Egyptian Museum). Maspero cleared away the sands that had once again buried the Sphinx to its shoulders and unearthed the large stone tablet, which is covered in hieroglyphics and sits at its breast above a small sacrificial alter between its paws.

The Sphinx reclines at the head of the causeway leading to Khafre's Pyramid, and in comparison, the Sphinx is small. Hewn out of solid rock with pieces of stone added where necessary, it looks like a recumbent lion and may have once been completely covered with limestone. During the Ptolemaic and eighteenth Dynasties, the Sphinx was an object of pilgrimage. Ornaments adorned the head and the crown, which no longer exists, and the face was coloured a reddish ochre—the colour used for kings. No traces of decoration remain today, but the red of the face was still visible towards the end of the 18th century. Herodotus called it 'Sphinx', meaning the head of a woman and body of a lion—and the name has lasted.

Though badly disfigured by time and abuse, it almost smiles as it looks out through all seeing eyes, conveying a sense of strength and mystery. In 1998 the crumbling icon was unveiled after a massive structural renovation had been completed at a cost of £1.5 million. The limestone body and paws were reinforced with 12,244 limestone blocks, some weighing over a thousand pounds. There was controversy on whether or not the fallen beard should be replaced, but the Sphinx remains clean-shaven with the original parts of his beard resting in the Egyptian and British Museums. The nose was lost in the 14th century—shot off by the Mamelukes who used it for target practice.

The Garden Ran Down to the Nile

The inscrutable Sphinx no longer stoically stares out over a landscape of undulating dunes around the glistening Nile. His view has been disfigured by an open-air laser-light theatre, sound speakers, a long line of dilapidated souvenir shops, the AA Riding Stables, and a parking lot. Does the Sphinx still seem to laugh at mortality while a new history unfolds before him—a stone's throw from his paws? Or does he wish he could sink back into the sand in disillusionment?

Wallis Budge wrote: "Egyptology has shown that it was a colossal image of Ra Harmachis, and therefore of his human representative upon earth, the king of Egypt who had it hewn, and that it was in existence in the time of, and was probably repaired by, Cheops and Chephren, who lived about three thousand seven hundred years before Christ."

In 1844 Sophia Poole saw the Sphinx when it still retained a certain degree of colour: "Its huge recumbent body, almost entirely buried in sand and rubbish. The head alone is twenty feet high. The face is much mutilated; the nose being broken off. This loss gives to the expression of the face much of the Negro character: but the features of the countenance of the ancient Egyptian. At first the countenance of the Sphinx, disfigured as it is, appeared to me absolutely ugly; but when I drew near, I observed in it a peculiar sweetness of expression, and I did not wonder at its having excited a high degree of admiration in many travellers. The whole of this extraordinary colossus was doubtlessly painted: the face still retains much of its paint, which is red ochre, the colour always employed by the ancient Egyptians to represent the complexion of their countrymen; yellow or pink being used by them for that of the

Egyptian women. All that is visible of the Sphinx is hewn out of a mass of limestone rock, which perhaps naturally presented something of the form which art has given to it."

The Rev. Samuel Manning also saw the traces of red on the face of the Sphinx: "At the eastern edge of the platform of Gizeh stands the Great Sphinx, a fabulous monster, compounded of the bust of a man with the body and legs of a lion. This combination is supposed to symbolise the union of intellect and power required in a king. The conception originated apparently in Thebes, and seems as intimately connected with that city as the pyramid is with Memphis. This gigantic monster is consequently some centuries later than the neighbouring Pyramids. The figure lies with its face to the Nile, with the paws protruding, in an attitude of majestic repose. The countenance has the semi-negro, or ancient Egyptian cast of features, but is much injured by the Arabs hurling their spears and arrows at the 'idol'. Fragments of the beard have been found, and some traces of red remain on the cheeks, which are perhaps of a later date. The head was covered with a cap, of which only the lower part remains."

When Gustave Flaubert and Maxine du Camp viewed the Sphinx for the first time in 1849, the only likeness they would have seen before, would have been artist's interpretations in the form of drawings. Flaubert referred to it as 'Abou-el-Houl' (Father of Terror): "We stop before the Sphinx; it fixes us with a terrifying stare; Maxime is quite pale; I am afraid of becoming giddy, and try to control my emotion." Maxime du Camp concurs: "Gustave gives a loud cry, and I am pale, my legs trembling. I cannot remember

The Garden Ran Down to the Nile

ever having been moved so deeply. When we reach the Sphinx . . . Flaubert reined in his horse and cried, 'I have seen the Sphinx fleeing towards Libya; it was galloping like a jackal'.

"We sit on the sand smoking our pipes and staring at it. Its eyes still seem full of life; the left side is stained white by bird-droppings (the tip of the Pyramid of Khephren has the same long white stains); it exactly faces the rising sun, its head is gray, ears very large and protruding like a negro's, its neck is eroded; from the front it is seen in its entirety thanks to a great hollow dug in the sand; the fact that the nose is missing increases the flat, Negroid effect. Besides, it was certainly Ethiopian; the lips are thick."

Eustace Reynolds-Ball recalls the fascination and mystery of the Sphinx in 1897: "The first view of the Sphinx is, undoubtedly, striking and impressive in the highest degree, but it must be admitted that the conventional rhapsodies of modern writers who enlarge on the beauty of its features are over-strained. Before the figure had been mutilated by Mussulman fanatics, it is possible that the mediaeval critics were justified in speaking of the Sphinx as a model of human symmetry, wearing an expression of the softest beauty and the most winning peace."

The artist, R. Talbot Kelly, though impressed with the Pyramids, found calm and mystery under the shadow of the Sphinx and regarded it in the same way that Amelia B. Edwards regarded Abou Simbel: "When seen in all the solemnity of night is inexpressibly weird, and gives the beholder an over-awing sense of eternal dignity and calm. Sit down and live with it hour by hour and night after night, and you will learn that the Sphinx is no mere monument of stone, but has a mysterious power of impressing itself upon your soul, as, looking backward through the ages, and into the dimness of the future, this most ancient and most incomprehensible of all Egypt's monuments forces upon you some slight understanding of what is meant by time and eternity."

Elizabeth Butler in 1909 felt an annihilation of time when in the presence of the Sphinx: "We next went down to the Sphinx and rested a long while in its broad shadow. The gaze of the eyes is exceedingly impressive, and though the face is so mutilated one would not have it restored. Strange that one should prefer the broken nose and the hare-lip! It would not be the Sphinx if it had the universal Sphinx face as originally carved. Originally! When? It was there long before the Pyramids, and it now appears that more than the 'forty centuries' looked down upon Napoleon's army from their summits. Sixty centuries, some say now. Time is annihilated as one stands confronted with the Sphinx, and a feeling of annihilation swirls around one's own microscopic personality."

Mabel Caillard experienced a curious disappointment in the Pyramids, having grown up with them. She felt her many childhood visits had destroyed the thrill of novelty and always envied people who could view them for the first time without what she called 'arriere pensee'. However, with the Sphinx it was different: "You seem to see it every time for the first time, and as you walk slowly away from it you resolve that this time must not be the last. The Sphinx never changes and is never twice the same. It has moods that mock its inscrutability even as they become absorbed in it. It is the symbol of survival. French soldiers might shoot away half its face but could not break its eternal calm; modern vandals may caricature it with rude familiarity but cannot alter its sublime detachment. As it confronts the rising moon in the clear quietness of a desert night, in its infinite solitude and its majestic serenity it is still one of the greatest wonders of the world."

When Robert Hitchins encountered the Sphinx in 1923, he also felt the urge to return time and time again to absorb its infinite wonder: "He who created it looked beyond Egypt, beyond the life of man. He grasped the conception of eternity, and realized the nothingness of time, and he rendered it in stone. Always as you return to the Sphinx you wonder at it more, you adore more strangely its repose, you steep yourself more intimately in the aloof peace that seems to emanate from it as light emanates from the sun. And as you look on it at last perhaps you understand the infinite."

Ever since people have been writing about the Sphinx, there has been a difference of opinion as to the sex. John Gadsby in 1860 thought the Sphinx represented a woman: "The head is that of a woman; and the lower part of the body of some animal. The claws are visible, but the nose is broken off. There was a boy in the group of Arabs around us who was without a nose; and my donkey boy said, 'Coll dis boy Spinx'."

Winston Churchill refers to the Sphinx as a woman where at 'The Big Three' conference held at the Mena House in 1943, to discuss the invasion of Europe; he took Theodore Roosevelt to the Pyramid complex where they stood looking up at the Sphinx: "Roosevelt and I gazed at her for some minutes in silence as the evening shadows fell. She told us nothing and maintained her inscrutable smile."

Thomas Medary Iden was sceptical that the Sphinx was a woman, not because of the appearance, but of the general opinion most men held of women in 1925: "The Sphinx is close by the Pyramids and is probably older than any one of them. Nobody knows who made it, or why. It has been generally thought to represent the worship of the sun, whose rising, in the east, it faces. Some have supposed it to represent a woman, but it has been facetiously declared that this could not be the case, as no woman could possibly have kept a secret so long; she would surely have found a way to reveal her identity before this time. Possibly her timidity about acknowledging her keeps her silent."

Probably the most well-known, and certainly the most evocative of all descriptions, is the literary prose written by Alexander Kinglake in 1835: "And near the Pyramids, more wondrous and more awful than all else in the land of Egypt, there sits the lonely Sphynx. Laugh and mock if you will at the worship of stone idols; but mark ye this, ye breakers of images, that in one regard, the stone idol bears awful semblance of Deity – unchanged fullness in the midst of change – the same seeming will and intent for ever and ever inexorable! And we, we shall die, and Islam will wither away; and the Englishman, straining far over to hold his loved India, will plant a firm foot on the banks of the Nile and sit in the seats of the Faithful, and still that sleepless rock will lie watching and watching the works of the new busy race, with those same sad earnest eyes, and the same tranquil mien everlasting. You dare not mock at the Sphynx."

At the foot of the Sphinx in the seventies, there was an open-air theatre where you sat on fold-down chairs and watched a *Son et Lumère*. Coloured lights played on the Sphinx and Pyramids as you were transported back across the ages by stereophonic music and a narrative of voices reliving Pharaonic history of Khufu, Khafre, and Menkura.

Soft breezes warmed the still night air and feral dogs barked in the distance evoking images of desert jackals in ancient times—while a million stars twinkled in the total black of the sky. Now and then a shooting star would arc across the limitless heavens and disappear into infinity, reminding you of your insignificance.

In 2008 behind the fold-down chairs, which had now increased in number, is a large raised terrace with a bar and more seating, where waiters serve drinks and potato chips. The floodlights have doubled, and an impressive, and much improved laser-light show, casts silhouetted pictures of the Pharaohs and their queens onto stone surfaces while interacting dialogue is dispersed through loud speakers. Although the sound has improved, the dialogue is the same, and now the pyramids are obstructed by the scaffolding that house the laser-lights and speakers.

Either side of the walkway leading up to the open air-theatre has been laid to turf and bordered with flowers and shrubs. An Egyptian Scottish band in full regalia, pipes everyone out when the show is over—but the Sphinx and its origin remain steeped in mystery, legend, and superstition.

The Garden Ran Down to the Nile

Behind the Ghiza plateau is the AA Riding Stables where I rode an Arabian horse every week around the dunes surrounding the pyramids—accompanied by my guide and teacher, Abdu Nabi. Sometimes we'd stop high above the plateau for a refreshing glass of mint tea served from a Bedouin's tent.

Six

Sakkarah

'Nefer-Setu'
(The most beautiful place)

In 1976 the road that led to Sakkarah was a narrow tarmacadam lane punctuated with enormous gaping pot holes that sent you weaving and swerving towards your destination. Lined with sycamore trees, it ran parallel to the Maryoutieh canal that wandered through antiquated mud-brick villages and lush fertile farmland, a pastoral tranquillity from the frantic pace and ear-splitting city where even the air became breathable.

Turkeys and chickens scavenged outside huts whose roofs were covered in dhoura stalks and television antennae—the only detail that dispelled a biblical image. Small boys would prod lumbering camels with sticks encouraging them to turn the large wooden sakiehs—an ancient cogged wheel device for lifting water—the eyes of the animal blindfolded while they circled monotonously. Camels slowly sauntered under the weight of sugar cane pilled so high and so wide that only four legs could be seen under the load.

The Garden Ran Down to the Nile

On the other side of the road was the village where women, balancing huge bundles of berseem wrapped in burlap on their heads, walked gracefully along the dusty road—their silver ankle bracelets clinking rhythmically at their bare feet—their brightly coloured dresses of orange, pink, and fuchsia, standing out against the green backdrop of the landscape. Old men on donkeys trotted by—their toes turned up to keep their slippers on—their faces like raisins beneath their turbans. Young children, dirty and barefooted, played by the rivers edge while their sisters and mothers washed copper cooking pots or laundry, slapping and rubbing them against the rocky banks. The women squatted on their heels—a position westerners find extremely difficult, if not impossible to achieve, their smiles and laughter dispelling any feeling of poverty that their living conditions might have conveyed.

Shadoufs, the most ancient method of lifting water lined the banks of the canal and every now and then an Archimedean screw could be seen, where men leathered by the sun crouched on the bank to turn the handle that rotated the 'screw' that lifted the water.

In the canal men bathed gamoosa (water buffalo), the animal's great head submerged in the water expelling streams of spray from its nostrils. Mile after mile the village life created a photographers paradise. Bedouin women in traditional black Ma'alayahs drove herds of goats through swirling dust. Their deep-set eyes peering over their yashmaks were blackened with kohl, the palms of their hands stained red with henna. In the fields small boys gathered berseem, a type of clover, tossing it into large baskets slung across the backs of docile donkeys. The fellaheen still used the method of farming that was used hundreds of years ago with primitive implements. Men naked to the waist, their bodies sweaty and glistening in the sun, tilled the rich black soil with gamoosa yoked to crudely made wooden ploughs called mihrat—the points crafted from iron. Children sat on one shaft of the plough to add weight, as dozens of snow white ibis stood motionless—patiently awaiting the spoils from the newly turned black earth. They resembled a relief from an ancient tomb painting. The men would wave—disguising backbreaking work.

In 2005 the shadoufs were gone, no longer lifting water to the fields that are no longer there. A noisy throng of humanity now resides where farmland once existed. The road traverses both sides of the canal that is strewn with rotting vegetables and smouldering rubbish from roadside vendors and the building rubble from the newly erected shops and hotels that have emerged. The city has now encroached where farmland once existed.

Three kilometres past the Sakkarah turning is the village of Mit Rahinah, founded by Menes (also known as Narmer) the first king before the First Dynasty. The ancient city of Memphis is rivalled only by Babylon as the greatest city of the ancient world. It is hard to imagine where splendid buildings and monuments once stood, because the stones were carried off in ancient times by builders of other monuments and edifices, and the area that was once desert, has been reclaimed by the Nile. The whole of Memphis has disappeared under centuries of mud and silt caused by the annual inundation that turned the one time metropolis into a forest of date palms.

The Garden Ran Down to the Nile

The Alabaster Sphinx that once guarded the Temple of Ptah reclined resolute surrounded, in 1976, by fragments of broken statues. Today it is roped off from would be defacers and climbing children, and a dozen gaudy kiosks line the surrounding area selling tourist tat.

Two colossal statues of Rameses II had lain face-down for centuries when discovered by Giovanni Caviglia and Hans Sloane. One of the statues now lays face-up and recently a purpose-built museum has been erected around it with a raised viewing gallery that allows visitors to gaze down upon the king in all his splendour. The statue is made from hard white siliceous limestone and is over forty feet long. Rameses wears the crown of Upper Egypt (the hedjet) and in one fist he holds a scroll. On his naked breast an amulet bears his royal name. The pair once stood at the eastern entrance of the Temple of Ptah, the largest and most important temple in ancient Egypt.

In 1955, President Nasser had the second statue restored and erected in front of the Bab al-Hadid, now known as Rameses Station where it stood in the middle of Rameses Square until 2006 when the colossus was becoming so polluted by the emissions from the traffic that traverse the vicinities roads and flyovers, and by the vibration from the recently built underground, it was removed to Ghiza where it is being restored. It will eventually be moved to the new Grand Egyptian Museum due to open in 2013.

To reach Sakkarah and Memphis in the 1800s, visitors took the daily train that ran to Upper Egypt boarding at Boulak and disembarking at Bedreshayn—about one hours ride through an almost continuous forest of palm trees. The journey commenced by carriage and then donkey, which would allow them to take in the site of Memphis on the way to Sakkarah—as long as the waters of the inundation did not cover it. In that case they would have to follow another route.

Messrs' Cook and Son would arrange the expedition, providing the carriage, the donkeys, a packed lunch, and the payments to the guides—which would leave the traveller free from haggling prices. Cook and Son would also provide tents if Sakkarah and the Pyramids of Ghiza were to be combined in a two day excursion. A large party would sometimes prefer to hire a steam-launch to take them to Bedreshayn and then continue the journey on donkeys. Murray's Hand Book 1888 suggests that: "Candles and matches, and some magnesium wire, for lighting up the Apis Mausoleum, should be taken; and provisions will be required for luncheon."

Baedeker describes the route via Bedreshayn to Memphis in 1914, which might have proved difficult to follow if the 'mounds of rubbish' and the 'broken pottery' had been cleared away: "We ride along the railway, turn to the right, cross a bridge, and follow the embankment towards the village of Bedrashein and a conspicuous grove of palms on the W. At the end of the embankment, 20 min. from the station, where the path divides, we keep to the left. The mounds of rubbish before us, the ruins of brick buildings, between which the lines of ancient streets may often be traced, scattered blocks of granite, and broken pottery mark the ancient site of Memphis."

"Irregular mounds of crumbled clay," is how Amelia B. Edwards remembers Memphis: "Memphis is a place to read about, and think about, and remember; but it is a disappointing place to see. To miss it, however, would be to miss the first link in the whole chain of monumental history which unites the Egypt of antiquity with the world of to-day. Those melancholy mounds and that heron-haunted lake must be seen, if only that they may take their due place in the picture-gallery of one's memory."

The Rev. Samuel Manning enjoyed the solitude of the Memphis landscape around 1871: "The road from the village leads through one of the most luxuriant palm forests to be found in Egypt. Our boat was moored for the night close to the point where an avenue of trees came down to the riverbank. The full moon was shining with wonderful brilliancy, pouring a flood of light over the landscape, of which we, in these northern latitudes, can form little conception. I went ashore and wandered for hours among the tall columnar stems and under the graceful feathery crowns of the palm trees. A party of villagers, too astonished even to ask for backsheesh, came out to gaze at the strange sight of a European wandering about after nightfall. There are few remains above ground of the splendour of ancient Memphis. The city has utterly disappeared. If any traces of it yet exist, they are buried beneath the vast mounds of crumbling bricks and broken pottery which meet the eye in every direction. Near the village of Mitrahenny is a colossal statue of Rameses the Great. It is apparently one of two described by Herodotus and Diodorus as standing in front of the Temple of Phtah. It lies in a pit, which during the inundation is filled with water . . . as we gaze at this fallen and battered statue of the mighty conqueror."

The Garden Ran Down to the Nile

Florence Nightingale made the journey in 1849 when she travelled through Egypt with her guardians, the Bracebridges. She describes her donkey excursion from Bedreshayn to Memphis: "We mounted (no ass having a bridle), and rode along a causeway till we came to the most beautiful spot you can imagine. I have seen nothing like it except in my dreams, certainly not in Egypt; a palm forest, the old palms springing out of the freshest grass; the ground covered with a pink flower, and the most delicate little lilac dwarf iris. Here and there a grassy pool and a flock of goats and kids, the long sun-light streaks and shadows falling among the trees. It looked as if nature had spread her loveliest coverlid, had grown her freshest flowers to deck the pall, and throw on the grave of Memphis."

Florence also laments of the statue of Rameses, which she came across, lying in the palm forest; "I have seen nothing like this palm forest in the East. And in the middle, in a grassy hollow, by the side of a bright pool of water, lies a statue of the great Rameses, the most beautiful sculpture we have yet seen. I never felt so much the powerlessness of words. There he lies upon his face, as if he had just lain down weary; you speak low that you may not wake him to see the desolation of his land, yet there is nothing dreary, but all is still. It is the most beautiful tomb-stone for the grave of a nation I ever saw. I felt as if God had placed it there himself, and said – 'Very dear to me thou were, my land of Memphis, and thou shalt have a fitting monument – the sweet green grass above thee spread, and one of the most glorious statues in the world to mark the place.' I could have cried when I heard them talk of turning it round upon its back, - as if God had placed it there, and it should not be touched by man."

Yet move it they did. I wonder what Florence would have thought if she could see Rameses today as he lies surrounded by lath and plaster. Would she have wept? Maybe the romance of Rameses fallen resting place has disappeared, but I can't help feeling that his dignity has been restored to him as he looks ever upwards to the Heavens, protected from the elements and graffiti.

A.B. DeGuerville, in 1905, seems to have had a very different experience than that of Miss Nightingale. However, his optimistic acceptance of the situation did not impair his enjoyment of the day's excursion: "All the flags soaked and hanging miserably, the Rameses started sadly on her voyage, and we leave Cairo, wrapped in a grey veil of mist, far behind. It is freezing! Seated on the bridge, smothered in coats and rugs we gaze on the flat melancholy banks. Here and there, enthusiastic fishermen watch their lines, oblivious of the drenching rain. In the fields the peasants, seated at the side of the cut cane, shiver and utter wild cries as we pass by.

"One o'clock. An excellent lunch has warmed and consoled us. We have just arrived at Bedrachen. From here a start is made to visit Sakkarah and the ruins of Memphis. Bravely armed with mackintoshes and umbrellas, we leave the Rameses, and men and women straddle the donkeys. The situation is so ridiculous, and there are amongst us some such curious specimens, that we end by laughing. To come to Egypt to be soaked, and to have the end of your nose red—this is indeed the height of pleasure. However, for once there is no dust!

"Two hours' donkey ride across flooded fields, past clumps of palm trees, that would be delicious if only the Egyptian sunshine would favour us, but, alas, no such luck; all the same we must be fair, such days are almost unknown in Egypt."

The once narrow Sakkarah road that ran along the canal has been turned into a wide two lane tarmacadam road with dozens of new carpet and textile schools with names like 'Cleopatra', 'Akhenaton', and 'Pyramids'.

The Sakkarah complex ticket kiosk, somewhat grander, is located at the bottom of the north plateau, which was once the necropolis of the Old Kingdom when Memphis was the capital of Upper and Lower Egypt. A proper road leads up to the plateau and just to the right, about half-way up, a museum and rest area has been built in smooth modern stone.

Annie Quibell, in 1925, penned a small guidebook for the excursion to Sakkarah by car: "Since the previous edition of this handbook was published, the advent of the motor car has made great changes in Egypt as well as in other places and now the easiest, quickest and most convenient and economical way to get to Sakkarah is by motor from Cairo.

"Cars can go right up to Mariette's house. Many people, however, like the ride from Mena House by camel or donkey and this has the advantage that it passes the Abousir Pyramids and Abou Ghurab, while the old way of going by train to Bedrashein and thence by donkey to Sakkarah is a pretty route and gives the opportunity of seeing the Memphis mounds and the colossal statue of Rameses."

The Necropolis of Sakkarah was the most peaceful place in Lower Egypt. Tranquil and calming, a place to sit with your thoughts and listen to the silence of the wind as it danced across the vast landscape that stretched in a sea of past excavations, now laid silent with time. Standing on the edge of the plateau near what I thought might have been Mariette's house; you looked out over fertile, verdant green farmland below nestling between Dom palms and sycamore trees. Looking to the south you saw the Pyramids of Dashir shimmering in the heat of the mid-day sun, and to the north, the Pyramids of Abousir.

The sky, a sphere of pastel blue smudged with white cumulus clouds could appear convex, touching the ground around you like the view through a fish-eye lens. Looking up at the sky one day in February the entire atmosphere changed. The sky lost its tranquillity and the cotton wool clouds turned grey and threatening. Darker and darker they became until their shadows turned purple, moving in time-lapse over the gradient sands. Then without warning, large droplets of rain began to fall. There was a rumble in the Heavens like a warning from the Pharaohs, then lightening cracked—cutting through the sky like a sword. I sat down between the dunes and waited for the phenomenal occurrence to pass and taking in all the beauty of nature's charismatic surroundings. The thunderstorm in the desert was over in fifteen minutes leaving a magnificent rainbow arching across the sky in fragmented colours and disappearing behind the Step-Pyramid of Djoser. I felt rather privileged at having experienced what must have been a very rare occurrence.

Imhotep, chief minister and architect to Djoser, Third Dynasty pharaoh of the Old Kingdom, built the Step-Pyramid. Constructed in a series of six stone mastabas (benches) in ascending levels, it is the oldest known pyramid in Egypt—400 years older than the Pyramids of Ghiza and dominates the mortuary complex. According to Murray's Guide Book, eleven other pyramids lay in desolated mounds surrounding it. On the north side is the entrance, which was blocked off as it was no longer safe to enter. Built above the entrance are three walls and a roof of granite blocks that house a life-size seated replica of the King. You peer through a small window in the front wall and see Djoser in stony silence peering back at you. The original statue is in the Egyptian Museum in Cairo.

Within the complex are the pyramids of Mereruka and Kagemni. They contain some of the most beautiful wall relief's throughout Egypt and deserve unhurried observation. They show scenes not of kings and nobles making the journey through the afterlife, but the Egyptian people themselves celebrating life. The walls are a marvellous expression of daily life. The scribes left nothing out; there are farmers, fishermen, herdsmen, craftsmen, goldsmiths, hunters, artists, tradesmen, even dwarfs.

A variety of birds, fish, animals, and reptiles are depicted and insects, grasshoppers, and dragonflies hide in the beautiful bas-reliefs. The condition is amazing and the colours are brilliantly preserved. In the Mastaba of Kagemni there is a wonderful 'ballet' where five dancers seem to defy gravity.

The magic that enveloped the whole of the complex of Sakkarah evoked images of the greatest civilization known to man. The vast Necropolis that was built by Imhotep to gather the Kings people around him after his death, mocks time.

The pyramid of Unas, the last king of the Fifth Dynasty, is one of the most accessible and easiest to enter. You walk straight in at a slight decline to the small antechamber covered with the famous Pyramid Texts. The wonderfully preserved hieroglyphs are the oldest known version of spells and prayers used to ceremoniously aid the dead king on his journey to the afterlife.

The Necropolis of Sakkarah has been excavated many times during the centuries and even today discoveries are still being made. Auguste Mariette, Director of Antiquities made the last great excavation in 1860 when he made a series of discoveries—including the semi-circle of poets and philosophers, and an Avenue of Sphinxes leading up to his most celebrated discovery in 1861, the Serapeum—the mausoleum of the Apis bulls. This vast subterranean tomb is entered by a wide decline of steps. In Mariette's time visitors would carry candles throughout the galleries that measure in excess of 230 metres in length.

Amelia B. Edwards and her party only ventured into the Serapeum about two hundred yards under candle light and magnesium powder: "which flared up wildly for a few seconds; lit the huge gallery and all its cavernous recesses and the wondering faces of the Arabs, and then went out with a plunge, leaving the darkness denser than before."

The party enjoyed lunch on the stone terrace of Mariette's deserted house where wooden tables and benches had been placed for the accommodation of visitors.

The Serapeum was the only site where the purchase of a ticket was necessary. A man sat at the entrance to the Serapeum and turned on a series of 40-watt incandescent lights that illuminated the most interesting of the twenty-four granite sarcophagi. The tombs, which measure 13 feet in length by 7½ feet in breadth and 11 feet in height, sit in recesses on either side of the gallery, but not opposite each other. The lids have all been broken or systematically pushed back, and the remains of the bulls are no longer there. One sarcophagus lid lays abandoned near the entrance. The Serapeum has been closed now for many years due to restoration.

Augusta Mariette lived in a house at Sakkarah with his wife and two children for two years during his excavations and welcomed passing visitors, including the German Egyptologist Henri Brugsch. Brugsch stayed with Mariette for eight months and describes the living conditions that did not seem to bother Mariette: "Snakes slithered along the floor, tarantulas or scorpions swarmed in the wall crevices, large spider-webs waved from the ceiling like flags. As soon as night fell, bats, attracted by the light, entered my cell through the cracks in the door and kept me awake with their spectral flights. Before going to sleep, I tucked the edges of my mosquito net beneath my mattress and put my trust in God and all the saints, while outside jackals, hyenas and wolves howled around the house . . ."

Sakkarah is a vast ancient burial ground possibly for the people who lived and worked in the Necropolis thousands of years ago, now desecrated by time and the changing sands. Wandering the dips and swells of the necropolis I came across a skull, half buried in the sand. The jawbone held an almost perfect set of teeth bleached white from the sun. The sands were littered with mummy beads and ancient relics scattered around the complex. Broken potshards and fragments of rock covered the surface of the sand where protruding fragments of mummy linen and bits of twisted and knotted rope were abundant. There were pieces of ancient wooden coffins, sometimes with round wooden fastening pegs and roughly hewn tool heads chipped from flint or granite.

On seeing a piece of mummy cloth protruding among the bits of bone, I attempted to pull it out. It was attached to something. I brushed away the sand and pulled up a large piece of gesso covered, painted mummy cloth depicting two reclining jackals; the God Anubis. They were nose to nose, painted yellow ochre on a blue background, and a standing figure of a woman with red hair or wig. There were several smaller pieces of typical border painting and tiny bits with gold leaf that shone in the sunlight. One fragment revealed a beautiful head, possibly of the God Ptah.

I thought of Amelia B. Edwards who had observed: "At Ghizeh one treads only sand and pebbles; but at Sakkarah the whole plateau is thickly strewn with scraps of broken pottery, limestone, marble, and alabaster; flakes of green and blue glaze; bleached bones; shreds of yellow linen, and lumps of some odd-looking, dark-brown substance, like dried-up sponge." That turned out to be fragments of what once was living flesh. "Presently some one picks up a little noseless head of one of the common blue-ware funereal statuettes, and immediately we all fall to work, grubbing for treasure."

Although I treasured my mummy cloth, my real pleasure came from finding mummy beads. I was hooked. I had joined the realms of souvenir hunters digging in the desert for mementos. I should have been ashamed of myself, but like Amelia B. Edwards, the experience of relic hunting had become infectious and the excitement of finding these small spoils far outweighed any remorse

The Garden Ran Down to the Nile

I might have felt. I justified my actions by the fact that it was no secret that the beads were there, they were simply too insignificant and too numerous for archaeologists to bother with.

A friend of mine had also caught the 'infection' and we would spend a full day every two weeks or so laying in the dips of the desert looking for these small treasures. We had a favourite place in a large crater shaped ravine somewhere west of the Step-Pyramid, where every now and again a guard would wander over the ridge and shake his finger at us. We would smile innocently, he would disappear back over the ridge and our archaeological endeavours would continue.

We learned to dig by the signs on the surface of the sand and the type of accumulated debris around the area, digging a small hole and then enlarging it by gently scraping away one side of the hole using the flat edge of a stone. This would reveal the mummy beads, if there were any to be found. Sometimes we would hit a real treasure trove, dislodging dozens of the faience beads in numerous shades of blues, browns and creams, many with the lustre still intact. The majority of the beads were round and flat, some were bugle shaped and sometimes we would find one made from cornelian or lapis lazuli. I found pieces of a small ushebti, which if intact, would have been about 4 inches high.

The children of the local village knew the existence of the mummy beads and small artefacts that lay just under the surface of the sand. Once two small boys persuaded my friend and I to follow them over the dunes to where an old man sat on his heels under a makeshift tent held up by a long stick. He was fanning the air with a fly-switch and greeted us with an unceremonious nod of his head.

The Garden Ran Down to the Nile

Beckoning us to sit, he reached into his 'tepee' and brought out a dusty old blanket that he spread out on the ground before us. With a twinkle in his eye, he laid out half-a-dozen tourist novelties; a chipped alabaster bust of Nefertiti, a pair of glazed earthenware candlesticks, a leather camel, and an assortment of necklaces and turkey-fed scarabs. When he realized that we were not to be fooled, he reached into the folds of his galabehya and pulled out several little intricate amulets, including a beautiful eye of Horus, a small delicate scarab beetle, and an old Kodak film canister filled with mummy beads. I purchased the eye of Horus, the scarab, and a tiny amulet of one of the god deities, I could not tell which.

Charles Dudley Warner wrote about the beads: "Great quantities of antique beads are offered us in strings, to one end of which is usually tied a small image of Osiris, or the winged sun, or the scarabaeus with wings. The inexhaustible supply of these beads and images leads many to think that they are manufactured to suit the demand. But it is not so. Their blue is of a shade that is not produced now-a-days. And, besides, there is no need to manufacture what exists in the mummy-pits in such abundance. The beads and bugles are of glass; they were much used for necklaces and are found covering the breasts of mummies, woven in a network of various patterns, like old bead purses. The vivid blue color was given by copper.

"The little blue images of Osiris which are so abundant are also genuine. They are of porcelain, a sort of porcelain-glass, a sand-past, glazed, colored blue, and baked. They are found in great quantities in all tombs; and it was the Egyptian practice to thickly strew with them the ground upon which the foundations and floors of temples were laid."

William C. Prime had a much more compulsive nature when collecting mummy beads, rather than being content with finding them scattered in the sands, he plundered the tombs and the mummies for what he called, mummy shawls: "The mummy was wrapped in shawls of more or less expensive character, the cloth being fine linen, sometimes ornamented with beads, while a very common form was a shawl made entirely of earthen beads strung on thread, and worked in graceful figures. Such shawls I found on two mummies which I unrolled at different times."

He had also procured some twenty mummy shawls from Arabs, who on digging at night had opened what they thought to be a tomb, but containing some two thousand mummy shawls. He purchased: "twenty shawls for three piasters each, being about three dollars for the whole. The character and quality of the articles determines their antiquity; and having unrolled some dozens of mummies, and become familiar with their clothing, I do not think I could be deceived in purchasing mummy cloth by even a Yankee speculator."

All good things must come to an end as one afternoon when my friend and I turned up at our 'cache' to find placards stuck strategically around the complex which warned, in English and Arabic, 'DON'T LOOK FOR BEADS!'

Sakkarah used to be empty of people at certain times of the year. Now coach loads of tourists descend on the plateau en mass. Hawkers, camel rides and so-called guides besiege the area. Wooden ramps have been built that lead to the tombs of Mereruka and Kagemni and areas have been cordoned off all together as armed guards police the area. More tombs have since been discovered; the tomb of Horemheb and a very interesting one belonging to two brothers, possibly twins, but you had to find someone with a key to let you in.

Seven

Khan el Khalili

▲▲▲

'Think, in this batter'd caravanserai, whose doorways are alternate night and day, how sultan after sultan with his pomp abode his hour or two, and went his way'
　　　　　　　　　　　　　　Rubàiyat of Omar Khayyàm

The Khan el Khalili is a section of the Muski, built in 1290-93 by Mameluke Sultan el-Ashraf on the Fatimid site of the ruined tombs of the Caliphs. It is one of the oldest bazaars in the world where you can lose yourself in its history. Around the perimeter was the spice market where quaint open fronted shops with wonderful old cedar wood cabinets displayed a multitude of spices. Concentrated scents of saffron, cinnamon, ginger, paprika, cardamom, and nutmeg hung in the air, reminding you that this was without a doubt, the Orient. Plastic bins scattered around the entrance held kilos of raisins, dates, figs, and dried apricots (mish-mish). Aromatic dill, tarragon, bay, and oregano challenged the bouquet of the spices, and saffron cost the same as cinnamon. The proprietor weighed the spices on an old apothecary's weight then laid each one on small papers which he folded into neat little cones.

The Garden Ran Down to the Nile

Crossing the main dirt road thoroughfare was like running a gauntlet—dodging a sea of local people, goat herds, and donkey carts over-loaded with terra-cotta pots. Entering the heart of the Khan el Khalili the heat and noise of the city subsides. Once the bazaar of the silk and carpet merchants, a labyrinth of twisting antiquated lanes and dusty alleyways form the present bazaar. In some places the lanes are so narrow they are not easily passed by two persons. Jutting rooftops form a canopy over the buildings creating a cool and secretive respite from the scorching afternoon sun. The intricate maze of crooked little alleyways cross and intersect so frequently it gives a sense of disorientation and confusion, and like Alice, losing your way becomes commonplace.

Colourful wares of every conceivable item of uselessness hang overhead and cascade down shelves and onto the lanes fronting the shops that pander to tourists. Proprietors stand amongst the confusion of their wares and you are suddenly caught in the cross-fire of sales pitches from adjacent competing shops enticing you in with promises of mint tea and a bargain with 'no hassle'.

The lane of the Goldsmiths was an incredible treasure-trove where 18 and 22-carat gold could be bought at a third of the market price in the western world. Another lane housed the Silversmiths whose work varied from exceptional pieces of quality craftsmanship to inexpensive trinkets of silver plate. Like gold, silver was weighed on small balance scales—as they were hundreds of years ago.

Omar, an olive-skinned Egyptian in his late twenties was a leather merchant. He had thick black hair combed back in shiny waves and a walrus moustache. He wore a heavy gold watch, gold chains, and Levis that were a size too small. He sold leather goods of every kind and the occasional snake skin or stuffed baby

The Garden Ran Down to the Nile

crocodile. In 2005 I visited his shop and found him still there, fortunately without the hippy persona. We had mint tea and lamented about the 'good old days.'

Further into the maze were the 'antika' shops where large windows displayed extraordinary curiosities, white elephants, and every manner of Egyptian curio claimed to be authentic. One particular shop, Moorish in style, was right out of the Arabian Nights. The lighting was subdued and there was the pungent smell of incense burning from joss sticks. Oriental carpets worn thin from a thousand footsteps covered the floor, and exotic chandeliers of burnished brass hung from the ceiling, illuminating the surroundings in subtle variations of light. Every inch of the shop was occupied by a kaleidoscope of confusion and colour.

The proprietor; a man of voluminous proportions advanced, waved a phlegmatic hand around the shop assuring that everything was authentic, and showed me a ushebti from Cleopatra's tomb—supposedly in her likeness. The eyes looked bossed. He tipped the contents of a small container onto the glass countertop and a dozen blue faience scarabs (good-luck beetles) spilt out.

I turned my attention to a small oriental carpet and enquired the price. He smiled through slit eyes and answered. I offered half, he replied in an uncompromising tone; hands turned upwards. We stared at each other, I grimaced, he shrugged. I indicated that for the price he wanted the carpet would have to fly, and left the shop with one of the scarabs—no doubt once fed to a turkey to produce the 'genuine' patina.

There were shops where finely crafted meshrabeya tables and screens were made, and shops selling semi-precious stones. Men sat cross-legged on the ground embroidering tablecloths, galabehyas and appliquéd tapestries depicting long vanished Pharaonic Gods in brightly coloured pieces of Egyptian cotton. One old man with gnarled hands was always there concentrating on his work through failing eyesight. His grandson now occupies the same corner. Young boys and men worked from rooftop dwellings above the shops handcrafting boxes with inlayed pieces of mother-of-pearl and bits of buffalo bone no wider than a needle.

Shops advertising exact replicas of French fragrances transported you into another world of scent and allure. A small, thin man swept across the room to greet me, his handshake light and cool, like a woman's. He waved bottles of scent under my noise before rubbing a bit of the oils on the inside of my wrist. After seven or eight, the perfumes took on the same sickly sweet odour. I chose two bottles of Egyptian oil, orange blossom called, Cleopatra, and jasmine called, Nefertiti. He poured the oils into small hand-blown bottles of green glass and screwed on red plastic caps. The faces of the Egyptian queens painted on the bottles had features more resembling the witches from Mac Beth. I wafted out of the shop clutching my bottles of Cleopatra and Nefertiti.

In the bazaar of the Coppersmiths an enormous man sat among his wares. The shop was alive with the shimmering illumination of polished brass and copper. Lanterns, lamps, and copper urns filled the room. Amber light subdued by dust and smoke reflected from every angle like a house of mirrors. Hassan, 'the Robber,' as he was fondly referred to by ex-pats, wore a flowing white kaftan and sat under a turban. His fingers were stained with nicotine and smoke encircled his head and then vanished like a disappearing iffrit. He looked like Aladdin in his cave. We sat on well-worn camel saddles and a young boy with dirty bare feet brought strong mint tea while we sealed a bargain for a large copper pot.

In 1876 Charles D. Warner's trip to the Muski was similar to mine, with the exception of 'the unsavoury throng', the picture does not seemed to have changed much: "This Oriental microcosm called a Bazaar is the most characteristic thing in the East, and affords most entertainment; in these cool recesses, which the sun only penetrates in glints, is all that is splendid in this land of violent contrasts. The shops are rude, the passages are unpaved dirt, the matting above hangs in shreds, the unpainted balconies are about to tumble down, the lattice-work is grey with dust; fleas abound; you are jostled by an unsavoury throng, you may be run against by loaded donkeys; grazed by beggars; followed by Jews offering old brasses, old cashmeres, old armour; squeezed against black backs from the Soudan; and stunned by the sing-song cries of a dozen callings. But all this is nothing. Here are the perfumes of Arabia, the colors of Paradise. These narrow streets are streams of glancing color; these shops are more brilliant than any picture – but in all is a softened harmony, the ancient art of the East."

Mildred Alice Oliver found the Muski a fascinating place in 1931: "The whole way of buying is most amusing. You are cajoled and bowed into one of these dens. Then you begin to bargain; in the middle of the bargaining they bring cups of Turkish coffee and you all partake and then you go on bargaining. You are seated on a sumptuous couch and at last the men get so affectionate they come and pat you and shake hands and ask all about your like and doings! The shop we spent a good deal of time in was one glitter of jewels and beads, paintings, mirrors, priceless carpets and draperies, brilliantly lighted by electricity, and yet when you go out you are in the narrowest slum you can conceive! We saw the gold and jewellery workers and some laying gilding on glass. We could have spent hours there."

Today the Khan el Khalili has quadrupled in size. The local artisans are nearly gone, their work now done in factories. Each shop is a replica of the one next to it and sells every kind of tourist curios. Confusion in the lanes is compounded by the congestion of tourist being dropped off by tour buses at the entrance of Muski Street.

Fishawis, the famous coffee house has been open 24 hours a day for two centuries. Brass lamps, gilded and cracked mirrors, and meshrabeya benches make you realize you are in old Cairo. It's still the best place to relax and soak up the atmosphere, smoke a shisha, and watch the microcosm of humanity pass by while you sip numerous cups of Turkish coffee brought by waiters in blue flowered Hawaiian shirts.

Just around the corner there is a modern restaurant named after the winner of the 1988 Nobel Prize for literature, Naguib Mafouz. Entered through a metal detecting archway, the cool interior of the restaurant is a respite from the throng outside where you can enjoy coffee and mezze while you have your shoes polished, or a three course meal served by waiters in embroidered galabehyas.

There is now an air-conditioned two story mall that houses quality boutiques within the maze of the old bazaar, where Uzi toting security guards protect the entrance.

The Garden Ran Down to the Nile

It used to be difficult to find any shop that sold bellydance gear, but in the past few years the popularity of the dance has gained enthusiasm, and now shop fronts are overflowing with beaded scarves, bra-and-belt sets (called bedla), and coin jewellery. If you can't find what you want in one shop, you can find it in another.

It is still possible to get away from the chaos by visiting the Sharia al Muizz across the bridge over the main Sharia al Azhar road to the Islamic quarter of the bazaar of the silk and carpet merchants. Here the Orient emerges. In the Mausolium of al-Ghouri, Sufi dancers and whirling dervishes perform twice weekly.

In the 1980s there were only two tarboosh (fez) manufacturers in Cairo. Now only one exists. The open-fronted shop in the narrow lane of Sharia Alghoria has been run by the same family for over 150 years. At the front of the shop the same ancient machine called a waga is still in operation, pressing the red Czechoslovakian felt into the familiar cylindrical shape of the tarboosh with the use of brass moulds and heat. The wearing of the tarboosh was abolished in 1952 by Muhammed Neguib. The shop now exists mainly through the patronage of restaurants, which in time could disappear. The proprietor maintains the business as his contribution to Egypt's cultural heritage.

Eight

Port Said

'Egypt is henceforth part of Europe, not Africa'
Khedive Ismail

During the time that Ismail was plunging his country into irretrievable debt, the Frenchman, Ferdinand de Lesseps was able to procure from the Pasha a concession to build the Suez Canal. The canal was built on the backs of forced labourers recruited through a tax known as the Corvée. The Corvée was comparable to national service where only the poorest Egyptian fellahin served under the guise of duty to the benefit of his country. These men were paid no wages and given no free food or housing.

Lucie Duff Gordon, while on her dahabeyah at Bibbeh, watched four huge barges sail by loaded with hundreds of men on their way to join the Corvée on the Suez Canal. In the eyes of most Europeans, Ismail Pasha was an innovator bringing progress and modernization to a backward country, but to Lucie he was a despot. In a letter to her mother she confides: "This appears to me a state of things in which it is no use to say that public works must be done at any cost. I daresay the wealth will be increased if meanwhile the people are not exterminated. What chokes me is to hear English people talk of the stick being 'the only way to manage the Arabs', as if anyone could doubt that it is the easiest way to manage any people where it can be used with impunity. These are not sentimental grievances, hunger and pain and labour without hope and without reward. The system of wholesale extortion and spoliation has reached a point beyond which would be difficult to go. Egypt is one vast plantation where the master works his slaves without even feeding them."

The building of the Suez Canal proved to be a ruinous expense for the country as Ismail borrowed money from European banks at hugely inflated rates of interest, and in the end Egypt was over one hundred million pounds in debt. As pressure was brought on the country to fulfil her obligations, Ismail, who was unable to repay even the interest, levied extortionate taxes on the fellahin; who were already overburdened by poverty.

In 1876 England and France formed a commission to take over the country's economy until the debt was paid. The two powers agreed to leave Egypt once payment was met. However, once in Egypt, the British found several good reasons for staying on. One being the Suez Canal, the new short route to her 'Jewel in the Crown', India. The other was the Sudan. Thus, the British occupation began, and three years later, Ismail was deposed and succeeded by his son Tewfik.

The opening of the Suez Canal took place on the 16th November 1869 with fireworks and gunfire to welcome the four thousand guests of Khedive Ismail, including: the Empress Eugénie of France, the Emperor of Austria, the Crown Prince of Prussia, and various dignitaries from around the world. Gas lamps and candles illuminated buildings, and ships were decorated in brightly coloured bunting and blazing fires on the decks. The ceremony was made even more spectacular when the fireworks dump blew up and nearly destroyed the town. The next day a procession of seventy ships headed by the Imperial Yacht *Aigle,* steamed through the Canal to Ismailia, where a party was given at the Palace of the Khedive.

No expense was spared as Thomas Cook remembers: "Champagne and other costly wines flowed like water; thousands met at the Palace of the Khedive to dance, talk and sup together; a wild military exhibition of Arabs and Bedouins was arranged for the gratification of the visitors; fireworks and illuminations closed the night, and thousands slept in tents specially provided for the occasion." Cook described his own passage through the Canal as: "One of the red-letter days of my tourist life."

The city of Port Said grew along with its reputation and in 1884 Richard Tangye remembers his first encounter with the town: "On arriving at our landing-place opposite the Custom House, a motley crowd rushed forward, some dressed in night-shirts, some in towels, others in their own black skins only. When we stopped, a score of them dashed into the water and began to seize our luggage, seeing which our boatmen called to us to beat them on the head with our umbrellas, and kick them off; but we managed to defend our property by loud words, which broke no bones. Then we were carried ashore amidst such shrieking, hustling, jostling, and shouting as I had never heard or seen before. The luggage was set down in the middle of the square to await the arrival of an official from the Custom House. After very slight examination we were permitted to pass, and then began another battle for the luggage; but we selected as our dragoman a tall, stout fellow named Hassan, who quickly routed the others; and then a file of these half-naked Arabs marched off to the hotel with the luggage on their backs. The Suez Hotel is a very comfortable establishment, with large, clean, and airy rooms, and bright and attentive native servants."

Father Thomas Medary Iden sailed up the Nile in 1925 in a houseboat called *Arabia*. He started the trip at Suez and describes it as such: "The Gulf was beautiful and the city of Suez was much larger and more attractive than we had supposed it could be. It was past five o'clock when we slowly steamed into the southern end of the canal, which was to shorten our journey between the Arabian Sea and the Mediterranean by some thousands of miles and by more than a week of time. The great canal is about one hundred miles long and one hundred yards wide. All boats go very slowly through it because it is relatively narrow and shallow. It is a most extraordinary experience – this plowing of one's way through the desert in a real ship. The process looks like a miracle to one who stands to one side in the desert and watches the great masts of one of these large vessels, calmly and majestically and easily and noiselessly piercing the desert sands, the water in the canal being entirely below one's vision. We thanked God, and De Lesseps, for it, and spent a good part of the night looking out of our stateroom window."

The Garden Ran Down to the Nile

On Father Iden's arrival, he was hurried through the streets of the town and put on the train to Cairo, thus avoiding contamination of what was said to be the wickedest city in the world.

In 1888 according to Murray's Handbook, Port Said had little to offer in the way of interest that a few hours walk would more than satisfy. Yet Port Said was the short cut to the East, the starting point of the Orient. Steamers of the P&O, the *Messageries,* the *Austrian Lloyd,* the *Russian,* and the *Rubattino,* snaked through the Canal. Ships on their way to India would lie in Port so the passengers would have time to visit the famous Simon Artz department store. Ladies disembarked under the watchful eye of a chaperon to purchase sun-hats covered with pelican skin and feathers, Curzon topees, and Turkish delight. They were judiciously steered out of the path of the 'Gully-gully' man who conjured with baby chicks. Gentlemen were warned of the dangers of going ashore where they might be enticed into brothels or by unsavoury characters selling French postcards.

The quay was a confusion of Oriental curiosities, beggars, fortune tellers, hawkers, and touts selling flywhisks and souvenirs. Children would dive for pennies thrown from the gunwale of the ship, and a throng of donkey boys and their braying donkeys with names like: 'Prince of Wales', 'Lily Langtree', and 'Champagne Charlie', waited on the dock.

Major C.S. Jarvis wrote about Port Said in 1937 referring to it as a small town set at the northern end of the Suez Canal: "By 1890 it had achieved the distinction of being called the wickedest town in the East, and vice and evil were rampant in its streets. Now a long line of British Commandants of Police have ruthlessly swept all this away utterly spoiling the old-world charm of the place, and vaguely suggests the interior of a Wasleyan chapel. At the present time it is exceedingly difficult to buy even a picture post card in the town, without having the police after you, yet in the good old days Port Said was famous all over the world for this type of art reproduction."

An Egyptian travel magazine described Port Said in 1956 as: "A clean, spacious little town of great charm quite different from any other in Egypt. The streets are arcaded, as Ismail's Cairo once was round the old Shepheard's, the side turnings look like something from New Orleans. The tiers of balconies are pure French overseas in quality. They are full of fascination and quiet pleasure. To stroll through these street, to look out over the harbour where the ships gather and pass from all the seas in the world, to sit under the arcades and sip your coffee or take tea, is a memory that is likely to last."

If the writer of that description had entered Simon Arzt in 1979, its ghost-like ambience would have charmed him, for as soon as you passed through the doors you entered upon a mislaid era. Standing on Palestine Street overlooking the quay on the Suez Canal, this Victorian genre department store was reminiscent of the Army & Navy store in Calcutta. It was truly one of the last remaining testimonies to Ismail's Egypt. Built in 1923 by Simon Arzt and Max Mouchally, it was the essence of faded splendour with creaking wooden floor boards, tall shelves brimming with glass and china, and countertops housing deep drawers of silk fabrics, textiles, and dry goods. A wide solid staircase with polished wood smelling of turpentine and wax curved its way up to balconies that overlooked the mélange below. Once the ceiling was made of glass, which allowed the natural light to flood in, illuminating the store.

Port Said remained a duty-free port of call where you could buy imported goods at very reasonable prices. Parts of the town looked like a war zone with crumbling and fragmented buildings bombed out in the 1967 war with Israel. Dogs of indeterminate breed and protruding rib cages roamed the area. Soldiers with drooping moustaches and ill-fitting woollen uniforms walked the dusty streets. Shopkeepers with piercing black eyes supported the walls of their shops, and rotund Coptic Priests in flowing black robes and wiry Rasputin beards, disappeared around corners.

Nine

Helouan

▲▲▲

'The fashionable and popular winter desert resort'
Black's Guide Book

    Nestled in the limestone hills just fifteen miles south of Cairo lies Helouan, once described as an artificial oasis with a dozen strong sulphur springs, continuous sunshine, and high tonic qualities. Helouan at the turn of the 19th century was reputed to be one of the world's most expensive health resorts. Invalids suffering from consumption, chronic bronchitis, asthma, anaemia, rheumatism, lumbago, sciatica, skin disorders, and gout, flooded into the Nile Valley for rest, recuperation, and the pure, salubrious healing atmosphere Helouan had to offer.

    Black's Guidebook of 1905 gives praise to: "Helouan, the fashionable and popular winter desert resort. Warm, dry desert air. Celebrated sulphur baths. English and Egyptian military bands in the park. Centre for excursions to Sakkarah, Memphis, etc., etc."

    John Gadsby who was fighting tuberculosis, came to Egypt no less than six times in the mid-1800s, when the weather turned cold in England. Gadsby, like many others seeking solace from the bleak wintry months would winter in Egypt.

Murray's 1888 Handbook promotes Egypt: "to the overworked teacher and student, the care-burdened merchant and man of business and those subjected to a hard daily routine, which has broken down their stamina, and induced a highly-excited state of nervous system; the confirmed dyspeptic and hypochondriacal (sic) invalid; the depressed and anxious-minded; the nervous and hysterical female; to all these the Egyptian climate may be beneficial. The bright and sunny sky is in itself an incentive to cheerfulness and pleasure."

In 1910 Helouan had the distinction of being the only modern town in the north of Egypt, and although it was mainly a resort for invalids, many people preferred it to Cairo—finding a variety of occupations to amuse them. There were race meetings, gymkhanas, dances, concerts, tennis, and a golf course. A large number of villas and apartments with baths were rented out. They came furnished or unfurnished and were built in the Oriental style, which was better adapted to the climate. Helouan was a favourite residence of Khedive Tewfik, who built the Tewfik Palace Hotel in 1899; a first class house situated outside of town boasting 100 rooms. It also had a racecourse and golf-links; though not a blade of grass was on the ground. It was in his Helouan residence that Tewfik died.

Around 1905, George Nungovich had two hotels in Helouan, The Grand, and the Hotel Des Baines. The hotels were advertised as such:

GRAND HOTEL, HELOUAN

First-Class Establishment standing in its own Garden.
Suites of Apartments for Families.
Electric Light. Lift. Hotel Heated Throughout.
American Bar. Billiard, Reading and Smoking Saloons.
SPLENDID VIEWS OVER THE DESERT AND THE NILE.
Golf-Club-House, Scotch Professional. Lawn Tennis.
Croquet Grounds. Library of 1500 Volumes. Baths. Telegraph Office. Telephone. English Sanitary Arrangements.
Excellent Cuisine. Home Comforts. Splendid Verandah.
Sandcarts for Driving in the Desert. Dog Carts for Hire.

HOTEL DES BAINES, HELOUAN

Situated close to the Thermal Establishment.
Entirely Renewed with All Modern Improvements.
English Sanitary Arrangements. Large Verandahs.
Splendid Views over the Desert.
Excellent Cuisine and Attendance.
Telegraph Office, Telephone, Electric Lighting.
Modern Rates.
Ladies' Drawing Room, Writing and Reading Rooms.

When Lucie Duff Gordon took up residence in Upper Egypt in 1862, she was suffering badly from tuberculosis and experienced regular bouts of blood-spitting. She was encouraged by her surgeon, Dr. Charles Izod, to continue smoking the cigars she had always used—in an effort to ease her cough, which she did until her death in 1869. It seems quite incongruous that at that time smoking was not only an accepted social formality, but believed to be beneficial to one's health.

Mary Whately could not see the benefits of smoking, yet thought the Egyptian tobacco less 'unwholesome' as it was milder than that of Europe: "Paper cigars are also in great use, and are now seen more frequently than the long pipe, or chibouk, as it was called, which older ladies still however prefer. In the harems the ladies smoke a great deal, and I think it injures their health. Even women of a humbler class often smoke cigars a great deal, but you seldom see countrywomen smoke, and they are the healthiest of the population. I cannot make out that these inveterate smokers are ever the better for it, and certainly they waste both money and time."

During the early part of the 19th century, before Egypt was developed sufficiently enough to cope with travellers, and until the enterprising Thomas Cook made Luxor, Assouan, and cruising the Nile a reality readily available, invalids had no choice but to stay in Cairo for their health. By the late 1800s the overcrowding of the city had, according to Eustace Reynolds-Ball, caused: "unsatisfactory hygienic conditions and appallingly primitive and unsanitary system of drainage. It is true that the sanitation of the Continental, Shepheard's, Ghezirah Palace, and other fashionable hotels is beyond reproach, but the visitor is not likely to spend all his time in the hotel. Besides, the innumerable urban amusements and social gaieties and dissipation's of this fashionable winter-city offer too many temptations to the invalid to neglect his health."

The Garden Ran Down to the Nile

Reynolds-Ball believed that the maximum benefit of the Egyptian climate was gained only from a prolonged Nile voyage as the Nile itself was more equable in temperature than its banks, and the "gaieties and dissipation's" of social life were almost nil.

William C. Prime highly recommended Egypt to invalids for its climate and calming atmosphere. He felt a voyage on the Nile a perfect dispensation to those suffering from pulmonary ailments: "Ladies of the most delicate constitutions need have no apprehensions in passing a winter in Egypt. The climate is delicious, the Nile boat is as comfortable as a hotel, and every luxury is provided by a careful dragoman that the most fastidious could desire. There is no such thing as 'roughing it' in Egypt."

Edward Lane believed the climate of Upper Egypt healthier than that of Lower Egypt, partly because the plague was prevalent in Cairo and Alexandria during 1835. It was believed that a possible 80,000 Egyptians fell victim to the disease in Cairo alone.

Alexander Kinglake travelled to Cairo in 1835, staying nineteen days: "During the whole time of my stay, the plague was so master of the city, and so plain in every street and every alley, that I can't now affect to dissociate the two ideas. . . . the funerals that daily passed under my windows were many. It so happened that most of the people with whom I had anything to do during my stay in Cairo were seized with plague; and all these died."

Kinglake became ill while in Cairo, but his unreserved optimism, self-discipline, and sheer will power probably saved him. Samuel Bevan remembered a red plague-seal over the door of the guesthouse he had stayed at in Alexandria around 1842, that had 'caused a shudder.'

There is a very old and widely known Egyptian superstition that says, 'Who-so-ever drinks the waters of the Nile, shall one day return to Egypt'. This is not to be taken literal, as drinking the Nile water today, will almost certainly have a negative effect. All the water in Egypt comes from the Nile—the Nile is no longer clean and pure. Tourists and residents are warned of drinking any water that is not bottled or boiled, and to stay clear of salads and fruits as they may have been washed in un-boiled water. The Nile is now so polluted that it can be quite dangerous to one's health. Bilharzia is prevalent along the banks of the river and stomach and intestinal infections such as 'Pharaohs revenge'—and worse, are common.

It was different before the age of industry brought pollution and the population explosion to Egypt. Every year the Sultan had shiploads of Nile water brought to Constantinople for his Harem. In 1842, Samuel Bevan noted the 'dirty brackish' water near Suez, but praised the water brought from the Nile in goatskins to be cooled underground in iron tanks for the consumption of passengers of the Overland Route.

John Gadsby in 1853 found the Nile water not as palatable as rain water, but perfectly drinkable when filtered: "The praises of the Nile water have been sung by travellers of every age, describing it as the most delicious in the world. The Arabs say that if Mahomet had once tasted it, he would have prayed that he might live for ever, so as to unceasingly enjoy its sweetness. To drink too much of the Nile water will relax the stomach, for it contains a large amount of salts;

and yet unfortunately, some travellers add to it an unusual quantity of oranges or other fruits, and thus often render the consequences serious. The Nile water has a turbid appearance as it rolls down its channel; but, after passing through an Egyptian zeer, a porous earthenware jar, it becomes perfectly free from impurities."

In the 1980s Helouan still had a thermal swimming bath and a variety of therapeutic facilities, and the climate was still warm and dry. However, the air was a far cry from the days when it could claim to be pure and salubrious as ever-increasing industrial development of the town and surrounding area was on the rise. Now, cement and lime factories, steelworks, automobile assembly plants, and a large power station defiled the area leaving the former tranquillity and beneficial amenities of Helouan gasping.

Ten

Thebes

The City of One Hundred Gates'
Homer

On my first day in Cairo I found myself dodging traffic and blaring horns as I made my way across Latin America Street past the Karnak Bazaar and rounded the corner to the Sunshine Travel Agency, next to the new Shepheard's Hotel to book my ticket to upper Egypt. Across the road a huge wooden barricade was hiding the demolition that had recently taken place. The celebrated 1907 Semiramis Hotel, the 'Queen of the Nile', as it called to commemorate the first Nile side hotel ever to be built, was being bulldozed to make way for the modern Semiramis Intercontinental. This was only the first of the demolition of several of Cairo's historical buildings that I was to witness.

I was flying Egypt Air—better known to ex-patriots as 'Inshallah (God willing) Airlines', that flew between Cairo and Luxor. I boarded the small twin-engine plane held about eighty passengers. The seats were narrow and the fuselage claustrophobic.

The Garden Ran Down to the Nile

The plane slowly made its way to the holding position with the aircraft pointing towards Thebes. The roar of the engines intensified as the plane started down the runway gaining speed and causing the cabin to vibrate and the wings to shake violently. The passengers ignored the no-smoking lights as the pilot lifted the nose of the aircraft off the runway, ascending at a steep angle before abruptly dropping down and levelling off—causing my stomach to hit my throat. A large Egyptian man wearing a short-sleeved safari suit, fumbled a length of worry beads, mopped the sweat from his brow, and lit another cigarette. I found myself prying my fingernails out of the arms of the seat to let blood flow back into white knuckles, as the stewardess served lunch; sandwiches wrapped in plastic paper, sticky cakes, and non-alcoholic beverages.

The plane flew at quite a low altitude allowing a non-descript view from the window as mile after mile of dun-coloured terrain, dotted with an occasional mud-brick village, passed by. There was not much to do but listened to the hum of the engines and watch the shadow of the plane cross the dips and swells of the landscape below. Every now and again the sun would reflect off the wing of the aircraft like a lazier, breaking the monotony. An hour later, as we prepared to land, the large Egyptian man again fingered his worry beads.

Safe on the ground I was met by Mr. Zakki, my guide from Sunshine Tours. He shook my hand like a long lost relative and whisked me off through the dusty roads which had once known Thebes to the beautiful Old Winter Palace Hotel—her terracotta coloured façade bathed in the pink light of the fading afternoon. The regal stone staircase fans both sides of the veranda where numerous Victorians wintering in Egypt must have sat and watched the colours of the sunset play on the hills across the Nile.

The interior of the Winter Palace had large stone pillars and clusters of sofas, tables and chairs placed strategically around the lobby giving the feeling that the interior had not changed dramatically over the last half-century; care-worn, yet charming. Palms and aspidistras in enormous brass pots lined the cream coloured walls of the huge room with its chintz draperies. An elaborate staircase with an Art Nouveau balustrade wound its way upwards to corridors of well-worn carpet passing heavily lacquered doors.

My room was on the second floor facing the Nile. It had a lovely high corniced ceiling, two single beds with soft mattresses, iron bedsteads, and delicate mosquito netting bunched around the back and secured with a cord. A large wingback chair filled one corner and there was a lovely old oak dresser with a bevelled mirror reflecting the charm of the room. The blue patterned wallpaper had faded sympathetically to harmonise with the once exquisite oriental carpet. Off the main room was a separate pink-tiled bathroom in need of repair, and an ornately decorated, but chipped porcelain suite in Victorian style.

French doors opened to the balcony where the view was imposing. The vast stretch of stark cliffs that cradled the tombs of the Kings loomed in a purple haze. To the right was an unobstructed view of the Luxor Temple. There were no hotels or modern buildings on the West Bank then, and only a few feluccas drifted silently on the Nile that wound its way under silver streams of sunlight. There were no luxury cruise ships lined five-abreast on the shore, no roar of cars and buses, and no bazaars or restaurants

The Garden Ran Down to the Nile

lining the banks of the river. Only the famous Gaddis Bazaar linked to the hotel, and a few kiosks along the Corniche that made galabehyas to order using old pedal-driven Singer sewing machines.

I stood motionless on the balcony, not wanting to break the spell of a civilization that time had forgotten. Staring out across the eternal river I knew that I was one of those romantic desert-loving westerners like Sir Richard Burton, Amelia B. Edwards and Gertrude Bell. I had tasted the waters of the Nile and I was not soon to forget it.

There is so much history steeped in this wonderful old hotel you can feel an entourage of famous people, if only in spirit; Gaston Maspero, Auguste Mariette, Sir Flinders Petrie, Howard Carter, and somewhere amid all the memories of the 19th century Egyptologists and extraordinary travellers, the Pharaohs themselves.

In the garden at the back of the hotel there were Mediterranean plants and flowers and a large aviary of tropical birds. Giant palms loomed in the moonlight and warm breezes stirred the fronds that played ghost-like shadows across the building.

The Old Winter Palace was built in 1886, and since I stayed there in 1976, has been refurbished with sympathy and due care to attention that denotes the historic splendour of this grand old lady. The main foyer with its parquet flooring is still host to large brass pots with weeping figs, and the sweeping staircase with its elaborate Art Nouveau balustrade, has been re-carpeted, making it a focal point.

The grandiose sitting room has also been redecorated in burgundy and pink with thick sumptuous curtains and table coverings edged with elaborate fringe and tassels. Mahogany furniture and oversized armchairs are grouped around the room illuminated by Chinese table lamps. The famous life sized portrait of David Roberts in Oriental dress hangs pride of place on one of the walls.

The gardens have been enlarged dramatically, and the aviary has gone. The palms loom twenty-five years higher, and there are many more exotic plants and flowers, and a shisha bar where you can recline on meshrabeya divans with brightly coloured cushions. At the end of the garden, nearly hidden by the foliage of a hundred different species of trees and plants, is an enormous swimming pool with an island bar, and a garden restaurant that overlooks it.

Mildred Alice Oliver stayed at the Luxor Hotel in 1930, but would have preferred the Winter Palace: "The little town of to-day is very crowded and picturesque, composed of mud houses, chiefly, narrow streets and most quaint little shops. As you get nearer the Nile bank you find much finer houses and some large hotels. Ours, the Luxor, is a well-established old one, rather low and like a big Indian bungalow with modern (higher) additions. It stands in a garden full of tropical trees and plants and in part of this immense garden stands (out by the edge of the river) the palatial Winter Palace Hotel, which is all under the same management. Personally I should have preferred to be there, for as you know, I don't mind gaiety! And there was a jolly little orchestra and heaps of most varied tourists to watch. A great terrace paved with marble on each side leads down to the Nile on one side and into the lovely hotel gardens on the other. Both terraces are used for tea and sitting out and have cane chairs, bright umbrella awnings, and every sort of gay luxury."

The Garden Ran Down to the Nile

The next morning I decided to live my propensity to the full and have breakfast on the balcony—bathing in the tranquillity of the moment. Down in the lobby Mr. Zakki was waiting for me and the rest of our party, five French tourists. He shook my hand once again in his vigorous water-pump manner and we all boarded the small ferryboat that was to take us across to the West Bank of the Nile and the Valley of the Kings. In Victorian times luncheon baskets would have been prepared by the hotel management and donkey sand-carriages waiting on the other side of the river. Unfortunately the only transportation that lay in wait for us on the west bank of the Nile, was a battered old mini-bus that careened up the slow twisting incline of the Wadyien to the rock-cut tombs of the Pharaohs.

The sun reflected off the white scree covered valley overlooked by its natural pyramid peak, the Cairn. I wanted to savour my few hours in Biban el Muluk (the Gates of the Kings), and was determined to go at my own pace and not be hurried from tomb to tomb. So as Zakki led the group of French tourists off in the direction of the much-celebrated Tutankhamun's tomb, I turned in the opposite direction to find tomb number seventeen.

Discovered by Giovanni Battista Belzoni in 1817, a long flight of wooden steps leads down into the cool entrance of the fourteen chambers of Seti I. At nearly 350 feet long, it is the largest tomb in the valley, and the most exceptionally beautiful. Although parts of the tomb have badly deteriorated due to flooding, the paintings are extraordinary—covering walls, pillars, and ceilings. Every chamber is elaborately decorated with scenes of the twelve chapters of the Book of the Gates; a mystical story of the journeying of the dead king in the form of the Sun God Ra through the dark underworld to be reborn again each morning. An assembly of various deities: Osiris, Hathor, Anubis the jackal, Isis and Nepthys, and the falcon-headed Horus, surround the procession as hovering vulture's look down from above.

At the time of the tombs discovery, hieroglyphics had not yet been deciphered and Belzoni could only have imagined what the strange scenes and picture writing could have meant. The burial chamber is dominated by an arched astronomical ceiling depicting gods, goddesses and constellations—many recognizable in today's heavens.

The alabaster sarcophagus of Seti is carved in incredibly fine detail showing the entire 'Book of the Gates'. But the sarcophagus is no longer there. Henry Salt, the British Consul General had a bent for trafficking in antiquities. He hired Belzoni, under the promise that all the treasures amassed would go to the British Museum—gratis. Salt, an unorthodox fame and fortune hunter, took credit for the discovery of the sarcophagus, along with many other treasures that Belzoni had unearthed; selling many of the items rather than donating them. Salt shipped Seti's sarcophagus to England and offered it to the British Museum—for a fee.

The British Museum however, turned it down, and eventually in 1824 it was purchased by the flamboyant architect, Sir John Soane, designer of the Bank of England and Dulwich College, for a mere £2,000 and relegated to the basement to join the hodgepodge and confusion of classical and mediaeval fragments at his London house at 13 Lincoln's Inn Fields—now a museum. I visited the house and remember feeling disheartened at seeing such an anachronism.

The Garden Ran Down to the Nile

I stayed alone in the tomb of Seti I for a long time trying to take in every square inch of the wonderful paintings, to burn in my mind's eye every brush stroke that had been so artistically executed. I felt as though I were eavesdropping on a culture I could not share, yet a feeling of acute awareness was overwhelmingly present. With the exception of Rameses III and Amenophis II, the other tombs in the valley seemed to pale into insignificance. The tomb of Tutankhamun is fascinating, not because of the beautiful sarcophagus that contains the boy kings mummy; which lays on view in the burial chamber, rather, the size of the tomb itself which is extremely small. It makes one wonder how the sheer volume of treasures, furniture, chariots, etc., came from within, let alone the three sepulchres that enclosed the two sarcophagi.

It also makes one reflect on the size of Seti I's tomb and the treasures it would have contained had it been found intact. Seti's tomb and the tomb of Nefertari, wife of Rameses II, have now been closed for nearly fifteen years. There are also plans to close the Tomb of Tutankhamun and others; due to the continual deterioration caused by mass tourism. A plan to create replica tombs in an effort to preserve the originals has been suggested.

Father Thomas Medary had the good fortune to meet Howard Carter in the Valley of the Kings in 1925, when Carter was still working at the site: ". . . we saw the tomb itself near Luxor, in the Valley of the Kings. It was brilliant, even gorgeous, with decorations as fresh and new in appearance as when the boy king's embalmed body was laid away in it some three thousand and five hundred years ago. The sarcophagus was a quadruple one. The immediate coffin, overlaid with gold a quarter of an inch thick and decorated with highly coloured, beautifully engraved figures, lies open to the gaze of the fortunate traveller who arrives on certain days of the week and who has paid for a special ticket of admission to the tomb. We had the good fortune not only of seeing the tomb, but of seeing also Howard Carter, the discoverer of it, and of getting a snapshot of him. Some doubt has been expressed as to whether the real mummy still rests in the gorgeous coffin shown to visitors, but it is reported that Mr. Carter declares he has actually had a peep at it and that it is in a fine state of preservation."

The Temple at Deir el Bahari was built by Queen Hatshepsut, the sister, wife and co-regent of Thutmosis III. The powerful female Pharaoh, a forerunner of women's lib, announced her right to the throne by claiming divine birth. The Temple of Hatshepsut is born from the semi-circle of rock-cut cliffs with sensitivity and harmony to nature. The platforms that rise to the entrance are like nothing else in Egypt and give the feeling of an open-air stage built for the gods under an audience of stars.

Today, in front of the restored temple there is a café that sells fast food and iced coke. A short distance away you can take a hot-air balloon flight at dawn, although the balloons don't actually soar over the Valley of the Kings as advertised, the prevailing air currents usually flow in the opposite direction, over canals and fields. But it is still an extraordinary thing to do in the early hours of the morning.

Just outside Medinet Habou is the Colossus of Memnon. Two immense seated figures of Amenophis III, which had originally stood in front of the king's mortuary temple and was the gateway to the Theban necropolis. Being the only part of the temple that is left, they too have suffered badly at the hands of time as the sandstone they are carved from is severely eroded.

It was said that the sandstone once contained beautiful agates, but Victorian travellers dug them out for mementoes. If you had visited the site a hundred years earlier, you might have heard the northern colossus emit a musical note at sunrise. But the gaps in the stone, caused by the ravages of time, which had produced the sounds, were sealed by the Romans in an attempt of preservation. Now we can only imagine and remember the wonderful myths that once existed.

Around the Colossus, local children seem to appear from nowhere to extract baksheesh, a custom no doubt made worse by the over extravagance of travellers.

Back in the mini-bus we passed the ancient community of Gurnah. The Gernawis derive from a Bedouin tribe that settled in the valley some hundred years ago and found it a convenient location for dealing in antiquities. The mud-brick village was the home of the infamous Ahmed Abd er-Rassul and his brothers who, during 1871-1881, exploited a royal cache of mummies they accidentally discovered at the base of a shaft in the catacombs of Thebes—while looking for a lost goat. The mummies, artefacts, and numerous papyrus scrolls soon found their way onto the black market to be snapped up by shady dealers and greedy collectors until finally found out and stopped by Agustus Maspero.

The ancestors of the Abd er-Rassul brothers still live there today and regard the brothers as folk-heroes. Today the villagers deal in modern 'antiques' for the tourists, along with soft drinks, fresh fruit, and taxi rides.

The robbing of graves continued into the twentieth century as the finest mummies were shipped to museums in the West. The less appealing specimens were used as Egyptian railway fuel over a period of ten years; their linen being stripped off beforehand and shipped to an American paper mill in Maine during the American Civil War to be turned into paper. Before any rational knowledge of medicine existed, mummies were also used as drugs and were exported from Egypt for that purpose. When demand exceeded supply, recently deceased bodies were dried using a preparation that gave them the same appearance and odour as the genuine article—a rather macabre reality.

There were few cars or taxis in Luxor in the seventies, and the popular mode of transport was a caléche, a horse drawn carriage. They travelled up and down the Corniche to and from the Temples of Luxor and Karnak. My caléche had a convertible top rather like the hood on a baby's pram. It was decorated with fringe and worsted tassels. The leather seat was cracked and worn-out from a thousand bottoms and squeaked with every movement.

The horse was also worn-out, tired and spindly looking with a protruding ribcage and a greying muzzle. His bridle was fringed between his ears and on his harness small silver bells tinkled as he walked. In spite of his appearance he had a spring in his step and seemed to know exactly where to go down the acacia lined Corniche to the temple complex of Karnak.

The Garden Ran Down to the Nile

One of the great wonders of Egyptian architecture is the Hypostyle Hall. One hundred and thirty-four columns—many of which are now missing, once supported the roof. The hall is divided into a nave that is seventy-nine feet in height. The twenty-two colossal columns are beautifully inscribed with bas-relief hieroglyphs on which light and shadow play. The columns on either side of the aisle are thirty-three feet in height and give a cool retreat from the burning sun. The capitals form the sepals of buds and lotus flowers. According to Baedeker the breath of this Great Hall is spacious enough to accommodate the entire church of Notre-Dame.

There was only a handful of tourist and the silence was overwhelming, almost intimidating. How lovely this temple must have been in Pharaonic times. If those pillars could speak what secrets they could tell. Not only the legacy of the hieroglyphs, but plain tales of everyday occurrences; the builders, the storytellers, the poets and scribes, the farmers, the market traders, and the boy that watched over the goats. Tales that are now buried deep beneath the sands of time. Walking between the columns gave privacy a new dimension, now it is difficult to find a private area to reflect—the contemplative silence has gone forever as there are now so many tourists.

The Son et Lumère show took place every evening around the Hypostyle Hall where searchlights threw angular shadows across the columns. The show is more grandiose today. Following the coloured lights and a running commentary throughout the temple, you finish at the Sacred Lake and sit on raised bleachers looking over the Lake that stands to the south of the Temple of Anon. The water is saline and undrinkable and watched over by the colossal, black granite Scarab of Amenophis III. The Temple of Karnak was built during the reign of many different Pharaohs, each adding his own temples and statues—making the sheer scale of the complex overwhelming.

G.W. Steevens refers to Karnak as the 'Jewel of Luxor': "I saw it first by moonlight as well. Along the dim, dusty road you suddenly come on a tall pylon – a square gateway, inclining slightly towards the top, narrow for its great height. Then Karnak begins. Soon you are in an avenue of couchant sphinxes, defaced lion heads, ghostly in the white light. In front of you tower what look like two fortresses, two mountains of masonry. They are so huge that you at first mistake them for real hills; yet they are only another gateway. Now you are in the great hall, standing like an ant between roes on rows of giant columns. Those at the back are half hidden in rubble that climbs to where the roof was; the nearest stand free, and it takes ten people's arms to encircle them. You stand abashed beneath them; wherever you look more tremendous pillars press in upon you; the blue-blacked, star-pierced heaven is only a little slit far, far above you. You are almost glad to escape from the impression of their majesty, and be out again in the moonlight you are accustomed to."

Douglas Sladen enjoyed seeing the temples by moonlight, riding to Karnak accompanied by three ladies from Cook's tour on board the 'Rameses the Great'. However, in 1908 there was no Son et Lumère, no lights to guide you through the ruins and the party explored the temple in a much more romantic, and no doubt just a little frightening illumination—matches and tapers: "Our white steamer looked as if she had been cut out of ivory as she lay at her moorings on the swift black Nile; a plank over the waters brought us ashore. There four large white asses were awaiting us, attended by tall Arabs. . . We rode through the gaunt black street. I fell back a little, the ladies wanted to beguile the way with idle chatter; to me that mysterious mile of moonlight was a precious bit of the Orient. The tops of the palm trees make black patterns against the moonlight: Wherever there was a gap I could see the hills of Thebes white as snow in the moonlight. The Arab village looked ghostly and Pharaonic with its grotesque outlines. . . . Even the ladies were transfigured, for, knowing that they were going to ride, they had come down to dinner in white summer frocks, instead of evening dresses. The worn Sphinxes in the darkness below the palm trees looked like sleeping monsters of the mysterious eld.

"Armed with the matches we stalked through the avenue of ram-headed Sphinxes, admirable in the moonlight. . . .To enjoy the romance of Karnak you must visit it by night, when you can hear the fans of the palm trees and the feathery tamarisks swishing in the breeze. In that half-light the eye wanders leisurely round the great court so tyrannized by the sun in the middle hour of the day; it notes the line of Sphinxes round the wall; the hill of stones poured from the fallen pylon; the mysterious gods emerging from the shadows outside the Temple of the third Rameses. These Egyptian statues of gods or men are all alive by night."

In 1976, looking out over the terrace of the Winter Palace across the river to the Valley of the Kings, and the steep stark cliffs that had kept their secrets for so many centuries, I wondered if Howard Carter had sat where I was now sitting, contemplating the same landscape. There were no bridges over the Nile—nothing to obstruct the view. Today, with the onslaught of tourism, the silence has gone and you can no longer gaze across the river to an unspoilt landscape or appreciate the sunset because a thousand lights from newly built hotels glare back at you and the noise from the street below is a non-stop cacophony. The Corniche is lined with hawkers and touts pushing felucca rides as everyone wants to sell you something with the promise of 'no hassle.' The river's edge can no longer be enjoyed in solitude as it's lined with tourist ships four levels high and five abreast resting at the water's edge in the permanent sludge of oil and rotting garbage.

Now if you want to see the temples of Edfu and Kom Ombo, or the Temple of Abou Simbel, you have to be transported in minibuses that drive in convoy under the protection of Kalashnikov toting soldiers.

Eleven

Assouan

▲▲▲

'She was an Amazon. Her whole life was spent riding towards the wilder shores of love'
Lesley Blanch

Assouan airport looked like a bombed-out air shelter. A small waiting room with peeling paint and filthy windows housed a mélange of people waiting for something or someone. Women and children were grouped together in a state of perpetual lethargy, spilling over the wooden benches and onto the concrete floor amid bundles of clothing, pots, pans, and crates of live chickens. A young man in a moth-eaten orange sweater and tight bell-bottomed trousers culminating over platform shoes was listened to a portable radio that blasted out Arabic music in broken airwaves. In one corner of the room old men played dominoes and smoked hand-rolled cigarettes through nicotine stained fingers—the smoke encircling their heads, and mixing with the flies that swarmed around the children—landing on their mouths and in the corners of their eyes.

The Garden Ran Down to the Nile

I moved outside and found a corner in the shade to wait for my guide from Sunshine Tours. It was hot and my bottled water had run out. I hoped that my hotel, the Old Cataract, had Evian or something similar. My guide, Mohammed, finally made his appearance looking as though he had slept in his suit. He mopped his brow, complained of the heat, and as we drove off, endeavoured to explain that there had been a mix-up in my hotel booking. While pointing out uninteresting points of interest, I was now going to be staying at the Kalabsha Hotel—two hundred metres and two stars down from the five-star Cataract Hotel.

At first glance the Kalabsha looked like a high-rise ghetto building on the outskirts of London with five floors of desert coloured concrete rising in straight angles. An uneven and unpaved road ran along the side of the hotel that led to the entrance. The dust swirled into the car and stuck to my perspiring skin as I thought of the lovely Old Winter Palace. When I saw the hotel my heart sank, but I was prepared to accept my fate as another adventure—besides, the Kalabsha boasted 120 air-conditioned rooms. Unfortunately the air-conditioning was out of order—so was the lift and my room was on the fourth floor.

Taking my leave of Mohammed, I followed a bent and sombre porter slowly up the dimly-lit staircase that he must have climbed countless times. Reaching the room, his key poised to unlock the door, we found that there was only a hole where the lock should have been. Confused by this, he bent down and peered through the hole before turning the knob and entering. He deposited my case on the bed, and with a nod of his greying head, closed the door.

I found myself in a small square room worsened by design, rather than time—linoleum flooring, hideous dingy wallpaper, one uncomfortable looking armchair of veined and cracked leather and a floor lamp with a brown stained lampshade dimming a 40-watt bulb. The lamp was placed in such a position as making reading in bed impossible. A picture hung on the wall and at first I couldn't make out what it was. On closer inspection I realized it was a print of a waterfall—hung side-ways.

Through a pair of shuttered doors the concrete balcony clung precariously to the side of the building and overlooked great stretches of sunburnt landscape dotted with dust-covered shrubbery. Every now and again swirls of smoke rose across the terrain from scattered dwellings. The angle of the building blocked the view of Elephantine Island and the river, but also kept out the scorching sun.

The mattress on the bed had given up completely, leaving a small indent in the center forbidding you from lying anywhere else. The telephone on the bedside-table had died, and as there was no lock on the door, I slipped my camera deep inside my tote and in pretence safety—locked it. After a quick wash in cold water with the miniscule sliver of soap employed by all hotels, I went down to lunch and hopefully bottled water.

The dining-room was a large open area decorated in a no-frills, functional fifties style with plastic seated straight-backed chairs and white cloths covering laminated pressed-wood tables. Whitewashed supports held up a ceiling that was dotted with pinhole lighting. The room hummed with polite conversation—bouncing off the stark walls and parquet floors where Nubian waiters in gold coloured galabehyas and white turbans stood in attendance.

The Garden Ran Down to the Nile

After lunch Mohammed appeared. A dusty taxi ride delivered us to the beautiful old Cataract Hotel (where I should have been staying) and we walked the long palm-shaded drive down the side of the hotel to the banks of the Nile where our boat was waiting. We stepped on board the careworn felucca as it set sail and glided past the famous Island of Elephantine—named after the smooth, large granite rocks surrounding the island that were said to resemble elephants bathing in the river.

Every now and again a felucca filled to overflowing with chatty tourists sporting white cotton beanies, would pass by and I felt grateful to be on my own. Dark skinned children played on the sand banks by the river's edge, absorbed in kicking around a deflated football in a game of soccer. Younger boys in small boats crafted from pieces of wood or old oil barrels paddled out to meet us. Their small makeshift masts were decorated with colourful bunting and they had strapped pieces of tin to their hands that served as paddles.

It would seem that very little had changed since 1925 when the Rev. Thomas Medary Iden recalled a similar picture: "American tin plated, obtained from Standard Oil (or other) cans, is used for multitudes of purposes all over the Orient. Yesterday we saw boats made of it. Boys on the lake at Asswan Dam were rowing about in small canoes of Rochefeller tin and these were propelling them with tin paddles, mere discs of the metal held between thumb and forefinger."

We docked at the Botanical Island, often referred to as Kitchener's Island as it was given to Lord Kitchener when he was

The Garden Ran Down to the Nile

Consul-General in Egypt. The Egyptian fellaheen loved Kitchener as he had been sympathetic to their needs as well as a devout securer of their well-being. He spoke classical and colloquial Arabic and had a passion for gardens—importing plants and trees from India, China, and the Middle East, to fill his Botanical Island. Palms, oleanders, and pomegranate trees overgrown and dusty, pay tribute to his efforts.

Sunlight and shadow filtered through the fronds of the swaying palms where birds sang and the sense of a hundred centuries permeated the air. There was an outdoor café that overlooks the river where we stopped to have what the locals call lemon—a drink made from small Egyptian lemons that look like limes. Two Nubian musicians weathered with age, entertained the visitors with traditional folk music played on the rababa; a two stringed viola played upright with a bow, and the daraboka; a drum similar to the Irish boron.

The Island is now owned by the Egyptian government.

We sailed on to a cove along the west bank of an island and docked by a steep sand hill that spilled down the bank to the water's edge. Huddled under the shade of a few palm trees half-a-dozen men were dozing with their camels.

I thought the camel a lovely looking animal from a distance. He is a proud, austere and a rather aloof looking creature with long sumptuous eyelashes. But on closer inspection there lurks ulterior motives and beneath those comical protruding lips lie enormous brown teeth resembling stained piano keys. He conceals them in a large mouth that is ready to spit, bite and make the most appalling growling noises. To ride one of these bad tempered beasts—which object to being ridden—could be described as misadventure and should be enough of a deterrent to any would be passenger. Nevertheless, I hired one of the less disagreeable looking animals, which the man called Mohammed—surprising originality.

Mohammed eyed me, growled his annoyance, and as I climbed 'on-board', heaved his way to his feet. His owner, a young man of undetermined age jumped on behind, bringing his body as close as he could to mine. To his disappointment I told him in no uncertain terms, to get off or we weren't going anywhere. Reluctantly he did.

Mohammed's large splayed feet slapped heavily on the sand as he sauntered off in a rolling-gait with the young man following behind. The only tourist for miles, I made my way over the sand-dunes without mishap to the mausoleum of the Aga Khan; the 48th Imam of the Shia Imami Ismailis, a Moslem sect dwelling mainly in Pakistan and Iran.

The Aga Khan had fallen in love with Assouan and decided to spend the rest of his life here. He built a villa that stands below the mausoleum in which he is buried. The mausoleum itself is a simple structure of desert coloured sandstone blending into the surrounding area like a watercolour painting. Sliding off Mohammed and leaving my shoes outside the door, I ventured in upon red carpets that showed thin and worn in the filtered sunlight—a cool retreat from the burning sun outside. A dim, incandescent softness complemented the strict silence that was observed.

The way back over the dunes seemed even hotter, the flies were persistent, and the camel's owner still pleading that he should be allowed to ride. As I was adamant that this was not going to happen, I gave way to better judgement, and feeling masterful over my 'ship of the desert,' gave him encouragement with the crop. This caused him to growl and break into a full gallop and I went charging off like Lawrence to Akaba—with Mohammed's owner running after me shouting and waving his arms in agitation.

Mohammed's trot had jarred every bone in my body, but his gallop was sheer suicide. His neck was stretched out in front of him, which left little to hold onto except my dignity. Fortunately I managed to stay on and he eventually slowed to his normal rolling gait and found his way back to the shade of the palm trees. The camel owner gasping at his heels.

Back in the waiting felucca I spent a blissful hour under billowing sails watching the magnificent panorama of Egyptian life glide by. The declining sun cast an amber glow across the fields and the lengthening shadow of the boat. The oars creaked in their rowlocks and made tiny ripples on the glass-like surface of the Nile, while luminous dragonflies danced and flickered as we came to rest at the resplendent pink and imposing Cataract Hotel.

There was not much to do or see at night in Assouan. Back then people disappeared like Monks to prayer. There was no street lighting or shops on the dirt roads that were more like lanes, so after a quiet dinner in the hotel dining room, I retired to my unsecured bedroom, wedged the cracked leather chair under the peek-a-boo doorknob, and rolled into the indent of the mattress where, covered in layers of mosquito repellent, I settled down with my Baedeker in the adverse lighting.

When I visited the hotel in 2006, all the roads leading to and around had been paved, and I found it had been converted to be a convention center for men—but they had forgotten to take down the worn and faded sign that still said—Kalabsha Hotel.

The Garden Ran Down to the Nile

A little way out of town, traversing on foot for nearly fifteen minutes through a landscape of sand, rock and date palms, was the granite quarries where the ancient Egyptian stonecutters obtained the stone that was used for building the monuments. Huge blocks of red granite were cut by boring a line of holes in the stone into which wedges of wood were driven before being soaked with water that caused the wood to expand and the blocks to split away from the quarry. The 137 feet long and 14 feet wide unfinished obelisk, reclined amidst silent, cool palm trees. I climbed the obelisk and walked the length where a massive crack runs down the center—the reason it was abandoned. It's estimated that it would have been the largest obelisk ever hewn and would have weighed 1168 tonnes. When the crack appeared the stonecutters had already dressed three of the sides.

A massive causeway was used to transport the blocks to the Nile. Today it's a road and the obelisk lies miserable and forlorn in its rock quarry that has been stripped of its date palms and peaceful atmosphere. Thousands of tourists now traipse round the man-made ramps that surround it. An enormous parking lot and ticket office have been built and you can no longer see the obelisk until you are directly above it.

Annie Quibell remembers the obelisk when she visited the quarry in the early 1900s: "Other characteristic sights of Assuan are the old quarries. The most famous object there, an unfinished obelisk, is not far from the town, just beyond the Arab cemetery. It is larger than any of the obelisks now standing and it was found to be too much flawed to be possible to remove it. Another attempt was made to cut it down to a smaller size, but again the granite was not of good enough quality right through and the whole thing was abandoned and lies as it was left there, sometime in the Eighteenth Dynasty."

At the beginning of the 20th century there were three excellent hotels in Assouan; the Grand Hotel d'Assouan, the Savoy, and the Cataract. These hotels were the center of society just as the prestigious hotels in Cairo. Under the management of M. Ferdinand Pagnon of the Upper Egypt Hotel Company, the Cataract Hotel underwent constant improvements. By 1902 it had all the comforts and amenities one could wish for. The interior of the hotel conjures images of the Arabian Nights with its large Moorish arches that give a Pharaonic feel. French cuisine is served in the dining room under a soaring domed ceiling—creating an atmosphere that obliges one to dress for dinner.

In 1902, as today, there were wonderfully furnished salons, long halls, and terraces that overlook the Island of Elephantine. A billiards room, a library, electric lights, and ornate iron worked caged-lifts are still in use. During the day there were sports of every kind to be had; with the occasional gymkhana, donkey and camel races. In the evenings there were bridge-parties, concerts, and balls.

Exploring the hallways one afternoon I was shown the 'Agatha Christy Suite' where the writer was supposed to have stayed. There is a brass plaque on the wall beside the door displaying her name.' The bell-boy let me into her suite which consisted of a bedroom, en suite bathroom, and sitting room complete with the desk she wrote 'Death On the Nile' at. The view from the balcony looked over the back of the hotel and the picturesque tranquil Nile. The bell-boy made me promise not to tell the management.

The Garden Ran Down to the Nile

The hotel is now owned by the Sofitel group and has been refurbished with sensitivity, keeping to the British Colonial Period and Victorian grandeur. It has been said that coming into the hotel is like walking into a painting or a period post card.

In 1905 while Améedé de Guerville was writing in his room with the windows to his balcony open, he heard a commotion and witnessed a spectacle that he was not soon to forget: "Hundreds of donkeys arrived at the gallop, donkeys of every colour and size, mounted by the most varied typed of riders that one could meet with under the same sky. Every one had come for a paper-chase, the start and finish of which were to take place at the Cataract. Never in my life have I seen such an extraordinary collection of men of all ages, their heads covered with sun-helmuts (sic), panamas, straw and felt hats, their legs encased in putties, gaiters, and riding-boot of extra-ordinary shape; the women adorned with strange head-dresses, from which streamed immense veils, with short skirts, excellent for walking but a trifle airy for the saddle. All this host, gathered from the four corners of the world, shouted and gesticulated in all the tongues, and I wondered at the quietness of the donkeys, excellent animals if ever there were. A little further on, squatted on the sand, their necks out-stretched, the camels looked on with the greatest interest at this stirring scene; and when the signal to start was given, and the immense cavalcade careered off with yells and cracking of whips, some of them, furious at being left out in the cold, emitted the most awful groans – and the groaning of a camel is none too musical."

Like the terrace at Shepheard's, the Cataract's large covered veranda at the back of the hotel is where people sit for hours in

The Garden Ran Down to the Nile

rattan chairs enjoying not the carnival of Cairean life, and a soporific view of the Nile across a landscape of palm trees and greenery where feluccas glide peacefully by.

You can sip your gin and tonic and watch the magnificent sunsets change from bright vermillion to deepest indigo over the rocks of Elephantine Island, but don't look to the left because the view is totally obstructed by the hideous high-rise New Cataract Hotel that throws its shadow over the gardens of the Old Hotel; it's swimming pool and the noise of the swimmers destroying the silence that once existed.

Assouan has now grown so large due to tourism that you can no longer stroll complacently along the Corniche enjoying the peace and quiet—as there is no peace and quiet. New hotels, restaurants, shops, increasing traffic, and the ever growing population is turning Assouan into little Cairo where you are accosted at every step by hawkers touting felucca rides.

An imposing Coptic Christian Cathedral surrounded by gardens and spot-lights occupies several blocks between the Cataract Hotel and the Kalabsha, and new roads have been built and existing dirt ones paved. Recently built houses in the American tract-style line the road that leads up to Nubian House, an outdoor café that serves up fresh fruit juices and picture postcard views; a last vestige so far bereft of tourists. From the high vantage point that overlooks Elephantine Island and the First Cataract, you can sip your mango juice and watch feluccas with soaring lateen sails meandering round the palm-covered islands on a serene azure blue Nile.

Twelve

Abou Simbel

'My name is Ozymandias, King of Kings:
Look on my works, Ye Mighty, and despair!'
                    Percy Bysshe Shelly

The great rock cut temple of Abou Simbel sits at the back door of Egypt. The sheer enormity of the colossal figures manifests a feeling of power, which amplifies the authority of the king. The three remaining faces of Rameses the Great stare out across Lake Nasser towards Nubia defying anyone to enter Egypt. When the High Dam project was launched in 1960 the rising waters of Lake Nasser would have completely covered the two temples—that of Rameses and the temple dedicated to his queen, Nerfertari—had UNESCO not stepped in. The temples were cut from one thousand and forty-two blocks—most of them weighing 20 tons each, and reset into artificial mountains on higher ground.

Baedeker describes Abou Simbel as one of the: "most stupendous monuments of ancient Egyptian architecture and challenges comparison with the gigantic edifices situated in Egypt proper. This temple produces a very grand effect by moonlight or at sunrise."

The Garden Ran Down to the Nile

It would have been wonderful, as Amelia Edwards experienced, to round the bend in a dahabeyah with the full morning sun reflecting off the faces of the magnificent King of Kings, or in the stillness of moonlight with a background of stars—the canvas sails flapping gently in the breeze. However, it was not be. I found myself on a non-air conditioned mini-bus crowded with overly enthusiastic German tourists; obviously unaccustomed to the intense heat of Upper Egypt. It was October, 108°F and rising. Bottles of water were passed around as corpulent women and portly men mopped their brows with large cotton handkerchiefs. The hum of German and broken English resounded throughout the coach as we bumped steadily into what seemed the middle of nowhere.

The German travellers appeared quite different from the way G.W. Steevens saw them in 1898: "Men in huge helmets, with puggary, (sic) huge blue goggles, knickerbockers, and chess-board stockings: women in the same helmets and goggles, vast blue veils, sunshade, short skirts, and vast hands and feet; both sexes crested with Meyer or Baedeker rampant – they make a picture at which native Egypt gapes in undisguised delight."

We disembarked and followed the guide in goat-herd fashion across a stretch of sand dotted with scrub and rock and rounded a hill where, on the left, one of four enormous seated figures of Rameses II emerged dominant. Looking out across Lake Nasser this stupendous monument is truly magnificent; one can see how Shelley was inspired to write 'Ozymandias'.

When first discovered in 1813 by John Lewis Burckhardt, the Swiss Arabist and traveller, only the colossal heads were seen rising from the sand drifts, which had almost completely covered them.

Burckhardt then related what he had seen to Giovanni Belzoni, who with the assistance of Charles Irby and James Mangles, two British Naval officers, painstakingly excavated the temple with little more than a few makeshift hoes and their bare hands—amid the constant quarrelling and hostilities from the surrounding inhabitants.

Shielding my eyes from the reflective glare of the sun, I studied the honey coloured features of Rameses the Great and thought about Amelia B. Edwards who in 1875 had spent fourteen days at the foot of this remarkable temple. She saw the three remaining faces transfigured every morning with the rising of the sun:

"It was wonderful to wake every morning close under the steep bank, and without lifting one's head from the pillow, to see that row of giant faces so close against the sky. They showed unearthly enough by moonlight, but not half so unearthly as in the grey of dawn. At that hour, the most solemn of the twenty-four, they wore a fixed and fatal look that was succeeded by a flush that mounted and deepened like the rising flush of life. For a moment they seemed to glow – to smile – to be transfigured. Every morning I saw those awful brethren pass from death to life, from life to sculptured stone. I brought myself almost to believe at last that there must sooner or later come some one sunrise when the ancient charm would snap asunder and the giants must arise and speak."

I had definitely been born too late. I felt cheated that I too, could not sleep under the shadow of Rameses, and felt resentful that I had to share my experience. 'One travels more usefully when alone, because he reflects more.' Thomas Jefferson.

The Garden Ran Down to the Nile

If I had known then what the site would be like in thirty years, I would never have complained as there were only about twelve other tourists there besides myself and my German companions

G.W. Steevens was another Nile traveller who in 1898 found the allure of Abou Simbel captivating: "It is the most original and by far the most impressive of the ancient monuments. We saw it first at night by flaring limelight. Here again, as in all the other temples, the mechanical wonder of the achievement is more than the beauty of it. Yet Abou Simbel, if not beautiful, is grand. For, two on either side of the doorway, sit four colossal statues, carved in relief out of the rock face. They are so well proportioned that they do not strike you as immense, but how immense they are you may judge from the fragments of one that has fallen. In the morning there they sat – one defaced three almost perfect, leaning in quiet majesty against the precipice, gazing across the river to the climbing sun. Nothing at all in sight but those four great, silent serene wardens by the door, looking changelessly out over the river to the desolation."

By 1843 the first steamers were appearing and the British consul in Cairo was complaining of a 'flood' of tourist into Egypt. Then in 1869 Thomas Cook embarked on what he called "a great event in the arrangements of modern travel." By 1902 the influx of sightseers on the Nile was noticed by Lee Bacon whose dahabeyah was moored at the foot of Abou Simbel: "Fortunately for us, the crowd soon steams away; many of the party having failed altogether to take in the grandeur of this wonder. We who are moored almost at its foot, seeing it at sunrise, at midday, in all the glory of the setting sun, then in the mystery of twilight, then lighted by the tremendous brilliancy of this moon of the far south, have decided that but for its having been too far away for the worlds experts to see easily, there would have been eight wonders of the world."

It seems that even at the turn of the century, G.W. Steevens found that tourists were being hustled passed monuments without much concern for concept: "We who stay so long and adore so profoundly can appreciate a little the feeling of the Egyptologist who heard a party of excursionists brag that they had finished Karnak in one hour. 'How fortunate you are, for I have been studying for many years and have not finished one wall!' But the sarcasm was lost on the gay excursionists, who continued on their way, to take in, anaconda-like, other temples in the course of the afternoon.

"The Upper Egypt silence is often broken by trivial and quaint remarks which linger long after in one's memory, where one would wish more important things could indelibly engrave themselves; remarks such as a traveller was heard to make, that she would have enjoyed Egypt very much but for 'so many dug-up things'."

For centuries the temple inside the rock cut monument lay buried under a mountain of drifting sand with the entrance covered but for a crawl space at the top of the doorway. In 1837 Amelia B. Edwards ventured inside through this crawl space to find: "It is a wonderful place to be alone in – a place in which the very darkness and silence are old and in which time himself seems to have fallen asleep. Wandering to and fro among shadows, one seems to have left the world behind. There was something so weird and awful about the place, and it became so much more weird and awful the farther one went in, that I rarely ventured beyond the first hall when quite alone."

In 1865 when William C. Prime visited—some twenty-eight years after Amelia, he too had slipped through the opening to the temple under the illumination of candles: "The sand hill was almost impassable. It was like climbing a snow bank fifty feet high, the feet going in deep and slipping far back at every step, so that we had to lie down and breath several times before we reached the top and descended into the doorway of the temple.

"Never since the days of Rameses has his great temple shone so brilliantly. Every statue held bright lanterns, and for two hundred feet through the long rooms we placed them – rows of every color, shining on painted walls and lofty statues. The altar was in the shadow – for so we arranged it – hiding the lights behind it that they might shine on the faces of the gods and not on the altar front. It was a gorgeous scene, worth visiting Egypt to look on that illumination; and we sat for hours in the hall, gazing with never – ceasing wonder and awe on the splendid statues and lofty walls. One can hardly imagine a place on earth where a man could be more emphatically alone than I then was at mid-night, two hundred feet from the air, in the deep caverns of Abou Simbal."

Thirteen

Alexandria

▲▲▲

'Tourists who come to Egypt are of two types – those who know what they have let themselves in for and those who don't'
                                              Major C.S. Jarvis

Once the greatest city in the world, nothing remains of the ancient Ptolemaic Alexandria, with the exception of Pompey's Pillar and the Temple of Serapis, an underground labyrinth of passageways beneath the modern city. It is said that Alexander the Great is buried somewhere in the catacombs, but his grave has yet to be found. Pompey's Pillar has nothing to do with Pompey—the 25 meter high column was erected in honour of the Roman emperor Diocletian. It is flanked on either side by two reclining Sphinxes and stands on the site of the ruined Serapeum. John Gadsby, when visiting Pompey's Pillar in 1847 found it: "much disfigured by the names of Europeans, painted upon it in all colors."

Gone are the Museum, the Hippodrome and the Gymnasium, and we can only guess at the location of the University—the academic nucleus that once housed some of the world's greatest minds and best-known scholars: Eratosthenes, Socrates, Archimedes, Hippocrates, and Euclid.

One of the greatest historical tragedies of all time was during the Alexandrian wars when Julius Caesar's army set light to the Egyptian fleet. The fire soon raged out of control spreading from the harbour destroying most of the city and the Great Library. The library housed the greatest accumulation of knowledge in the world—the most ancient collection of books and manuscripts known to man. All arriving ships that contained books were directed to submit them while they were copied, swelling the library to no less than 700,000 books—over twice the number of people living in Alexandria. They included volumes of the works of: Aristotle, Homer, and Plato, collections of poetry, philosophy, art, and music, studies of the principles of mathematics, the sciences, medicine, astronomy, geometry, geography, physics, chemistry, and engineering. The original Septuagint translation of the Old Testament was lost in the fire along with ancient writings on the history of Egypt—history which could have revealed many of the mysteries of a culture that must now remain obscure.

Manetho was one of the first great historians of Egypt. He wrote of Ptolemy Philadelphus in the 3rd century B.C., which was also amongst the records destroyed in the Great Library fire.

In 1987 a new library, the Bibliotheca, was approved by UNESCO and in 2002 it opened. The building was designed in the shape of an enormous discus embedded in the earth to represent a second sun rising beside the Mediterranean. It is more of a museum than a library.

The Garden Ran Down to the Nile

One of the few remaining original hotels left in Alexandria is the Cecil. Built in 1929 by the Metzger family; of French, Egyptian, and Jewish origin, it sits on the Corniche overlooking the Mediterranean and Saad Zaghloul Square where Cleopatra's Needle once stood. The hotel was seized by the Egyptian government after the 1952 revolution, where after a lengthy court battle, was returned to the Metzger family. It is now owned by the Sofitel Group and has maintained with sympathy, its original romantic quality. Shaded by looming palm trees, you step into 1920s gentility where Laurence Durrell and Agatha Christie were amongst the famous residents. The central staircase with its period black and gold wrought-iron balustrade, sweeps around the original mahogany caged lift with concertina doors and matching wrought-iron gates.

To the west of Alexandria on the Mediterranean coast is Agami. It was built as a resort in the 1950s by innovative rich Egyptians. Bathed in sunshine and salty breezes, in summer it became the St. Tropez of Egypt with a section of villas known as millionaire's row. In the off-season the town appeared as an amalgamate community of past decades merging together in a complex of summer villas empty of people.

Once a prosperous community shaded under a canopy of trees, Agami was a pleasant break from hectic Cairo. It was sometimes so languid it bordered on lethargy and seemed a little decadent and lost under layers of dust and fading paintwork—a forgotten holiday community where verandas with worn wicker chairs covered in a variety of non-matching chintz and canvas faded from the sun, awaited the summer tenants. Windows shuttered

The Garden Ran Down to the Nile

against the sun and potted plants long since dead from lack of water, gave an abandoned look to the area.

Our villa was about one kilometre up the beach from the Hanoville Hotel. A hotel frequented by foreign ex-pats in the winter, but closed down in the summer months as the heat was so intense you could not lie on the beach—and there was nothing else to do in Agami but lie on the beach that was often deserted. The sunsets were magnificent and the blackness of night total. The sand stayed warm from the heat of the day, and looking up from a lying position, a million stars were palpable and intensely visible due to the lack of artificial lighting in the surrounding area. Mars a visible glowing red mote, Orion and Nebula, the Big Dipper, all the constellations you learned in school and then quickly forgot because you were never able to see them from the city skies. They twinkled solitarily or in clusters in the parabola of night sky that disappeared into the black of the Mediterranean. Shooting stars would arch across the expanse and disappear into infinity. The depth of the sky was disorienting and the silence so intense it made your ears ring.

The villa was an unattractive large six-bedroom stone built and box-shaped building with a flat roof, high corniced ceilings and tiled flooring that kept the inside cool. A sun-trap balcony off one of the bedrooms overlooked the sea that was about fifty meters away. The stale smell of damp and salt disappeared when the heavy wooded shutters were flung open to the warmth of the afternoon, flooding the rooms with sunlight.

The proprietor was a Swiss-born spinster in her eighties called Mary. She had huge feet that were always covered in Lyle stockings and carpet slippers and her shabby attire included a hand-knitted, grey cardigan that had seen more moths than soap. She cared for two stray puppies with deformed legs; keeping them in the cellar under the house justifying, that they would not survive out of doors.

When she was not renting out the villa, she stayed in two of the rooms off the kitchen. Once, when collecting the keys, I realized why the house had so many cigar-sized cockroaches. Her small kitchenette was filthy with unwashed dishes, cutlery, and pots and pans. Food had hardened to concrete on the countertops—the smell was overpowering. Her sitting room was darkened by closed shutters. The room housed a small bed with crumpled bedclothes, and a table piled high with books and stacks of yellowing magazines from Europe. A large overstuffed chair that had long since lost the battle to Mary's corpulence sat vacant. A sideboard revealed dozens of prescription medications in dusty containers—most of them years out of date.

Mary looked like the bad fairy from a Grimm's tale with long grey wisps of hair escaping hairpins, and a back bent round from unkind years and osteoporosis. But she was a kindly old soul who lived within the memories of her past life. She and her sister had come to Egypt as girls, abandoning the rules of polite society to live a liberated life in a foreign country in a time fraught with dangers and hardships for single women. Her sister painted, and in the large living room overlooked by a balconied hallway, the walls held numerous oil paintings that testified to her talent. Now Mary was alone with her two crippled dogs.

I had been told that farther down the beach was some kind of army barracks. I never knew for sure, but groups of men would come down the beach, to where we always sunbathed, to swim and muck-about in jocular adolescence. Whenever my friend and I sat on the beach, several young men would lodge themselves within reach of us, even though there were miles of empty beach on both sides. My friend would take with her a large length of wood, in case a situation should arise. It never did.

The Desert Road was a desolate barren highway 220 km long that linked Alexandria to Ghiza and took four boring hours to traverse—depending on how fast you drove. There were no petrol stations and nothing of any interest on either side of the road but an ocean of sand, the wind, and an occasional spinney of trees or group of scrawny wild camels nibbling invisible vegetation. The only respite was a dreary café at the half-way point called, Half-Way House. You parked your car under a corrugated tin awning where a throng of village boys with dirty rags congregated—waiting to wipe the desert off your windscreen in hope of a few piasters.

There was always the same ragged beggar who, having no legs, sat on a board to which small iron wheels similar to a child's roller-skates were attached. He pushed himself around with calloused rag-wrapped hands ignoring with dour recklessness, the moving cars. With the bonnet of the car opened to cool the engine, you could have a meal at the Half-Way House—if you dared, or indulge in very nice ice cream, and use the washroom where the doors had no locks.

Time slips away in the desert and before long the sun is sinking like a golden orb in a vermillion sky. Nobody wanted to find themselves on the un-lit and unmarked narrow Desert Road at night. Racing the sun down the highway towards Cairo was hazardous, weaving in and out, dodging potholes, and burnt-out rusting hulls of what once were cars, and army lorry's abandoned on the roadside. When night came it was treacherous. Oncoming cars with no headlights would hurl themselves at you like missiles and then flash their high-beams on their approach—blinding you with dazzling light. Kamikaze drivers in Toyota pick-ups and taxi drivers in high velocity Peugeot's known as 'flying-coffins', descended on you from behind in total darkness only to career past with a fixed determination to be in the lead. The Desert Road was nowhere to be at night.

There has been a dramatic change on the once barren Desert Road. It is now a duel-carriageway lit and lined with petrol stations, buildings, farms, fast-food restaurants, hotels with swimming-pools and tennis courts, a two-story shopping mall called Dandy Mega Mall, and a Carrefour—French supermarket.

Fourteen

The Overland Route

*'Man cannot discover new oceans unless he has
the courage to lose sight of the shore'*
Ancient Chinese Proverb

Before the Overland Route was conceived, mail and passengers bound for India were transported on steamers of the Peninsula Steamship Company by way of the South American coast. With the Doldrums to port—to avoid the monsoon and north going current around the African Cape—it took three months to reach Calcutta from Southampton. The Ships were sailing once a month between Malta via England to Alexandria when the company obtained a mail contract between Suez and Calcutta, which meant if they could get across Egypt, it would cut the travel time considerably—but there was still 150 miles of desert to cross from Alexandria to Suez.

Thomas Fletcher Waghorn, an enterprising young man whose name was soon to become synonymous with the Overland Route, worked for the East India Company. He was a pioneer of his time, resilient, determined, and a prolific letter writer and traveller.

Waghorn was obsessed with getting the mail from one point to the other in the shortest time possible—often putting himself through extraordinary hardships to find the fastest course.

There were two routes across Egypt to Suez at the time, both starting at Alexandria and stopping at Atfeh in Cairo by way of the freshwater Mahmoudieh Canal. The canal was forty-eight miles long, nine feet wide and in some parts eighteen feet deep. It was built in sandy soil by a Corvée of 200,000 men under the auspices of Mohamed Ali.

Egypt up until then had merely been a convenient transit stop for people travelling to India. When the East India Company established a service of horse-drawn barges and native boats along the canal, the additional choice of route afforded the tourists a visit to the pyramids and travel up the Nile to Luxor—before crossing the desert to the Red Sea port known as Cosseir, 250 miles south of Suez. The choice usually depended on how strongly the current was flowing down the Nile.

Samuel Bevan was one of the first employees of Thomas Waghorn—and his book, *Sand and Canvas*, gives a fascinating and descriptive account of the Overland Route by a very well informed author. The year was 1842 when he responded to an advertisement in the London Times: "Wanted immediately, for service in a foreign country, a gentleman of business-habit and good address. Salary £250. per annum. All expenses paid."

Bevan was duly engaged as an accredited agent of Wagon's India and Overland Route. His job was to transport mail, baggage, and passengers via the horse-drawn barges up the Mahmoudieh Canal and then on calabses (horse-drawn covered carts with two enormous wheels) to Suez; stopping at rest houses along the way, and acting as guide in charge of the travellers and their comforts.

When he first arrived in the port of Alexandria, his first impressions of the modern Egyptians, the: "half-naked fellows on the shore," proved to be quite an experience for him: "I shall never forget the scene that awaited us on landing at the hard. Camels, donkeys, merchandize of every description, shrieking women, boys, and greasy Arabs, were jumbled together in indescribable confusion; the men fighting and cuffing one another, with the most violent gesticulations, in their anxiety to appropriate the luggage of the newly arrived passengers, in order to convey it to the city. Furner, armed with a huge whip, which I learnt to call by the name of 'Korbash', dealt his blows right and left on the heads and shoulders of the natives, and speedily cleared a way for us to where a group of donkeys were standing, all saddled and bridled.

"Five minutes hard riding brought us into the middle of a crowded bazaar, and we were forced to relapse into a trot, our boys clearing a space before us by repeated cries of 'Shimalek! Aminak! Ariglak!' ('To the left; to the right; mind your legs!'). The scrambling about of the poor Arab women, in their efforts to get out of the way, was at once ludicrous and painful; and I was unfeignedly glad when we suddenly emerged into the great square of Alexandria, and pulled up at the door of 'Waghorn's India Agency'."

The Rev. Samuel Manning arrived in Alexandria in 1874 on the Austrian steamer, *Urano*. He was met with the same pandemonium and the korbash was still in use: "Scores of boats came round us, manned by half-naked Negroes and Arabs. I was seized by half-a-dozen fellows at once, each endeavouring to drag me into his boat. A similar conflict was going on over every article of my baggage, and it was only by a vigorous application of the dragoman's whip that I and my belongings were rescued from them and stowed away in one of the boats.

"We only escaped from the hands of the boatmen to fall into those of the donkey-boys, who effectually dissipated whatever feelings of reverence yet remained. At length we extricated ourselves from them and made our way to the hotel."

Samuel Bevan commenced his official duties on the 18th July 1842, when the mail steamer *Tagus* arrived from Southampton with about two-dozen passengers for the Overland, and a prodigious quantity of baggage. Once in Alexandria the mail was loaded onto a barge that was destined for the mouth of the Mahmoudieh Canal. Bevan and the passengers assembled at Rey's Hotel, the point of departure for the passenger boat, where they were to proceed on donkeys and rendezvous with the mail barge.

Travel in the 19th century had its downside. Getting from one place to another took an excessive amount of time, was arduous, and often fraught with danger and mishap as Bevan recalls: "Half a mile's ride brought us to the avenue of trees upon the banks of the Canal, where covered passenger-boats were waiting to receive us, that containing the mails and luggage, having already gone on a-head. The choice of seats, for berths there were none, was of course given to the ladies, the rest accommodating themselves where best they might. Four strong horses, mounted by as many Arab riders, were attached to the one long iron boat, which contained us all. The dew was falling like rain, soaking every thing that was exposed to it, but this did not deter some of our party from throwing themselves at full length upon the roof, where, snugly shrouded in their cloaks, they ran a much better chance of getting a little rest, than when squeezed into a sitting posture below. When a sudden shock and instantaneous stoppage of the boat, found that our precious Maltese captain had run us into the bank, having quietly followed the example of those around him, by dropping to sleep at his tiller. Fortunately for the horses, the rope had parted with the sudden check, or they would have been pulled into the Canal, which I afterwards found was not an uncommon occurrence."

When John Gadsby made the Mahmoudieh Canal journey by steamer, he gave a detailed and picturesque account of the people and country and the way things were in Egypt in 1847: "Along the banks of the canal, for some distance from Alexandria, are many neat palaces and villas, belonging to the Turkish Beys and the European merchants. The gardens, being well watered, are exceedingly productive, as well as pleasing to the eye. Lake Mareotis lay to our right, and looked like the sea, as we could not scan over it. The whole of the country through which the canal runs is covered with water when the Nile overflows its banks."

In 1853, the orientalist, writer, explorer, etc., Sir Richard Burton, was travelling incognito as a Pathan (Afghan) during his Pilgrimage to the Holy Cities of Islam. He found the Mahmoudieh Canal the: ". . . ugliest and most wearisome of canals. I saw the canal at its worst, when the water was low; and I have not one syllable to say in its favour. Instead of thirty hours, we took three mortal days and nights to reach Cairo, and we grounded with painful regularity four or five times between sunrise and sunset.

"You see nothing but muddy waters, dusty banks, a sand mist, a milky sky, and a glaring sun: you feel nought but a breeze like the blast from a potter's furnace . . . and thus you proceed till with a real feeling of satisfaction you moor alongside of the tumble-down old suburb 'Bulak'."

John Gadsby was far from comfortable on his journey but was still able to appreciate what he was experiencing and paints a colourful description: "As the country all around continued to be exceedingly flat, there was little for some time to disturb my reveries. Were it not for frequent palm groves and occasional minarets, there would be little on shore to relieve the eye. The villages, which are situated about a mile apart, are all built of mud, and are about as wretched as anything that can be well conceived. Almost the only exception to this, between Afteh and Cairo, is Fooah, a town of some importance, in which is a manufactory of the fez, a woollen cloth of which the red caps, or tarbooshes, worn by the people, are made. Here I counted 12 minarets. Every inch of land on both sides was richly cultivated. Now and then, on the west, we got sight of the desert, and saw the sand blowing about in clouds, obscuring the desert from view by its own particles.

"Half-naked Arabs, the color of unburnt bricks, left their work to gaze upon us at every bend of the river. Pelicans, cormorants, eagles, and other large birds, with wild ducks and geese, were as numerous as sparrows are in England. Mr. B. shot an eagle as it was flying over the steamer. It measured about 7ft. from tip to tip. Everything now was truly oriental. Nothing European was to be seen, except the steamer and what was on it; and this is the time at which a traveller's interest becomes truly awakened.

"I shall, I believe, ever look back upon this Nile trip with satisfaction. Altogether it formed one of the most pleasing excursions I ever made."

Between 1835 and 1837 Waghorn's Original Transit Company laid the foundations of the Overland Route. Waghorn spent a good deal of his time in the desert amongst the Arabs, building a series of rest-houses from Cairo to Suez for the use of transit passengers traversing the desert in calabses.

In 1840 Arthur Anderson, who was the managing director of the Peninsula Steamship Company —soon to become P&O (Peninsular & Oriental Steam Navigation Company), bought out the East India's canal route and established a service of steamers; the *Lotus* and the *Cairo*, drawn by the tugboat *Atfeh*. It proved to be a vast improvement over the horse-drawn barges. The new passenger steamers carried a trumpeter on board whose job it was to warn off the many approaching barges laden with wheat, beans, and barley. Yet every now and then one of the barges would run into difficulty and the captain of the steamer would jump on-board the intruding vessel shouting and cracking his whip over the backs of the crew.

As the canal had a difference of level from the Nile at Atfeh, Anderson had a lock built to raise the boats for the continued journey up river. At that time Waghorn had a steamer called the *Jack O'Lantern*—reputedly full of vermin, that made the Nile journey. Until then baggage had to be lifted off the barges and transported by camel for 200 yards before being put onto the Nile steamers for passengers taking the second route to Suez.

Anderson then improved the first route that ran across the desert between Cairo and Suez by repairing the thoroughfare and installing a semaphore telegraph system between the two places. It was at this time that the enterprising Waghorn and Messer's Hill and Raven amalgamated their services under the name Hill and Co. and the Overland Route flourished, bringing a surge of travellers to the Nile Valley.

The Overland Route operated in both directions across the desert. Passengers returning from India would be advised to write months in advance to say what ship they were coming in on and whether they would be landing at Suez or Casseiu. Waghorn or Hill would then arrange for donkeys, camels, and guides; or if the passengers were travelling on up the Nile to Luxor, a suitable number of boats. The passengers were warned that they must bring with them several boxes of rusks or biscuits—as the local bread was inedible, a supply of wine, ale, and spirits, and four to five dozen bottles of drinking water—as the water could be quite brackish—even making tea undrinkable.

Thomas Waghorn's undertaking of the Overland Route lasted from the 1830s through most of the 1840s, reducing the three-month journey from England to India by half. Waghorn's energy and enthusiasm for improving his timetable, and his ability to organize transport at both ends, gave him a reputation for being able to be in two places at once as William Thackeray warmly praises: "Lieutenant Waghorn is bouncing in and out of the courtyard full of business. He only left Bombay yesterday morning, was seen in the Red Sea on Tuesday, is engaged to dinner this afternoon in Regent's Park, and (as it is about two minutes since I saw him in the courtyard) I make no doubt he is by this time in Alexandria or at Malta, say, perhaps, at both."

At the starting point when crossing the desert to Suez, was the newly opened British Hotel, run by Samuel Shepheard, whom Mr. Hill had employed in 1835. The hotel was destined to become the legendary Shepheard's Hotel. Once the travellers reached Atfeh they would form themselves in parties of six and were given a number. When they arrived at the British Hotel there were notices posted on the door informing each party of the departure time for Suez. It proved not to be a very good system as one party arriving at midnight might be told they were leaving in several hours' time, or parties arriving earlier might find themselves with a day's wait.

If travel was an arduous affair, luggage was another obstacle to overcome, as it was at some point transported by camel. The camels were hired by the amount of luggage to be transported and his load was seldom more than two packages. Bedouins had the ordeal of sorting out and distributing the luggage onto the camels. They had little idea of balancing weight and it was not unusual to see a portmanteau strapped to one side of the beast, and a large, but lightweight hatbox on the other side; which did nothing to improve the animals' already disagreeable disposition.

The journey from Cairo to Suez ran in a straight line east to west across the desert for eighty-four miles and usually took about twenty hours to traverse achieving about five miles per hour and stopping at the rest houses for refreshments, respite from the scorching sun, and to change animals.

The journey was not a comfortable one on the rough gravel. The caravan would inevitably come across hazardous rocks, carcasses of dead camels, and soft sand in which the wheels of the calabses would become buried to a depth of a foot or more. This caused loss of time and a great deal of labour for the horses, the Seis (running footman), and sometimes the passengers who had to disembark and lend a shoulder as Samuel Bevan recounts: "Every now and then a wheel would come in contact with one of these, (large round stones) giving us a shock sufficient to drive the breath out of us. As we exchanged the stony track for the fine hard sand, I slept long and uninterruptedly, until I was suddenly aroused by a shock which had well-nigh thrown me out of the vehicle. Raising myself, I looked out and missed my only companion, the driver. The shaft horse had fallen over the body of a dead camel, and had brought the other down with him, whilst poor Hassan had been pitched clean off his perch, and was picking himself up with many lamentations."

Accompanying her husband Viscount Canning, to India in 1855, Charlotte Canning recalls the Overland course in the horse-drawn calabses as being: "marked with the skeletons of dead camels." She gave up counting the carcasses at 162 in four hours.

Seventeen-year-old Harriet Tyler made the crossing in 1845 in a convoy of six horse-drawn calabses and remembers it as: ". . . an awful journey." She eventually fell asleep, her head slumping on the shoulder of a fellow passenger, Mr. Wiltshire, a tea taster on his way to China, whom it seems had to use the greatest restraint from kissing her.

The Garden Ran Down to the Nile

There were six rest houses or stations along the route, the first being just nine miles from Cairo. It was a mere stable where the horses were changed if needs be. The second was a large building with three bedrooms where the passengers could rest. Supper was provided and a full change of horses made. The third station was a stable like the first, and Station four was the half-way point and much more pretentious than the rest.

Samuel Bevan recalls: ". . . having an upper story, with a rickety flight of stone-steps, and a tolerably spacious court-yard below, where, at the time of our arrival, a queer-looking sheep, and some lean shrivelled fowls were sniffing and pecking about, and scraping up their last earthly meat, whilst a turkey-cock, perched on an empty cafass or hamper, was dismally sounding his death-rattle."

All the supplies, including water, were brought from Cairo by camel caravans with enough food to supply all the stations for several weeks. The standard meals served were roast chicken, curries, Irish stew, boiled eggs, rice puddings, and numerous cups of tea. If on occasion there had been a large influx of passengers to and fro, a sort of famine took place and it was not unusual to find a loin of camel staring up at you from your dinner plate. One Englishman remembered the good meal he had at the second station in the 1840s, which included: eggs, Irish stew, beer, ale, cold turkey, other fowl, and: "a modest looking *'carte des vins'*."

The Overland Route amused John Gadsby, but in 1854 when he experienced the journey for himself, it became something other than amusing: "It was always to me an interesting sight to watch the passengers for India leave in the vans, to cross the desert to Suez.

Half a dozen two-wheel vans, each with four horses, drive up to the hotel door. The names of the passengers are called over. Six persons seat themselves in each van, and off they go. Those who leave at night are accompanied some distance by men with torches.

"I once went from Cairo to Suez in one of these vans, but it was the most horrid journey I ever had in my life. Being in the night, and having no beacons to guide us, our driver frequently lost the track, for there is no regular road in the desert, and then the jolting was terrific. Now we are pitched one upon another, and then banged back again; now we run bump upon a huge stone, which makes us roar again; knocked right and left, shaken in every direction, causing us to laugh at first, but to nearly cry at last; and now we come to a dead lock in the sand. Then the driver halloos to the other drivers, 'Where is the road?' And we hear the answer, 'I don't know; I'm lost myself.' Off we go again, bump, bump, bang, bang,—it really is terrific. And thus we go on from station to station. My stomach did not, for several days, recover from the effects of the shaking."

Signals were sent from a semaphore telegraph system from one tower to the next across the divide informing the stations of the pending arrivals. The road to station five was barely distinguishable as the ground was so hard that tracks did not leave marks, and the area was strewn with the bleached bones of dead camels that often proved hazardous to the vans.

Station six was the last stop where a good meal and a most welcomed nap could be had before continuing the last leg of the journey to Suez, and Waghorn's hotel—managed by an English woman and her nephew. There the passengers would await the East India Company steam frigate that would take them to India.

In 1858 the Overland Route was soon to join the archives of history as an artist from the Illustrated London News writes: "When I was homeward bound the whole distance from Suez to Cairo and visa versa was performed in vans. Then five vans, each containing six 'insides', started in a set – changed cattle at posthouses, at stages of six or seven miles, through the desert, and accomplished the journey in some seventeen or eighteen hours. Four hours after the departure of one set, another set started, and so on until the number of passengers was exhausted. Now a railway crosses the desert from Suez. All the cattle are collected on this space, and almost any number of vans start at once: a rare sight it is. I would not have missed the little bit of 'vanning' for a great deal; but it won't be had much longer. Soon the rail will be opened all the way to Suez; and the enterprising traveller will be able to sleep as soundly across the desert as he would from London to Brighton."

Around the same time, a private soldier painted a lively picture of travellers making the crossing on donkeys and seeing the caravan of calabses—which he likened to bathing machines: "After partaking of an excellent breakfast, served in a canvas tent, we were provided with donkeys to cross the desert to Suez, a distance of 25 miles. Fancy about 200 Europeans in white clothing, on donkeys, followed by Arabs on foot in their many-coloured and motley garments, surrounded by vast plains and hills of nothing but sand, and you have a scene which must be witnessed to be fully appreciated. The animals jogged along between a walk, a run, and a trot, without great labour, till we had proceeded about fourteen miles, when we halted about an hour for refreshment. There were also several caravans similar to English bathing-machines, and drawn by horses and mules, but very few chose this method of crossing the desert."

The early travellers might have felt less than comfortable with their mode of travel, but if they had made the journey before the nineteenth century when the Ottoman Sultan was in power they would have found the route from Cairo to the Red Sea fraught with much more serious hazards. Marauding bandits were the biggest danger. Passengers *en route* to India would gather together in Cairo and travel in large groups accompanied by Arab soldiers. The women would be transported in sedan chairs—each slung between two camels and completely covered over by a canopy with curtains. The air was stifling and the poles that supported the litter would occasionally slip away from their fastenings bringing the passenger crashing to the ground.

By the 1860s tourism was slowly taking hold in Egypt with a few handfuls of the Overland travellers taking side trips to visit the pyramids. But travel in the country still had its dangers from nomadic Bedouin and it was advisable to carry a gun and have an escort when travelling the desert.

It wasn't until 1869, when Thomas Cook embarked upon what he called, "a great event in the arrangements of modern travel," that people poured into Egypt. Some were attracted by the climate, others the history or antiquities and some came just to absorb the beauty and tranquillity of the country. John Murray published his *Hand Book for Egypt* in 1835, and it was said that the people visiting Egypt and the Holy Land were doing so with the Bible in one hand and Murray's in the other.

Fifteen

Dahabeyahs, Effendis, & Dragomen

▲▲▲

'Happy are the Nile travellers who start thus with
a fair breeze on a brilliant afternoon'
Amelia Blandford Edwards

Egypt in the 18th century saw only a handful of travellers who had ventured into the country of unseen landscapes *en route* to India. But when Thomas Cook opened restrictions to an unknown land in 1860, Egypt soon became an essential stop in the itinerary of the Grand Tour often preserved in history by the literary archaeology of those travellers.

As early as the late 1800s guide books were filled with suggestions for travellers and invalids coming to Egypt. Suggestions like wearing flannel next to the skin and for men to bring at least two tweed suits. The medicines suggested for minor ailments were extreme by today's standards: quinine pills, chlorodine, Dover's powder, zinc eye-wash, ammonia, lint, silver nitrate, copper sulphate, oil of peppermint, morphine, and sticking plasters. For best treatment of a headache it was suggested to bathe the head with cold water while keeping the feet in hot water containing a teaspoon of mustard. If very severe, eight or ten leeches could be applied to the temples. For simple diarrhoea a blue pill, Dover's powder, or a small tablespoon of castor oil with ten drops of laudanum. For severe diarrhoea, fifteen drops of diluted sulphuric acid in a small wineglass of water. For dysentery, a blue pill followed by two tablespoons of castor oil and four egg whites—beaten in water with a little powdered gum Arabic, or a slight aperient followed by tincture of opium or concentrated tincture of camphor. For fits of shivering, one to three doses of quinine followed by rest and copious perspiration.

It would seem most of these treatments were far worse than the complaint. Chlorodine was a combination of chloroform, opium and cannabis. Quinine came in crystal form and was made from chloroform, sulphuric acid and ammonia. The little blue pill that was so widely used for toothache, depression, parasitic infestation, and tuberculosis, contained arsenic and a dangerously high quantity of mercury.

Charles Dudley Warner had a sense of humour about the necessity of being prepared for the worst and admits that they overdid it by bringing an Aboundance of drugs, poisons, foul smells and bitter tastes: "It is such a cheerful prelude to it (the voyage), to read that you will need blue-pills, calomel, rhubarb, Dover's powder, Jame's powder, carbolic acid, laudanum, quinine, sulphuric acid, sulphate of zinc, nitrate of silver, ipecacuanha, and blistering plaster. A few simple directions go with these. If you feel a little unwell, take a few blue pills, only about as many as you can hold in your hand; follow these with a little Dover's powder, and then repeat, if you feel worse, as you probably will; when you rally, take a few swallows of castor-oil, and drop into your throat some laudanum; and then, if you are still alive, drink a dram of sulphuric acid. The consulting friends then generally add a little rice-water and a teaspoon of brandy."

Sir John Gardner Wilkinson recommended another 'useful thing' for the comfort of the traveller, a sleeping apparatus to dissuade mosquitos and other pests. But most of the Victorians who ventured up the Nile did so with all the comforts of home at their fingertips.

The items recommended as necessary were as numerous as the medicines—so travelling lightly was never an option. There was also the ordeal of finding the right dragoman, reis, and crew—and the agreements and drawing up of contracts. When the paperwork was completed they had to obtain and hire a suitable boat—which often had to be completely submerged to rid it of rats and vermin.

The fitting out of the cabins then had to be done, and buying enough supplies to see them through their journey. Once again the guidebooks were of great help in suggesting some of these very useful things: A first-rate fowling-piece, gunpowder and shot, thermometer, barometer, compass, field glasses, measuring tape, pocket knife, twine, a leather or metal drinking cup, a flask, coal, wood, candles, matches, postage stamps, frying pans, hammers, hatchets, flatiron, a supply of magnesium wire for lighting tombs and caverns—and a lamp for burning it in. A tent, a ladder, sextant, chronometer, sewing kit, iron rat-trap, green-lined umbrellas, a remontoir, coloured glass spectacles with gauze sides, two portmanteaux, carpets, mats, blankets, travelling bags, washing soda, a pith helmet with a blue or green veil, or a muslin puggaree that covers the hat and falls over the back of the neck and ears.

Then there were the curtains for the boat, containers for water, crates of turkeys, coops of chickens, and enough food and cooking staples that would last the length of the journey—as many food items could not be had along the way.

For the artist: writing, drawing and painting materials, camp stool and drawing table. For the sportsman: brown leather Wellington boots and stout waterproof shooting-boots. For relaxing: pipes, tobacco, and red Turkish slippers. A library of about 30 books, including suggested ones, was also deemed essential, and if the boat was big enough, a saddle, bridle, and a donkey.

Sir John Gardener Wilkinson's list suggesting books for the artist/draughtsman setting up amongst the tombs and temples: "Larcher's Herodotus, Champollion's Phonetic System of Hieroglyphs, Pococke, Denon, Hamilton's Aegyptiaca . . . to which may be added Brown, Belzoni, Burckhardt, Ptolemy, Strabo and Plinty; but of course these last three, as well as of Diodorus, extracts will suffice, if he considers them too voluminous."

Wilkinson assumed that anyone going up the Nile was doing so in a scholarly capacity rather than for pleasure. He also suggests—in a more practical sense, having the cracks in the boat filled in with putty and then having the boat washed and painted with red ochre bound with egg, and an iron rat-trap brought on board.

Florence Nightingale preferred cats in preference to the rat-trap: "We have brought two cats for the rats in my cabin are so fierce and bold, that I am obliged to get up in the night to defend my dear boots. You cannot keep clear of rats with all your care when you are anchored near to grain boats at night." Later, when journeying up the Nile she recounted: "A noble cat has come aboard of its own accord, and killed two rats: I believe it is a god! We have now four cats, the god and three others; the god is the only one who does the work, but he has cleared us of rats, and with an ornamental border of boots all round the tops of our beds we do very well."

Harriet Martineau gave advice on women's attire when travelling in Egypt—paying close attention to the fashion of the day: "Brown Holland is the best material for ladies dresses; and nothing looks better, if set off with a little trimming of ribbon, which can be put on and taken off in a few minutes. Round straw hats, with a broad brim are the best head-covering. A double-ribbon, which bears turning when faded, will last a long time, and looks better than a more flimsy kind. There can hardly be too large a stock of thick-soled shoes and boots. The rocks of the Desert cut up presently all but the stoutest shoes: and there are no more to be had. Caps and frills of lace or muslin are not to be thought of, as they cannot be 'got up', unless by the wearer's own hands. Habit-shirts of Irish linen or thick muslin will do: and; instead of caps, the tarboosh, when within the cabin or tent, is the most convenient, and certainly the most becoming head-gear: and the little cotton cap worn under it is washed without trouble. Fans and goggles of black woven wire are indispensable."

It was a popular practice with travellers going up the Nile to take along fire-works, rockets and flags to announce their presence, and Warner was no exception: "Abd-el-Atti (the dragoman) should have been born in America. He would enjoy a life that was a continual Fourth of July. He would like his pathway to be illuminated with lights, blue, red, and green, and to blaze with rockets. The supreme moment of his life is when he feels the rocket-stick tearing out of his hand."

The wonderful thing about being a traveller in Victorian times was that time itself was of no consequence. The Victorians literally wintered in Egypt. Their itinerary was flexible. They spent months cruising on the Nile in their own personally hired dahabeyahs complete with all the luxuries of home at their fingertips. They stopped where they liked and when they liked and for as long as they liked, seeing the sites with sensitivity and an adventurous nature. Their days were spent sketching, writing, reading, exploring, shooting or simply drifting along the Nile watching from wicker chairs, the panorama of the countryside in the open air of the upper deck. They were not controlled by time-watching guides, hurried along in a systematic site-seeing regime.

Amelia B. Edwards journeyed up the Nile in a style of formality and romance that most travellers—even in her own day, could only dream of. The luxuriously appointed *Philae I* in which she sailed, left none of the conveniences at home, not even the pianoforte. Amelia had a gift for being able to describe in a picturesque and romantic way an impression so colourful and detailed you felt as if you were there: "A dahabeeyah, at the first glance, is more like a civic or an Oxford University barge. It carries two masts; a big one near the prow and a smaller one at the stern. The cabins are on deck and occupy the after part of the vessel; and the roof of the cabins forms the raised deck, or open-air drawing-room, which is furnished with lounge-chairs, tables and foreign rugs, like a drawing-room in the open air.

"Her total length from stem to stern being just one hundred feet, and the width of her upper deck at the broadest part a little short of twenty . . . four sleeping-cabins, two on each side . . . measured about eight feet in length by four and a half in width, and contained a bed, a chair, a fixed washing-stand, a looking-glass against the wall, a shelf, a row of hooks, and under each bed two large drawers for clothes. At the end of this little passage another door opened into the dining-saloon – a spacious, cheerful room, some twenty-three or twenty-four feet long, situated in the widest part of the boat, and lighted by four windows on each side and a skylight. The panelled walls and ceiling were painted in white picked out with gold; a cushioned divan . . . ran along each side; and a gay Brussels carpet adorned the floor. The dining-table stood in the center of the room, and there was ample space for a piano, two little book-cases, and several chairs . . . the prevailing colors being scarlet and orange. Add a couple of mirrors in gilt frames; a vase of flowers on the table . . . plenty of books; the gentlemen's guns and sticks in one corner; and the hats of all the party hanging in the spaces between the windows, and it will be easy to realize the homely, habitable look of our general sitting-room."

Florence Nightingale and her companions, the Bracebridges, had one of the best and largest boats on the river owned by the Bey, and only ever used by the Harem, but Florence much preferred exploring the country on foot than relaxing on board: "The sitting cabin is quite a pretty little room, painted with green panels, and a divan all round it; the B.'s are in the second cabin, then comes a passage with large closets; the third is mine. The Levinge mosquito net is put up, and is a capital invention; as to being chokey, the cabin of a dahabieh at night runs no risk of being too warm. All our gimlets up, our divans out, our Turkish slippers provided, and everything on its own hook, as befits such close quarters.

Our larder hangs overhead in the shape of a basket full of bread, and two cages full of oranges and meat; our kitchen is immediately beyond . . . so that we have kitchen, scullery, still room, larder, safe, and pantry, all in a nutshell, or at least in a walnut."

Florence and her companions kept chickens, turkeys, and pigeons on the deck of the boat. Milk was available everywhere as was bread and butter. Florence much preferred exploring the countryside to sitting on deck or having to travel the river when the wind was up: "Now, if you ask how I like the dahabieh life, I must say I am no dahabieh bird, no divan incumbent. I do long to be wandering about the desert by myself, poking my own nose into all the villages and running hither and thither, and making acquaintances. I dearly love our dahabieh as my home, but if it is to stay in it the whole day, as we are fain to do when the wind is fair, that is not in my way at all."

It was customary when living on the Nile in a dahabeyah to give the boat a name and to fly the flag of your country, which you were obliged to register at Cairo. The Union Jack flew at the stern of her boat, and the Bracebridge's colours, skilfully stitched by Florence, flew half-way up the rigging: "All my work since I came on board has been making the pennant, blue bunting with swallow tails, a Latin red cross upon it, and ΠΑΡΟΕΝΟΙΙΗ in white tape. It was hoisted this morning at the yardarm, and looks beautiful. It has taken all my tape and a vast amount of stitches, but it will be the finest pennant on the river, and my petticoats will joyfully acknowledge the tribute to sisterly affection."

A.B. DeGuerville felt that the most important person on board was the dragoman, as it was he who arranged the excursions and gave all the explanations desired. The dragoman was held in high regard, like the director of a film, without him there would be no tour. He was a man of reputation and dignity, usually having been educated in Europe. He spoke several languages and knew how to transact with the local people. There was no continual disbursing of baksheesh for entrance fees, gratuities to attendants, donkey boys or camel drivers. The traveller's dragomen saw to these petty annoyances. The Reis (Captain) was second in command.

Baedeker describes the dragoman as useful to those who wish to see as much as possible in a very short time, but warns that only a well recommended dragoman should be engaged, preferably those for whom the hotels assume responsibility.

The valuable advice given in Murray's Hand-Book for Egypt on the hiring of a dahabeyah, was to hire the vessel through Thomas Cook and Son or direct from the owner in which case a contract should be drawn up. It was also advantages to make a separate contract with a dragoman for the catering and the general running of the boat: "All who can should get a dragoman recommended to them by friends who have had experience of him: it will save them a great deal of trouble, and they will feel more sure of the sort of man they have to deal with. Those who are new to the country should apply to Messrs. T. Cook & Son, who have an office close to Shepheard's Hotel in Cairo."

A word of warning was also given: "There are dragomen of every sort and kind, good, bad, and indifferent; and the traveller who has to choose from among the numbers who present themselves at Alexandria and Cairo, must take his chance. But it is seldom that the really good ones, who confessedly are at the head of their profession, fail to give satisfaction."

One roguish dragoman told A.B. DeGuerville of his 'natural power' which God had given him: "He has made us all males, powerful males, besides whom you are nothing but weak little children. That is why your women when they come to Egypt despise you and make gods of us! It is she who, whilst we are on earth, give us glimpses of heaven!"

DeGuerville was appalled as he listened to stories of foreign women whose details the man had written down in a little pocket book: ". . . he showed me letters from women, with well-known names and of good family, which if published would give the world something to talk of."

When William C. Prime and his party travelled up the Nile in *The Phantom*, a contract was drawn up between the parties and their dragoman, Mohammed Abd-el-Atti.

CONTRACT

We, the undersigned, J. Hammond Trumbull, and W.C. Prime, with Mrs. Trumbull and Mrs. Prime, have this day agreed with Mohammed Abd-el-Atti for a trip up the Nile, on the following conditions:

Mohammed Abd-el-Atti engages to provide a comfortable boat, with awning and jolly boat; to furnish said boat with beds, bedding, tables, china, glass, water filters, and all and every requisite necessary for the convenience and comfort of first-class passengers.

1. Mohammed Abd-el-Atti agrees to provide all stores, provisions, candles, lights, etc., as shall be necessary for the entire voyage. Also to provide as many courses for breakfast, dinner, etc., as shall be required by the above parties.
2. Mohammed Abd-el-Atti agrees to provide and pay for one cook, one servant, and one assistant, to wash clothes, etc., during the entire voyage.
3. Under the above conditions Mohammed Abd-el-Atti agrees to take Messrs Prime and Trumbull, and party, to EsSouan, and back again to Cairo, for the sum of two hundred and twenty-five pounds in gold, giving then fifteen days' stoppage on the voyage, at any place or places they may wish to stop or remain at, and providing donkeys and guides for visiting any such places.
4. For the first fifteen days of stoppage, exceeding the above period, that they may wish to remain below the first cataract, they will pay to Mohammed Abd-el-Atti the sum of three pounds fifteen shillings per diem.
5. For any period they may wish to remain below the first cataract, after the expiration of the above provided period, they shall pay Mohammed Abd-el-Atti the sum of three pounds per day for each day.

6. Should the above parties, after their arrival at the first cataract, wish to proceed to the second cataract, Mohammed Abd-el-Atti agrees to take them on in the same boat, and same style, and they shall then pay him the sum of sixty-seven pounds ten shillings for the trip between the two cataracts and back, and they shall have three days for stoppage, for visiting such places as they may desire. And if they shall desire to stop more than three days above the first cataract, then, for every day of stoppage above three, they shall pay him at the rate of three pounds per day.
7. It is, moreover, fully understood that Mohammed Abd-el-Atti is to pay all presents on the voyage; to pay all donkey hire, guides, guards, etc.; to present crew, sailors, reis, pilot, or persons on shore, during, and at the end of the voyage.
8. It is understood that, if the party should go to the second cataract, then the provision for days of stoppage over fifteen days below the first cataract is altered, and they shall pay Mohammed Abd-el-Atti in that case, only three pounds per day over the first fifteen days provided for, for every day more than such fifteen that they may wish to stop.

Dated, at Cairo, this 27th day of October, 1855.

N.B. The boat is to be procured and equipped, and the trip to commence as soon as possible.

Signed by the Americans
Sealed by Mohammed Abd-el-Atti.

The Garden Ran Down to the Nile

Prime selected his boat, examined and approved it, fitted it out with oriental furnishings and two Yankee rocking chairs he had obtained in Alexandria, and hoisting the American flag, set off on a journey of a lifetime.

Mohammed Abd-el-Atti was one of the most accomplished dragomen in Egypt in the mid to late 1800s. He had lived some years in England and France, spoke the languages of those countries as well as Italian, Turkish, and of course his own language, Arabic. He could read and write, and was a good storyteller, so it was only natural that in 1876 Charles Dudley Warner, another American travelling up the Nile, should seek out and hire Abd-el-Atti as dragoman for his party: "Abd-el-Atti, our dragoman, is riding ahead on his grey donkey, and I have no difficulty in following his broad back and short legs, even though his donkey should be lost to sight in the press. He rides as Egyptians do, without stirrups, and uses his heels as spurs. Since Mohammed Abd-el-Atti Effendis first went up the Nile, it is many years ago now, with Mr. Wm. C. Prime, and got his name prominently into the Nile literature, he has grown older, stout, and rich; he is entitled by his position to the distinction of 'Effendi'."

Warner described the crew and the interior of the boat they christened *Rip Van Winkle*: "We have taken possession of our dahabeehya, which lies moored under the bank, out of the current, on the west side of the river above the bridge. The flat, open forward deck is capable of accommodating six rowers on a side. Then comes the cabin, which occupies the greater part of the boat, and makes it rather top-heavy and difficult of management in an adverse wind. First in the cabin are the pantry and dragoman's room; next a large saloon, used for dining, furnished with divans, mirrors, tables, and chairs, and lighted by large windows close together. Next are rows of bedrooms, bathroom, etc.; a passage between leads to the after or lounging cabin, made comfortable with divans and Eastern rugs. Over the whole cabin runs the deck, which has sofas and chairs and an awning, and is good promenading space. The rear portion of it is devoted to the steersman, who needs plenty of room for the sweep of the long tiller. The steering apparatus is of the rudest. The tiller goes into a stern-post which plays in a hole big enough for four of it, and creakingly turns a rude rudder."

In 1899 about thirty years after Amelia B. Edwards had sailed up the Nile, Lee Bacon and his wife engaged a dahabeyah to make the leisurely Nile trip to see the sites, write, paint, and welcome in a new century. Their houseboat was christened the *Terrapin*.

"The cabin carpet is bright red Brussels, with such large flowers that one bouquet is sufficient to fill the saloon and part of the passageway, while there is enough blue chintz with yellow fringe at all the cabin and saloon windows to smother us, or to open a second-hand furnishing establishment. The couches or sofas of the saloon are so high that we are forced into the Eastern cross-legged attitude in order to sit on them at all, and after we are all seated – for there are only two of us – there is room left in one of the sofa corners for our library of about twenty volumes, while in another are wraps, hats, opera-glasses, and all the things which are needed a hundred times each day. There are no shelves to put anything on, and no time to put things away or to get them out.

"The upper deck of our houseboat is a delight; it is like a roof with an awning spread over it. All day long the sun keeps it bright and attractive, and at night the lights from the saloon below shine up through the netting's and colored glass of the skylight. The sofas and tables of the deck are covered with Eastern cotton draperies, which are well fastened at the corners, for otherwise the sudden gusts of wind would snatch them away without warning."

The Bacon's dahabeyah became more than just a houseboat as they seemed to have settled into their new way of life on the river with interest and enthusiasm: "Our big saloon serves as dining-saloon, gentlemen's smoking-saloon, ladies' sitting-room, library, and writing-room. When we sit in the middle it is for meals; when we sit in one corner we can easily reach all the volumes in our thirty-volume library; when we sit in another corner we are geologists, handling and marking strange bits of stone, and specimens of potsherds. When we go to one end of the saloon we are in our armory, with its one revolver and two guns to hand; while still another corner is the hat and cloak department and wrap centre, in which there is quite a varied selection. Another corner is reserved for a bottle of good Kentucky whiskey and some eau gazeuse. Another side looks as if the aim of our voyage was to collect botanical specimens, for here we have henna-berries, castor-oil beans, small green gourds, the vegetable ivory of the dom palm, and a branch of doorha, which looks just like the wand which Baccus had often in hand."

In 1871 W.H. Davenport Adams describes his trip up the Nile: "We engage a Dahabeeya, or Nile-boat, and prepare for our voyage up the 'sacred river'. And a more delightful excursion it is difficult to imagine! The scenery through which he is carried easily and not too rapidly is of a striking and varied character. Villages of mud huts, embowered in groves of palm; sandy shoals, alive with wings, and gay with the plumage of the flamingo and the ibis; quaint native barges, of all sizes and types, carrying dusky passengers in brightly-coloured attire; a yacht or two, belonging to some adventurous European or wealthy Moslem; men paddling along on rafts; little busy cafes, nestling in the shade of far-spread sycamores; creaking sakias, or water-wheels, used for the purpose of irrigation; and beyond the emerald strip of fertile valley the yellow boundary of the Desert; - all these combine to form a picture as splendid as it is rare."

Amelia B. Edwards takes us back through the years and deposits us on a dahabeyah in the middle of the Nile: "We sit on the high upper deck, which is furnished with lounge-chairs, tables and foreign rugs, like a drawing-room in the open air, and enjoy the prospect at our ease. Long belts of palm groves, tracts of young corn, only an inch or two above the surface, and clusters of mud huts, relieved now and then by a little whitewashed cupola or a stumpy minaret, succeed each other on both sides of the river, while the horizon is bounded to right and left by long ranges of yellow limestone mountains, in the folds of which sleep inexpressibly tender shadows of pale violet and blue. Thus the miles glide away."

William C. Prime felt that: "Ladies of the most delicate constitutions need have no apprehensions in passing a winter in Egypt. The climate is delicious, the Nile boat is as comfortable as a hotel, and every luxury is provided by a careful dragoman that the most fastidious could desire. There is no such thing as 'roughing it' in Egypt."

G.W. Steevens description of his voyage evokes a picture of charm and tranquillity: "You are not to worry, not to arrange about anything; you are just to sit easy and be happy. You come up in the morning, and there, steel-blue in the sun, shines the benevolent Nile. You forget how many days you have been looking at it; you could look at this miracle forever. Rural Egypt at Kodak range—and you sitting in a long chair to look at it."

Not all Nile travellers came for the same reasons, like missionary Mary Whately. Although she found beauty and tranquillity in the 'wonderful colours' of Egypt, she had no interest in what she called pagan temples and curious ruins: "I and my friends go for the sake of bringing the gospel to some of the villages on the river, our employment is so deeply interesting that no ruined temples could delight us so much, for man is a ruin himself, ruined by sin and Satan, and only the knowledge of a Saviour can raise him out of that ruined condition."

There were times when John Gadsby, wintering in Egypt for his health, found dahabeyah life monotonous: "We go round and round, as it were, like a windmill. As it was yesterday, so it is to-day, and so we may expect it to be to-morrow. The same yearnings after home, the same palm groves, the same desert in the distance, and the same dry weather."

However, most travellers never found the river boring. According to A.B. DeGuerville it was quite the opposite: "I cannot understand those who say that the Nile is monotonous; for me, every minute, it has a different charm, and I could voyage on its waters for weeks without fatigue. There is no more ideal way of passing the winter months than by slowly ascending the famous river on board a dahabeyah. But dahabeyahs are not within the reach of every purse; according to the number of persons travelling

The Garden Ran Down to the Nile

together they cost from £400 to £600 a month, everything included. Fortunately there are Cook's famous services of express boats between Cairo, Luxor and Assouan, besides their tourist steamers. The later are very popular and deservedly so, for it is impossible to wish for greater comfort. The *Rameses,* the *Rameses III,* and the *Rameses the Great,* which undertake the service, are fine boats . . . Besides sleeping accommodation, dining-room, library and smoking-room, there is on the upper deck . . . a fine open space which forms a large hall. Tables, arm-chairs, easy-chairs, soft Eastern carpets and green plants make a charming resort and a favourite one with all the passengers. It is there that after meals coffee is served, there that afternoon tea is taken, there where one can chat or play cards or enjoy music, whilst able at any moment to glance out on the banks of the river. If the evenings are chilly, large awnings are let down round the deck, and by means of these an immense salon is quickly made, brightly lit by numerous electric lamps, and where impromptu dances can be held. The food is excellent and unlimited.

"Wherever there is something of interest to be seen the boat stops, and donkeys, guides, or, if desired, chairs with porters, await the passengers, the cost of which is included in the ticket."

Yet with all the comforts of home at his fingertips, there was one thing DeGuerville had not expected: "This morning I experienced a shock, a violent shock, and it was the waters of the Nile which caused it. There are on the *Rameses* excellent bathrooms, and I had promised myself matutinal (sic) ablutions pleasant and comfortable. Waking early I ordered my bath from the Arab servant at six o'clock. A few minutes later I entered the bathroom, and it was then that I received the shock. The magnificent bath was full of dark yellow mud, very dark, almost black, thick and repulsive. Questioned, I heard the Arab vaguely murmur as he closed the door behind him, 'Nile water, very clean.' Very clean! I turned the tap and from it oozed the same liquid mud; 'Shall I be not cleaner, but less dirty, by going without my bath, or by steeping myself each morning in this mud? I calculate that we shall not arrive in Assouan for twelve days . . . in the first case I shall have on my skin the accumulation of two hundred and eighty-eight hours, and in the second, I shall have twelve superimposed coatings of fertilising mud. The idea of the latter rather amused me; knowing its wonderful properties. I hesitate no longer, and make the plunge."

Again to DeGuerville's surprise it wasn't all sunshine and lazy blue skies on board the *Rameses* in December of 1904: "What weather! Can this be Egypt? The heavens are black, and rain descends in torrents. In spite of the carriage hood I have been drenched between the hotel and the landing stage. Why the devil don't they have closed carriages in Cairo?

"All the flags soaked and hanging miserably, the Rameses started sadly on her voyage, and we leave Cairo, wrapped in a grey veil of mist, far behind. It is freezing! Seated on the bridge, smothered in coats and rugs we gaze on the flat melancholy banks.

"One o'clock. An excellent lunch has warmed and consoled us. We have just arrived at Bedrachen. From here a start is made to visit Sakkara and the ruins of Memphis. Bravely, armed with mackintoshes and umbrellas, we leave the Rameses, and men and women straddle the donkeys. The situation is so ridiculous, and there are amongst us some such curious specimens, that we end by laughing. To come to Egypt to be soaked, and to have the end of your nose red, - this is indeed the height of pleasure. However, for once there is no dust!"

It was not just rain that could be an inconvenience—wind, dust, and sandstorms proved just as much an irritation as felt by John Gadsby in 1850: "We were one day at dinner, when, looking through the cabin window, I saw a thick yellow cloud over the sky. I said to my companions, 'If I were now in England, I should say we were going to have a thunder storm.' Almost at the same instant I remembered what I had read about the Simoom, that is, a hurricane, which rushes furiously over the desert and sweeps all before it. I called out to our dragoman, 'Hajji, the Simoom!' In an instant every man was on his feet. The mainsail was taken in, and the small sail literally torn down, and thrown on the deck. In 10 or 12 seconds more the blast rushed upon us, and blew us violently on the opposite bank. The men quickly jumped on shore, and held the boat by ropes. The river became greatly agitated, and the waves rose to an incredible height. I could not have believed it had I not seen it. And then the sand – how terrific! It seemed as if the wind had brought with it half the desert. The wind howled, and the sand, in yellow clouds, battered against the boat. We were literally enveloped in it, notwithstanding that we shut ourselves up in the cabin. It got into our nostrils like snuff, and found its way into our pockets, and even into our watches."

Florence Nightingale had a frightening experience during the Khamseen; the fifty days a year the wind blows in from the desert: "We had had heavy clouds for two days, and yet no wind; the sailors did not know what to make of it, they had never seen such a sky before without a sirocco. Soon the wind increased so much that they could not pull against it. We got into a little bay, where the eddy became quite a whirlpool. Five times we tried to tow out of this corner, and five times we were swung round and back again by the whirlpool, till we were obliged to give it up. This we thought the more provoking, as five dahabiehs, which kept in the middle of the stream, passed us, going very near the wind; and one with her sail flapping.

"About three, the khamsin increased; it was a wind like this which destroyed six years ago a caravan of 300 camels belonging to Mehemet Ali. The air became filled with sand. The river seemed turned upside down, and flowing bottom upwards, the whirlwind of sand from the desert literally covering it. It grew dark, and the blast increased so, that we drove a stake into the bank and fastened a rope to it for the night.

"I saw one of the dahabiehs which had overtaken us in the afternoon, floating past us, bottom upwards; nothing to be seen of her passengers. She struck in the sand just astern of us, and remained fast there. I did not go to bed – we bumped incessantly, and at the stern especially so hard that we thought we must spring a leak. It was so dark that we could see nothing, but in the morning we found that our boat had been astride of the poor wreck all night, which had been whirled round by the eddy under us. At dawn I looked out, she had entirely gone to pieces – nothing was left of her but a few of the cabin planks, which our boat picked up, a chest of clothes which we saved, and her oranges floating in the whirlpool. I never saw anything more affecting than those poor oranges, the last luxury of their life in the midst of death. We learnt that of the five boats which passed us yesterday to windward four had gone down, and of their passengers, twenty (including women and children) had been lost."

G.W. Steevens made the Nile journey in one of Cook's steamers *Rameses the Great* in 1898 reaching Bedreshayn in much better weather conditions: "The dragoman a fat figure in green robe and wonderful silk skirt, a fat brown face below a gold-worked turban entered the dining-room, faced his flock with proud modesty, and clapped his hands. Instantly the clatter of lunch sank to expectant silence. 'Ladies and shentleman', he began, in the long-drawn accents of the muezzin who summons the faithful to prayer, 'in one half an hour the steamer will stop at Bedrechein. Then we shall take donkeys and ride three-quarters of an hour to the gre-eat statue of Rameses the Second. Then we shall ride three-quarters of one hour to the gre-e-eat pyramids of Sikkara, and we shall enter the gre-e-eat tomb of Thi. Then we shall return one hour and one half to the steamer, where you shall have tea'. There were exactly eighty of us – English, French, Germans, Belgians, South Africans, Americans, and Australians, from the uttermost ends of the earth. Our mood was devotional. We regarded the dragoman with respect, and the great tomb of Thi with awe. Our trusty cameras were slung at our backs: our diaries lay in our cabins with our stylographs at half-cock beside them.

"Already Mohammed was on the sandy beach, selecting donkeys. Out we streamed after him into a sea of waving brown arms and legs surging furiously over the little island of feasts. Some of the elder ladies mounted chairs, and were borne off, palanquin fashion, on the shoulders of four boatmen. The rest climbed with delicious quavers on to donkeys, the donkey-boys screamed, and yelled, and whacked, and we were off."

Sophia Poole journeyed up the Nile in a dahabeyah that she thought admirably constructed for the navigation of the river: "Their great triangular sails are managed with extraordinary facility, which is an advantage of the utmost importance, for the sudden and frequent gusts of wind to which they are subject, require that a sail should be taken in almost in a moment, or the vessel would most probably be overset. On many occasions one side of our boat was completely under water, but the men are so skilful that an accident seldom happens, unless travellers pursue the voyage during the night."

It was usual, when meeting another boat of travellers to salute each other with a mutual discharge of firearms as John Gadsby recalled: "The boatmen, on such occasions, are particularly noisy, as they are sure to recognise some friends in the other boat. The clearness of the air adds to the distinctness of their voices."

The crew of a dahabeyah maintained a custom that was always observed on the commencement of a voyage, which Sophia Poole was pleased by: "As soon as the wind had filled our large sail, the Reyyis (or captain of the boat) exclaimed 'El-Fat-Hah'. This is the title of the opening chapter of the Kur-'an (a short and simple prayer), which the Reyyis and all the crew repeated together in a low tone of voice."

A favourite pastime while travelling on the Nile was shooting pigeons and other game, which was permitted as long as they were not near a village. Most travellers on the Nile took advantage of the numerous game birds for their consumption, but there were always those who would kill just for the sake of improving their marksmanship.

A.B. DeGuerville met one of these 'sportsmen' while on his Nile journey: "This morning has been perfect, and on the deck of the Rameses we are enjoying to the full the beauty and the joy of life with every breath we draw. Numbers of wild birds, thousands of duck, disport themselves on the water or pass overhead in dense masses. That maddens a young Belgian, a great sportsman it seems, who passes his time in repeating, 'Ah! If I only had my gun'! Well, I said to him, what would be the use of your gun if you had it? The *Rameses* would not stop to allow you to pick up your birds. He looked at me astonished, and replied in the most natural way, 'But I should have had the satisfaction of killing them. Look! What a grand shot!' There was the real man, with his inborn instinct to kill and destroy for the satisfaction of killing them!"

John Gadsby remembers the flights of numerous birds along the Nile: "Pigeons cost us nothing but powder and shot, for all we had to do was to go on shore and shoot them for ourselves. In some parts, they fly in clouds, the rays to the sun being reflected from their beautiful plumage. Some idea of their number may be formed when I mention that eight or ten may often be killed at one shot. We were frequently able to supply the boatmen as well as ourselves."

In 1868 the far-seeing Thomas Cook opened a branch of his travel organization in the gardens of Shepheard's Hotel. He hired two Nile Steamers, the *Benha* and the *Beniswaif* from the Khedive at £40 each. 'The Napoleon of Excursions' as he was dubbed, was to embark on what he called "a great event in the arrangements of modern travel." Expanding his already popular tours to Switzerland, France, and Italy—with excursions to Egypt and the Holy Land, his first steamers appeared on the Nile in 1869 opening up exotic travel to the middle-classes.

The dahabeyah had generally been a form of travel for the more affluent genteel, most having an income of £300 to £600 a year. So when the availability of the larger steamers came along, more people could be accommodated. Not perhaps in the same lazy and lingering lotus eating way, but in relative comfort and more importantly, in affordability.

Cook was charging a party of seven, £850 to £900 for three months on one of the oldest dahabeyahs. While a modern dahabeyah luxuriously fitted out might be anything from £1,100 upwards for the same period of time and number of passengers. He could now offer a twenty-day tour from Cairo to Luxor to Assouan and back— including all sightseeing, at £50 each or fourteen days excursion at £35 each.

Thomas Cook was the first to replace the tiller, the long cumbersome steering apparatus on the early steamers, with the paddlewheel. He built the first flat-bottomed boat, the *Prince Abbas*, and piloted her up and down the Nile himself to prove its stability. He opened Egypt to Europe and the rest of the world as a holiday destination, where before the British and Americans were dominant.

By 1905 Cook had seven steamers on the Nile offering weekly and bi-weekly services from Cairo and Assuit, calling at all points of interest on the way to the First Cataract. He also offered a service of smaller private steamers and dahabeyahs especially adapted to the requirements of families and private parties accommodating from eight to sixteen passengers.

Charles Dudley Warner reflected on the advantages of the leisurely mode of transport on a dahabeyah, which afforded one to take 'three to four weeks', as opposed to the 'four days' in which the Cook's steamer took: "Toward night a steamboat flying the star and crescent of Egypt, with passengers on board, some of 'Cook's personally conducted', goes thundering downs tream, filling the air with smoke and frightening the geese, who fly before it in vast clouds."

It was Warner who coined the phrase: 'Sociability decreases on the Nile with the increase of travel and luxury'.

Florence Nightingale had no love for the newly found way of travel in the steamers, and declared that she would not travel in one if she were "never to see the Nile without them."

The Reverend Samuel Manning also found a negative aspect in the steamers as opposed to the dahabeyah: "In a public conveyance it is not possible to choose one's fellow travellers. A yet more serious objection to the steamers has been their scandalously dirty condition, and the swarms of vermin with which they were infested. For those who have ample means and leisure, and who have resources within themselves, or in their party, to bear the monotony of some days or weeks on board a boat with nothing to do and little to see, the Nile trip in a dahabieh is one of the most delightful excursions in the world. To others the steamer offers a very tolerable substitute."

Regardless of whether one preferred the steamer or the dahabeyah, the cuisine offered on board the steamers, however, could hardly have been better and were, according to Eustace Reynolds-Ball: ". . . varied and plentiful, if not actually luxurious, and should satisfy the most exigent traveller."

A Menu on a Nile Steamer 1st December 1896.

LUNCHEON

Hors d`Oevres.

Rougets au Vin Blanc. Poulets au Sauté au Madère.

Roast Beef – Pommes de Terre.

Salade. Fromage.

Dessert. Café.

DINNER

Consommé Pâté d`Italie.

Poisson à la Orly.

Noix de Veau à la Livernaise.

Espinards aux Oeufs. Bécassines Roties.

Salade. Baba au Péches.

Dessert. Café.

The Garden Ran Down to the Nile

Reynolds-Ball may have favoured the dahabeyah for a prolonged Nile voyage, but he also realized the practicalities of the steamers for the majority of the people: "Formerly, the only orthodox way of doing the Nile voyage was by means of these native sailing-boats, universally known as dahabeyahs, and the costliness of this means of locomotion practically confined it to the English Milord. Of late years, however, the wholesome competition of the great tourist-agencies has brought about a general reduction in the rents of these pleasure-craft. With a party of four or five, the inclusive cost of the two months' voyage to Assouan and back need not exceed £110 to £120 per head, granting, of course, that the organiser of the trip knows the river, has had some experience of Nile travel, has a nodding acquaintance with Arabic, and is able to hold his own with his dragoman."

When the Prince of Wales (Edward VII) and Princess Alexandria visited Egypt on a state tour in 1869, it was a luxury tour that far exceeded any others—with the possible exception of the Empress Eugenie of France. The Prince and Princess toured Egypt as the guests of Khedive Ismail. They travelled in a royal flotilla in the manner befitting a future king of England. The first of the small fleet of boats was a large steamer with a comfortable deck and an extravagant luxurious salon fitted out with solid English furniture and deep pile carpets where the party took their meals.

Towed by the steamer was the *Alexandria*, the dahabeyah that served as elegant living quarters for the Prince, the Princess, and Mrs. William Grey, the personal companion to the Princess. The sitting room housed a large pianoforte and divans covered in blue silk. A second steamer towed a second dahabeyah for the staff—

followed by two kitchen steamers towing barges laden with provisions: 3,000 bottles of Champagne, 20,000 bottles of soda water, 4,000 bottles of various wines and liqueurs, chickens, sheep, turkeys, three French chefs, and one French washerwoman. Two more steamers followed the towing barges with every kind of requirement, including four riding horses and a donkey for the Princess. The final boat in the convoy was the *Pride of the Two Seas*, Ismail's personal steamer for the accompanying party; the Duke of Sutherland, Mr. William Howard Russell, and Sir Samuel Baker, a reputed explorer and sportsman who served as special guide on the trip up the Nile.

The royal flotilla made its way up the river stopping to visit ancient temples, points of interest, excursions to bazaars, and visits to various important local officials. The Prince often went ashore to shoot crocodile and birds—although the former almost always eluded him. The Princess and Mrs. Grey, when not visiting temples, spent their time painting and drawing on the deck of their dahabeyah.

The Prince, on two occasions, once with the Princess, visited Lucy Duff Gordon on her dahabeyah just weeks before her death from tuberculosis. Lucy wrote of their visit: "The Prince was most pleasant and kind, and the Princess too. She is the most perfectly simple-mannered girl I ever saw. She does not even try to be civil, like other great people, but asks questions, and looks at one so heartily with her clear, honest eyes, that she must win all hearts. They were more considerate than any people I have seen, and the Prince, instead of being gracious, was, if I may say so, quite respectful in his manner; he is very well-bred and pleasant, and I am sure has a kind heart. My sailors were so proud of having the honour of rowing him in our boat and of singing to him."

Sixteen

Dividing the Spoils

▲▲▲

'I am ashamed to say that all the best paintings and sculptures have been destroyed by travellers'
                                    Lucie Duff-Gordon

The famous Italian hydraulics engineer and circus strongman, Giovanni Batiste Belzoni, was one of the first men to make significant archaeological discoveries throughout Egypt. He was once described as a 'colossal man built like Hercules who touched the tops of doorways with his head.'

Along with names which can be seen scrawled across monuments and sites the length and breadth of Egypt, is Belzoni's.

In the second court of the Ramesseum, fragments of a black granite statue—the toppled colossal of the King, lay in ruin on the ground. On the throne are the names of Rameses II—and Belzoni.

Belzoni discovered numerous tombs and temples and left a comprehensive record for history—although his methods of archaeology were crude and more than often destructive. Belzoni had used a battering ram at the Valley of the Kings to gain entry into the tombs. His system was certainly due to subliminal ignorance as archaeological methods, as we know today, were non-existent in the early 1800s. Yet, it was because of ignorance that incalculable damage has been done at the hands of pick and shovel diggers.

When Belzoni became interested in finding an entrance to Khafre—the second pyramid at Ghiza, the French Consul Bernardino Drovetti, with whom he had long competed, threatened to open it before him—if necessary with gunpowder. Fortunately, Belzoni beat him to it to stake his claim, without the use of gunpowder. He scribed his name in bold black letters on the south wall of the burial chamber where you can clearly read today—BELZONI MARCH 2ND 1818.

The French writer, Gustave Flaubert, was disgusted by the disregard in which people treated the monuments throughout Egypt: "On the top of the Great Pyramid there is a certain Bufford, 79 Rue Saint-Martin, wallpaper-manufacturer, in black letters; an English fan of Jenny Lind's has written her name; there is also apear, representing Louis-Philipp. Also scratched in the stone are little holes forming an Arab abacus; it's a game – pebbles are put in the holes for calculation."

Inside the pyramid of Khafre, Flaubert notes that: "Under Belzoni's name, and no less large, is that of an M. Just de Chasseloup-Laubat. One is irritated by the number of imbeciles' names written everywhere. "In the temples we read travellers' names; they strike us as petty and futile. We never write ours; there are some that must have taken three days to carve, so deeply are they cut in the stone. There are some that you keep meeting everywhere – sublime persistence of stupidity."

The Garden Ran Down to the Nile

The French traveller Edward de Montule, while wandering through the tomb of Seti I in 1817 accompanied by Belzoni, was deeply concerned by the looting of tombs and the destructive way in which they were entered and plundered—including Belzoni's own methods: "If any perfect tombs still exist, I sincerely wish they may escape the research of the curious antiquary; to them the learned are become objects to be dreaded as Cambyses, for the sarcophagus's (sic) and mummies which they contain, would inevitably take the road to London or Paris."

When reaching the summit of Abousir, Amelia B. Edwards found: "The summit of the rock is a mere ridge, steep and overhanging toward east and south, and carved all over with autographs in stone. Some few of these are interesting; but for the most part they record only the visits of the illustrious – obscure. We found Belzoni's name; but looked in vain for the signatures of Burckhardt, Champollion, Lepsius and Ampere."

In *Le Nil,* written by Maxime Du Camp, travelling companion of Flaubert, Du Camp had categorically condemned the defacers of monuments. His later editions contain an irate footnote: "The preceding lines have brought me bad luck. A facetious tourist who apparently read them has amused himself by inscribing my name, in large capital letters, on several temples in Egypt and Nubia. I protest against this profanation, and I beg readers of this book who may travel on the Nile in future to be good enough to rub out those inanities, which I am incapable of having committed."

The Garden Ran Down to the Nile

In the name of diplomacy ambitious diplomats had more interest in stockpiling and selling antiquities than in conducting foreign administration. The British Consul Henry Salt, whose contributions to epigraphy were considerable and must not go unnoticed, spent most of his time collecting artefacts for his own gain. He hired Belzoni under the pretence that his discoveries would go to the British Museum—and then claimed the finds for himself.

Salt's eagerness to participate in new discoveries and to publish his findings found him digging at the ancient sites, blasting open tombs, and hacking away paintings and reliefs, and then selling the spoils to competing foreign countries. Salt's principal rival in the passion to possess was Bernardino Drovetti. An ambitious dandy, he also trafficked in African animals—mummified and alive. Drovetti supplied a menagerie of exotic birds and beasts to crowned heads and eccentric collectors around the world. Some of the animals he dispatched overseas were: gazelle, antelope, onyx, ostrich, Arabian stallions, Nubian sheep, and milk cows.

He once had a request for an elephant, but the most exotic animals he ever shipped were two giraffes. They travelled 2000 miles up the Nile from Sennor to Alexandria, where, after a three-month rest on the grounds of Mohammed Ali's palace, they were shipped separately across the Mediterranean Sea—one to Paris, the other to London.

Mohammed Ali was one of the most unscrupulous offenders Egypt has ever known. He handed out the country's treasures on a grandiose scale using government labour to plunder and even transport statues, obelisks, and priceless papyri to foreign countries and private collectors of whom he found favour. In 1918 Museums in Europe and America were overflowing with Egyptian antiquities, and to keep on good terms with their governments, Mohammed Ali's cavalier attitude in dividing the spoils, simply became good manners.

Throughout the 19th century, the demand for souvenirs continued to grow and the trade in antiques was flourishing. A campaign of looting and destruction by profiteering vandals for the greedy collector was rife. Galabehya clad touts hovered around dahabeyahs moored at the banks of Thebes and local inhabitants sold hundreds of precious objects from exploited tombs to private collectors. The tombs were being stripped of their antiquities daily.

The ever increasing number of tourists to Egypt brought with them a desire for artefacts so much so that they were not content to purchase them from the bazaars and local touts, but took to chipping away fragments of monuments and hieroglyphic reliefs wherever and whenever possible. When they were not able to carry off their booty they left their graffito on tombs and temples the length and breadth of Egypt. Most of the earlier discovered tombs in the Valley of the Kings are etched with names, quotations, and even poems whose dates span the entire period of the Roman rule. The tomb of Memnon alone contains over 1,000 of these idioms.

An artist of the *Graphic*, an illustrated journal in the late 1800s, captured with pen and paper the wanton destruction by several young American women chipping away pieces of hieroglyphs from the magnificent columns of the Ptolemaic Temple of Hathor: "This temple is one of the best preserved and grandest monuments of Egypt. This imposing edifice is noted for having on its outer walls the supposed portrait-representations of Cleopatra and her son by

Julius Caesar. This fact apparently inspires those tourists suffering from the mania for collecting mementos of their peregrinations to possess themselves of pieces of the stonework, hence, month by month, during each season the mutilations exhibit increasing depth and breadth."

At Abou Simbel, Lucie Duff-Gordon was appalled by the graffiti carved on the monuments and especially that of Prince Puckler-Muskau, her mother's former 'postal' lover: "The scribbling of names is quite infamous: beauty defaced by Tompkins and Hobson. Worst of all, Puckler-Muskau has engraved his in huge letters and size on the naked breast of the august and pathetic giant who sits at Abou Simbel. I wish someone would kick him for his profanity."

Puckler-Muskau's name survived the relocation of the temple by UNESCO in 1965, and is clearly visible today. Lucie goes on to say: "I am ashamed to say that all the best paintings and sculptures have been destroyed by travellers. "In 1852, Belzoni's tomb (Seti I) was literally strewed with fragments. I grieved to see it, and I felt that I could cheerfully have assisted in sending the depredators back, handcuffed, to their own country, whether on this side of the Atlantic or the other."

John Gadsby when on top of the Great Pyramid in 1847 was confronted by boys with paints, brushes, hammers and chisels asking if he wanted his name 'mortalising.' (sic) Gadsby was one of the more conscientious travellers: "I was not ambitious that way, so declined both the brush and chisel." Not so Sir Thomas Lipton who in 1882 paid one of the fellahin at the Pyramids to incise the name LIPTON into the stone above the entrance to the Great Pyramid.

On the eastern side of the Step Pyramid are two houses, the house of the north and the house of the south—symbolizing the unity of Upper and Lower Egypt. The house on the south features examples of 12th century BC graffiti where the admiration of Djoser is depicted in a cursive form of hieroglyphs and is now protected from modern day defacers under Plexiglas.

Auguste Mariette, curator at the Louvre in Paris had been sent to Egypt in 1856 to collect antiquities for France. Realizing the enormity of the growing problem arising from the destruction and removal of ancient monuments in Thebes and elsewhere along the Nile Valley, he appealed to the Khedive Said to establish an organization for the protection of standing monuments. The French Consul-General and French businessmen in Cairo fervently backed Mariette, who was given a house on a rocky platform in Sakkarah along with a grant to start a national museum in Bulak to house antiquities that were in need of protection.

During Mariette's flourishing career he excavated thirty-five major sites, and although his archaeological excavations were destructive and unscientific, he virtually stopped wide-scale looting in Egypt.

The trafficking of mummies alone was staggering. Shiploads of mummies were sent to America, the wrappings to be turned into paper during the Civil War. The Royal Cache plundered by the infamous Abd er Rassul brothers—sold to collectors over the years, and the prying open of sarcophagi to rip apart the mummies in search of gold, jewellery and amulets, gives question to how many of the mummies may have been the bodies of significant kings now lost for eternity.

The Prince of Wales, Edward VII, was not above plunder. In 1869 he took home to England thirty-two mummy cases, one sarcophagus, a number of antiquities, a papyrus, and a menagerie of live birds and animals—including a monkey, two goats, two flamingos, a parrot, and a snapping turtle.

The discovery of the Turin Papyrus provided a list of kings and their precise reigns in years, months and days beyond historical record. By the 19th century it had been so badly handled that over half the contents had been obliterated. This document almost certainly had been used by the classical writers to obtain information which is now lost to us.

Herodotus travelled the Nile Valley in 460-455 B.C. and was the first historian to write about the ancient Egyptians. Alan Gardiner thought Herodotus the 'Father of History.' Auguste Mariette was less favourable, calling him a criminal for revealing only stupidities: ". . . he tells us gravely that a daughter of Cheops built a pyramid with the fruit of prostitution. Considering the great number of mistakes in Herodotus . . . would it not have been better for Egyptology had he never existed?"

Herodotus had visited Egypt when the ancient language was still spoken and left detailed descriptions of the country and culture, but he never learned the language; which could have revealed many historical mysteries—including the key to hieroglyphics that was still in use during his time. He wrote in great detail about the people's lives, their religion, their customs and their occupations. But he accepted what he heard as fact, never questioning what might be hearsay, thus making his records a mixture of truths and myths to be deciphered by modern scholars.

Before a moral responsibility emerged within Amelia B. Edwards, making her realize that Egypt's history was disappearing at a rapid pace before her own eyes, she too revelled in the pursuit of the more portable antiquities: "We soon became quite hardened to such sights and learned to rummage among dusty sepulchres with no more compunction than would have befitted a gang of professional bodysnachers. These are experiences upon which one looks back afterward with wonder and something like remorse; but so infectious is the universal callousness, and so over-mastering is the passion for relic-hunting, that I do not doubt we should again do the same things under the same circumstances."

On one occasion in Thebes, Amelia was determined to obtain a papyrus that had been discovered along with other treasures, including a mummy from what she thought was a royal tomb. Another party of travellers, the Misses Broclehurst, were keen on acquiring the same papyrus that was accompanied by the mummy. Amelia, not wishing to buy the mummy at any price, nor the papyrus unseen, lost out to the Misses Broclehurst who: ". . . bought both mummy and papyrus at an enormous price; and then, unable to endure the perfume of their ancient Egyptian, drowned the dear departed at the end of a week."

The Ancient city of Heliopolis, known as the 'House of the

The Garden Ran Down to the Nile

Sun,' had been the seat of learning for philosophers such as Plato and Eudoxus until it was destroyed by the invasion of the Persians. Heliopolis had all but disappeared by the time Strabo visited in 24 B.C. In the district of Al Matariyyah, a single obelisk dedicated to the Sun God 'Re' remains. Beside it stood two other red granite obelisks erected to Tuthmosis III, which were removed to Alexandria by Agustus Caesar to decorate the Caesarium. In 1881 one of the obelisks was moved to New York's Central Park and the other to London to stand on the Victoria Embankment by the Thames—more 'gifts' to the west from Khedive Ismail.

Mabel Caillard, as a small girl, lived with her family in Ramleh near Alexandria. She remembers walking down to the seashore with her father to see Cleopatra's Needle (as one of the obelisks was called). It stood close to the Ramleh railway station and was one of the last monuments of Ptolemaic Alexandria to be transported to America—its companion had already been carried off to England. Mabel recalls: "In due course a ship arrived with a space cut through the middle to accommodate the monolith, and a scaffolding was set up, surmounted by the American flag, to enable it to be lowered to the necessary level. I remember now the predictions that the needle would certainly go to the bottom on the voyage across the Atlantic, and so imbued was I with the idea that for a long time I believed that it had actually done so."

Vandalism of the temples and monuments did not start in the last few centuries, although this is the time when the worst of it seems to have taken place. The ancient Pharaohs thought nothing of destroying a predecessor's monument in order to obtain building material for their own use. Defacing the rulers' names on Bas-Reliefs and painted figures were commonplace. Cartouches were hacked out in order to have the new reigning kings' name immortalized on the existing temples and obelisks. Seeing how easily the bas-reliefs could be obliterated, Rameses II had the foresight to have his hieroglyphs carved deep into the monuments, thus preserving his name forever.

When visiting the Island of Philae, Amelia B. Edwards was loathed to see several centuries of inscriptions belonging to the period of Greek and Roman rule: "They have cut their names by the hundreds all over the principal temple, just like tourists of to-day. Some of these antique autographs are written upon and across those of preceding visitors; while others – palimpsests upon stone, so to say – having been scratched on the yet unsculptured surface of doorway and pylon, are seen to be older than the hieroglyphic texts which were afterward carved over them." She mentions that while the Priests of this period tried to imbue Christianity: "Hundreds of temples were plundered . . . Forty thousand statues of divinities were destroyed at one fell swoop."

The American traveller Charles Dudley Warner's irreverence at the destruction left by previous generations in the name of religion is marked by his description in 1876: "It is indeed marvellous that so much has been preserved, considering what a destructive creature man is, and how it pleases his ignoble soul to destroy the works of his forerunners on the earth. The earthquake has shaken up Egypt time and again, but Cambyses was worse; he was an earthquake with malice and purpose, and left little standing that he had leisure to overturn. The ancient Christians spent a great deal of time in rubbing out the deep-cut hieroglyphics, chiselling away the heads of strange gods, covering the pictures of ancient ceremonies and sacrifices, and painting on the walls their own rude conceptions of holy persons and miraculous occurrences. And then the Moslems came, hating all images and pictorial representations alike, and scraped away or battered with bullets the work of pagans and Christians."

Another American, William C. Prime was a law unto himself. He had no compulsion whatsoever in unwrapping dozens of mummies in an attempt to find what he called 'mummy shawls', a covering made from fine linen and ornamented with cornelian and lapis lazuli strung beads.

Prime also enjoyed shooting game, not just for food, but for his own amusement and seemingly attempted to rid Egypt of as many partridge, plover, pigeons, pelicans, geese, ducks, hawks, vultures, fox, wild pigs, and crocodile as he could. He boasts of having shot 306 pigeons in one day, and the amount of ducks he brought down as being "absolute murder."

Prime was an interesting man when it came to plunder. He had absolutely no scruples when it came to procuring artefacts. He seemed to have considered it his right as a superior howajji: "Abd-el-Atti had been making a purchase of an antique, on his own account, from an Arab of Goornow. He had learned that a mummy of the most ancient, rare, and valuable kind, had been found, and he had negotiated for and bought it. He directed the Arabs to bring down the daughter of Pharaoh to the shore of the Nile, three miles below on the west bank, near a tree which we all knew, at midnight on the night of our starting. He went down early with the small boat and four men to receive the freight. On our appearance with the *Phantom* (the name of his boat) he was to board us. So the daughter of the Pharaoh (who dares say she was not the daughter of Amunoph himself?) commenced her voyage from her ancient resting place and the graves of her fathers. Three thousand years of repose – then, the Nile-boat of a wandering Howajji – then, a curiosity-room in Cairo – and then the sea, the Pillars of Hercules, the Fortunate Islands, and a new world! There is verily no rest even in an Egyptian grave. This royal lady slept quietly on our cabin deck during the voyage down the river, and Abd-el-Atti transferred her to Dr. Abbott at Cairo, who, I suppose, will ship her to enrich the collection in New York."

Florence Nightingale had been disappointed with the 'souvenirs,' which were becoming increasingly hard to find with all the collectors and archaeologists coming to Egypt in the mid-eighteen hundreds. She wrote home: "As for the Egyptian rubbish, you may do just what you like with it, keep it, or give it away. There is nothing that reminds me of what I have seen, nothing that savours of my Karnak, except the bronze dog, the brick seals which sealed the tombs at Thebes, and the four little seals in the light box – two of which are of Rameses – you must not give away what is in the great Nubian basket, because some of that rubbish is Trout's. (Trout was Florence's maid). The Darfur bracelets are for you – I got them at Philae. Louisa must have a pair of the little figures found in the tombs, but I shall make her a little collection out of the rubbish, when I come home.

The Garden Ran Down to the Nile

"I thought in England one had nothing to do but walk into the tombs and dig out the newest jewellery! Whereas there never was a place like Thebes for the impossibility of getting anything. As for Egyptian things, unless you carry away Memnon's head, like Belzoni, I don't know that there is anything to be had."

Samuel Bevan remembers an American physician that lived in a large commodious house in a quiet area of Cairo that was fitted out in the oriental style: "When not occupied by his Esculapian duties, the doctor devotes a part of his time to the formation of a cabinet of Egyptian antiquities, and he is so well known to the Arabs as a collector of rarities, that relics of all descriptions find their way to him, the bearer being generally rewarded according to the outward appearance of the article, by a sum often strangely disproportionate to its real value. Among other objects of great interest, is a ring of solid virgin gold of great weight, which from its hieroglyph, is supposed to have belonged to one of the Pharaohs. By this, the doctor deservedly sets great store, and has repeatedly refused to part with it, although a very high price has been offered. Mummy ornaments of all descriptions, with holy beetles and scaribei, form a prominent portion of the collection, which is visited by most travellers as one of the sights of Cairo."

For the most part the Egyptian people who took part in the plunder and trafficking of antiquities did so for the sole purpose of bettering their existence. They were not in a position to afford the luxury of art appreciation, nor were they interested in a heritage that was not theirs and one they knew little about. They plundered because there was a market for plunder—a European market.

The Garden Ran Down to the Nile

Auguste Mariette's attempt at protecting standing monuments had come to nothing, but in 1882, Amelia B. Edwards formed the Egypt Exploration Fund; a society backed by a powerful group of men. The society was designed to carry out scientific excavations of which serious research was the primary objective.

Sir Flinders Petrie excavated for forty-two years and made more major archaeological discoveries than any other archaeologist before him. Unfortunately he was trapped under an incompetent administrative bureaucracy in Cairo that forced him to sell artefacts to competing American and European museums to support his excavations.

Petrie realized the importance of accurate dating and measurements and his publications improved the standards of archaeology in the field bringing forward a whole new generation of Egyptologists. His list of students who went on to become prominent archaeologists is imposing, including Howard Carter, who improved methods so much that he became one of the finest archaeological draughtsmen of all time.

Proper care was now being taken in the excavation of archaeological sites. When a discovery was made, only after recording the objects by cataloguing every detail, by drawing or painting, and by that time, photographing, did they proceed with the excavation.

When Egypt became a sovereign state after the Protectorate had been abolished, changes in the antiquity laws were made. From that time on any discovery of antiquities automatically became the property of the Egyptian government. This change came about just six weeks before Howard Carter discovered the tomb of Tutankhamun in the Valley of the Kings on the 4th of November

1922. Until that time, the majority of the contents of the tomb would most certainly have gone to the Metropolitan Museum in New York. Fortunately, the passion for looting and collecting antiquities has slowly evolved into a discipline of scientific techniques and specialized methods of field archaeology to the benefit of future generations.

Howard Carter's burial, on the 6th of March, took place at Putney Vale Cemetery, London. There were only nine mourners, including his brother, two assistant archaeologists, and Lady Evelyn Beauchamp, Lord Carnarvon's daughter. Like so many other great people of history, his achievements are only now being fully recognized.

Seventeen

Living Among the Egyptians

'The West can teach the East how to get a living, but the East must eventually be asked to show the West how to live'
Tekyi Hsieh

Getting to know the Egyptian people is getting to know Egypt. It seems bizarre that westerners sometimes look on non-western societies as having a cultural and linguistic ignorance where in Cairo, the typical educated Egyptian speaks on average three languages. English is the second most widely used language in Egypt as it is the first language in business and almost everywhere you go the people speak or have knowledge of it. Boys learn English to prepare them for the outside world. Girls are taught French for social etiquette. The Egyptians taste in literature and furniture widely favour the French. Most homes were full of carved gold-leafed reproduction furniture made in the so called 'Louis Farouk' workshops around the city. Buildings and houses are heavily influenced by French design and have the same style of shuttered windows as seen all over France today.

The Garden Ran Down to the Nile

Egyptians are optimists, their promises coming easier than their deliverances, which are usually *boukra inshallah* (tomorrow, God willing). Time is of no importance in Egypt and though exasperating, it is virtually impossible to get anything done in a hurry. I sometimes wondered why watches were worn at all and came to the conclusion that they were more of a fashion statement than a necessity.

Modern day Cairo is one of the most exciting and fascinating cities in the world, but it also has the power to enclose and frustrate you. This malady is often referred to as culture shock and more often affects the wives of long-term diplomats and businessmen when they find themselves left to cope alone in a daily environment they are not familiar with.

Unlike a European country, where the difference is primarily the language, the customs in Egypt can be as much a barrier as the language itself and no matter how well intended you are, when the charm wears off, anxiety and frustration can occur. The difficulty arises when everyday things once taken for granted, became a concern. Nothing worked as quickly as you were used to—if at all. Power shortages were frequent and could last for hours. The main source of contact would normally have been the telephone, but most people didn't have one as there was a long waiting list, and once installed, they were usually unreliable. At the time, no one had mobile phones.

In the home it was essential to boil drinking water and the horror stories about which foods were safe to eat and which foods were not, quickly circulated causing over concern about eating anything at all. Repairs to the general running of the house were always carried out *boukra inshallah*. The mosquitoes were voracious, the flies relentless, and the heat insufferable during certain times of the year. There was an ever-present layer of dust that covered everything no matter how often you cleaned, and one of the biggest worries was employing a reliable and honest housekeeper, cook, and *Bowab* (caretaker).

Hot water was provided by butane cylinders known as Buta Gaz, and always seemed to run out just when you were in the shower. There were numerous trivial irritations of daily life to contend with that made some people hostile and aggressive towards their host country. There were those who took refuge by alienating themselves in the company of their own countrymen, not bothering to learn a little of the language or to get to know the Egyptian people or the country.

The Egyptians have a word to compensate for the 'shortcomings' of their country—they simply say *ma'alesh*, which means, 'never mind, it doesn't matter.' If the western world had a word like *ma'alesh* it would probably mean less heart attacks and stress, two adversities the Egyptians do not seem to suffer from. A patient attitude and a sense of humour are two requisites essential for living in Cairo.

The Caireans eternal optimism can be difficult for the westerner to reconcile. They will tell you the affirmative only because they want to please you. It is of no use to get him to see the relative importance of the matter at hand. He is compelled by formalities and politeness and ceremoniously conducts his business through the usual methods of unlimited justifications and cups of coffee. The fundamental difference between east and west cannot be overcome by similarity in dress nor the use of a common language. We have to realize differences of disposition in able to establish a basis for understanding and acceptance that will enable us to form a lasting relationship.

Compassion for animals is for the most part a western trait not shared by the Egyptians, though they are not entirely unsympathetic. Misfortune is looked upon as the will of God and therefore gracefully accepted. Animals are part of the workforce in Egypt and you will rarely see a working-class Egyptian family with a pet dog or cat. Coming from a society where animals are kept as pets and companions, rather than out of necessity for one's livelihood, it was hard to turn a blind eye to some of the things seen in the back streets of the city. It was illegal to put a horse or any large animal down at the scene of an accident, no matter how badly injured. The animal would have to be moved to a veterinary hospital. It sometimes appeared that animals were regarded with a cavalier attitude considering the weight and burdens they were expected to pull—often under impossible circumstances.

Carts with enormous loads of unbelievable cargo were dragged through the streets of careering traffic by dwarfish and neglected donkeys—ribs protruding, eyes closed to the dust and flies, their heads always bent downwards as they struggled against their burdens through the hostile streets that showed no patience. They had difficulty stopping the momentum of the load at intersections as there were no brakes and the driver would jump off and brace himself against the animal. When continuing, they had a new challenge trying to gain traction on the hot asphalt surface—their hooves slipping under the weight of their tasks and sometimes bringing them to their badly calloused knees.

The Garden Ran Down to the Nile

Egyptian donkeys are extremely small, yet they were used for every kind of work imaginable. The fortunate ones worked in the countryside carrying loads of maize, fodder, berseem, and sugar cane. They were usually ridden by small boys or old weathered men who had to turn their toes up to keep their slippers on.

The donkeys of the Zabayeen, a tribe of Copts that lived and worked on the rubbish heaps in the City of the Dead, would haul a heavy and precarious load sixteen miles a day in temperatures over 100°F and on little food and water every day for as long as they lived, usually about four years. The long grade that led up to the city dump was the hardest task as they struggled against their harnesses—most of which were made from ropes wrapped with dirty rags—their hides rubbed raw with never a chance to heal. When I left Egypt in 1981, the government was trying to eliminate this type of transport by introducing rubbish trucks throughout the city. When I visited Cairo in 2005, I saw no rubbish carts pulled by donkeys.

But the majority of the working people cared enough about their animals to realize that they were the source of their income and needed to be looked after. More and more people were becoming aware of the Brooke Institute, a hospital for sick horses and donkeys a few miles from the city center.

The hospital was started in 1934 by an English woman, Dorothy Brooke, as a mission service to rescue 100,000 cavalry horses after World War I, that had been imported to the Middle East and sold as working animals. She was appalled by the miserable conditions of these animals and devoted the rest of her life to the hospital, which relies entirely on donations. It is a registered charity and was still managed in 1981 by her son, Richard. The hospital could accommodate up to 150 animals at any one time with clinics in Luxor, Assouan, and Alexandria. They rescued animals that were badly in need of help, replacing them with a healthy animal until the owners animal had recovered, and educating the owner in the care, attention, and needs of their animal.

Religion is fundamental to the Egyptian Muslims way of life. Devotions are daily and can be seen and heard all around the city. The dark brown spot on the forehead of many Egyptian men is called the *zabib*, or raisin. It is a testimony to years of devoting in prostrated prayer. The Mohammed Ali Mosque, known as the Alabaster Mosque (when Saladin built the Citadel—he used the alabaster facing blocks from the pyramids) forms one of Cairo's most famous landmarks and affords one of the best views over the old city due to its magnificent situation at the top of the Citadel.

The mosque is Turkish Imperial in style, built in 1824 by a Greek architect from Constantinople. It gives a truly romantic picture when viewed from a distance where the charming oriental quality of the glistening domes and towering minarets are sharply defined against a background of cerulean sky. In the centre of the courtyard there is a Turkish baroque basin where devotees perform their ablutions before entering the mosque. A 'gingerbread clock' looks down from the central court; given to Mohammed Ali by King Louie-Philippe of France in exchange for an obelisk of Rameses II. The obelisk was from the Temple of Luxor and now stands in the Place de la Concorde in Paris. The clock has never worked and is somewhat of an anachronism alongside the Moorish arabesques.

The Garden Ran Down to the Nile

Looking out over the rough stone surface of the parapet, there is a magnificent view as the shimmering heat dances over a thousand centuries, and radiates off the crenulated walls of the fourteenth century Madrasa of Sultan Hassan, and the nineteenth century Rifai Mosque, seen in the foreground. Over the great stretches of the city—cut in two by the Nile, Cairo spreads towards the desert and the Pyramids of Ghiza. On the opposite side, the Mokattam Hills appear grey against an orange haze as the smell of history filters through the air.

Tour buses and taxis wait at the lower enclosure that houses the infamous gate-passage where Mohammed Ali conducted his massacre of the Mamelukes in 1811. Coaches release hordes of tourists several times a day for the obligatory tour. Two men sit just inside the upper level gate to the entrance of the mosque and hand out cotton socks to slip over shoes. The interior is impressive due to its enormity rather than its decorations. A dignified silence resounds within the coolness of the walls. To the right of the entrance is the elaborate tomb of Mohammed Ali.

In romantic years gone by, the rising of the sun would be accompanied by the solemn call of the Muezzin from a distant minaret, clear and faint, obliging the faithful that prayer is better than sleep. Across the dusty rooftops of the city's houses and the paint box green of the Delta his voice would permeate the air. Unfortunately in most mosques today the melodious voice of the Muezzin has been replaced by the harsh, acrimonious blare of loud speakers that attack the silence at full volume. They can be heard five times a day reminding you of the Muslims devotion to his religion, and at no time is this more apparent than during the month of Ramadan—the month of heat. At the first sign of the crescent

The Garden Ran Down to the Nile

moon Ramadan begins and lasts for twenty-eight days. It is the time in which the soul is purified and all Muslims, with the exception of children and the aged or infirmed, fast from the first thread of dawn until the last rays of the sun. It is also a time of charity and a time to form new bonds of understanding between people.

Being the month of heat makes the burden of the fast even greater and as the day progresses, tempers grow short as people hurry to finish their daily tasks and return home in time for the setting of the sun and the *Id al-Fitr*, the feast of the breaking of the fast. The streets are virtually empty by six o'clock and it is a joy to be able to drive through the city without the usual carnival of traffic. During Ramadan, devotees make their Pilgrimage to Mecca. It is one of the five pillars of the faith; the fundamental requirements of being a Muslim. Believers are expected to visit Mecca at least once during their lifetime if they can afford to and if they are in good health. When a man has made his Al-Hajj (Pilgrimage) he is allowed to wear green. Fairy lights are sometimes strung around his house on his return.

Nobody slept during Ramadan, Muslims or Howajji (Christians). The streets outside the flat could be very noisy in the evening, especially during Bairam, the three-day feast following Ramadan when festivities would go on into the early hours of the morning. At the end of our road fairy lights were strung, floodlights glared and Arabic music could be heard throughout the night dispersed through loud speakers at top volume, piercing ears with a series of high-pitched electronic screeches. It was a time of jubilation as people gathered for the evening's festivities of elaborate banquets and entertainment. Cafés, shops, and mosques were open all night.

The Garden Ran Down to the Nile

Next door to us was an Egyptian family that we became neighbourly with. They kept chickens in the back yard. We would always know when they were having chicken for dinner. The cook would chase one of the scrawny birds around the yard in a whirl of dust and feathers with a great deal of noise and clucking until the death rattle subsided. Several days before the end of Ramadan a sheep would be tethered by the chicken coop awaiting its demise; where it would be taken in the house and slaughtered in the bathtub.

Ibrahim was a round-bellied, galabehya clad Bedouin who worked 'free-lance' for the Embassy's ex-pats. He had once cooked for the British Army and would now cook for a *fête champetré* or an elaborate dinner party. His speciality was chicken, lamb, and beef curry. Ibrahim would appear on my doorstep on the morning of the dinner party and I would give him seven Egyptian pounds; enough to purchase groceries that would feed two dozen people. With an acknowledged nod of his turbaned head he would disappear up the road in a cloud of dust on his rickety old push-pedal bicycle to return an hour later laden with meat and freshly plucked chickens— whose heads drooped from the basket on his handlebars, and bunches of wilting vegetables and other miscellaneous sundry teetering in a box roped to the back fender. The kitchen door would slam shut and that part of the house was then off limits to me until the ultimate feast. The sound of clattering pans and the wonderful smells of bubbling sauces would waft throughout the house and lead me stealing to the kitchen to see Ibrahim peering into saucepans and chopping vegetables with tempestuous deliberation.

An hour before the party two suffrages (waiters) would appear to serve pre-dinner drinks and snacks, staying on to clean up the aftermath of the *Cordon bleu*; although it would take several days to completely return the kitchen to a workable order. Days later I would find hardened sauce drips inside drawers and between counter tops and cooker. Great lumps of rice glued to the ceiling and unrecognisable foodstuffs in inconceivable places. Pans were burnt beyond redemption and cooking utensils bent and blackened, but Ibrahim's *pièce de résistance* was much enjoyed by all and he was always invited back for an encore.

Eseldine was the longest serving member of the embassy staff. He was the Ambassador's chauffer—driving one of the five Rolls Royce's at the time in Egypt.. He was small and angular, a Nubian of indeterminate age with taught skin stretched over high cheekbones. Polite and soft-spoken, he had an amenable demeanour that was born out of years of service to the British Embassy and its diplomats. Eseldine was highly respected amongst the Egyptian and British staff alike. He used to salute the Ambassador—a vestige gesture from a former era. I always imagined him wearing a tarboosh—which he probably had at one time.

The Rev. Thomas Iden liked the red tarboosh worn by the Egyptian's, as he felt it was: "a very dignified headgear. I have decided that a man cannot look slouchy in a fez. It is much cheaper than a hat; it lasts a long time; the style never changes; and you never have to take it off. Your shoes you remove . . . but your hat you leave on when you enter a house or a mosque."

Rifai was in charge of the local staff. He was a considerate man that still had a thick crop of black hair—now flecked with grey.

His round moustachioed face was deeply lined and tanned by a half-century of Cairo sun. A true gentleman, he was helpful in many situations— including interpreter and head bartender at embassy functions. Acquiring a maid, cook-*sofragi* or *bowab* was best done by letters of reference or by word of mouth from a trusted Egyptian.

Rifai was responsible for engaging my maid, Samira. She was a trustworthy and dependable woman, about thirty something who was the wife of a cousin of an uncle of a friend of Rifai's brother, or something like that. Everybody in Cairo seemed to be related in some way or another.

Samira would appear at eight o'clock in the morning, Monday through Thursday to clean and dust the dim, cool interior of the flat. She was thin and dark, a gentle woman with five children. Her kohl-lined eyes accentuated a pretty face still visible through the labours of her accepted roll in life. She went silently about her chores, slapping dust from shutters, airing bedding over railings, washing windows with vinegar and old newspapers, and cleaning floors and staircase with worn out rags and cold water.

Every other Wednesday the *makwagi* would come to collect the ironing and take it away to an open fronted, hole-in-the-wall laundry where he plied his trade on an enormous wooden table— that served as an ironing-board, and an ancient flat iron filled with burning coals—kept hot on a Primus stove. I made him promise that he would never dampen my clothes by spraying water from his mouth. He promise, and I pretended to believe him, but never gave him anything he could ruin. Men's shirts and tablecloths he was a master at, but women's clothing seemed to be a mystery to him. My jeans would come back with knife-edged creases. The next day he would appear with the finished ironing and a beaming smile of satisfaction and I could not help but give him a few extra piasters.

Rubbish was collected six days a week by Omar, a Copt of the Zabayeen who parked his rubbish cart in the road outside the building while he made his rounds; his patient donkey waiting while the feral cats scavenged in the cart. He was a tall man with dark curly hair and a uniform of khaki coloured shirt and trousers. I saved all my vegetable scraps for his donkey, which he came to expect and always accepted with a grateful smile.

When my father was visiting one year, he noticed that Omar's donkey had an open sore on his shoulder that was not healing, as the rag-wrapped ropes that served as a harness was continually rubbing against it. My father cleaned the donkey's wound with antiseptic and covered it with a gauze bandage. He checked the donkey every day and Omar would smile and agree that the donkey was improving. Within a week the wound had healed. Several days later, two men who had been working on a building site across the road came to my door and asked to see the hakim (doctor). One of the men had cut his hand and wanted my father to bandage it. My father became well known that summer by the people in the area. He liked taking long walks and would stop to chat to the locals, even though they didn't speak each other's language. He once bought a case of Coca Cola from a corner kiosk for a group of men that were working on the road by our house. He thought they could use some refreshment in the heat of the day. From then on, every time the men saw him they would wave and shout greetings.

After several unsuccessful *bowabs*, it was once again Rifai who introduced us to Mohammed, a Nubian who had travelled down to Cairo from somewhere near Abou Simbel—leaving his wife and family in order to find work. It was hard to tell Mohammed's age, I thought somewhere in his sixties. He was as dark as ebony with fading grey-brown eyes and remnants of greying hair beneath his white skullcap. He had about half his original teeth and those were stained with nicotine. He would speak to me in Arabic gesticulating with long, bony fingers as if I understood every word he was saying, his racking cough frequently interrupting his speech. There was always mint tea brewing or the smell of lentil soup and boiled potatoes with garlic bubbling away on the Primus stove within his hut. He used to like helping me water the potted plants and the blood-red canna lilies in our garden. I became extremely fond of the old man.

Bobo had a small butcher shop on 26th July Street, the main street in Zamalek where mutton was sold as lamb. His shop was decorated with sheep carcases that hung from hooks down the front window. Every so often a live lamb would be tethered outside the shop awaiting its demise. All his meat was tough, but inexpensive. Beef was only available on Thursdays, and the deliveries were made through the open-fronted shop. Customers would duck so as not to be clobbered by the swinging carcase slung over the man's shoulder. Beef cost E£1 per kilo (approximately one pound sterling). Pieces were hacked off in great chunks from a carcass that hung suspended from a large hook in the ceiling. In one corner of the shop, stood an ancient iron meat grinder. As the meat was ground to mince, it pushed out the remains of whatever else had been in the grinder beforehand.

Being a butcher was a hazardous trade as the blood-stained bandages and previous scars on Bobo's hands testified. In a Muslim country pork is not easily available, even in a Copt's butcher shop, but there was one shop in Mohandessin that had a European style meat counter where you could buy bacon.

Not far down the road from Bobo's was 'Vasalakis', the green fronted grocery store owed by a Greek Cypriot who sold fresh eggs and a good selection of cheese and sliced ham. At Christmas he had chocolate Santa's in colourful foil wrappers, and at Easter, chocolate eggs and chenille chicks.

Down Hassan Sabri street in Zamalek, was the Japanese owned 'Sunny Supermarket' that sold Birds Eye frozen peas, Knorr soup mixes and vacuum-sealed fruit juices. Supermarkets were springing up all over the city and just about every food was available. The exception was fresh cows' milk, as there were no dairy cows in Egypt. Un-pasteurised buffalo and goats milk was available, but unadvisable to drink.

In the early 1800s the Englishman John Gadsby thought the buffalo milk delicious and that it had a 'relaxing tendency'.

Imported goods in the supermarkets were expensive, but at the *gomeyah* (government store) food and household goods were sold at subsidised prices. If you were prepared to queue amongst dozens of local women draped in black ma'alayahs, and could speak some Arabic, as no English was spoken in these shops, you could purchase American frozen chickens at E£1.50 each, and sugar, flour, dried beans, and rice at very low subsidized prices. They were scooped out of open bins, weighed on ancient scales, and wrapped in brown paper. Egyptian soap powders and cleaning agents were also available if you knew what to ask for.

The Garden Ran Down to the Nile

Egypt has the largest variety of fruits and vegetables anywhere in the world and because of the hot climate vegetables grow quite large throughout the year. Local bakeries specialized in cakes, biscuits and sweet Egyptian pastries, but some of the premises were not always hygienic. The bakery shops located in the Nile Hilton and the Jollie Ville Hotel by the pyramids made very good bread. The renowned Groppi's in Ezbekiyeh Square had a garden where you could have coffee or one of their delicious ice creams. Egyptian ice cream was made to a very high standard. There were two brands, Groppi and Dolci.

In the winter there were men with brightly decorated pushcarts selling piping hot sweet potatoes and corn on the cob. In the summer they sold watermelon from flat-bed trucks parked by the side of the road. They were large and round and usually injected with Nile water to make them weigh more.

In the evening around Zamalek, young street vendors peddled boxes of the Egyptian brand tissue, Carmen. They would walk among the cars waiting at traffic lights, peddling their wares. Also walking among the cars were children selling night blooming jasmine and honeysuckle that they had strung into lei's, and despite the fumes of the traffic, the air was sweet with the fragrance of the flowers. At ten or fifteen piasters it was hard to say no.

We attended a wedding reception given by a wealthy Egyptian family in the ballroom of the Nile Hilton Hotel. No expense was spared for the Bride and Groom or the buffet dinner for the guests that numbered around four hundred. The father of the bride was a Coptic Egyptian businessman from an educated class of Europeanised bourgeoisie. The Hilton was one of the popular venues on such occasions, probably due to its cantilevered staircase that rises up from the foyer in a dramatic sweeping spiral.

A piper in full Highland dress led the newlyweds up the stairs followed by a candlelight procession of young girls dressed in white and carrying two-foot candles. Women warbled the *zagharit* (cry of joy) and the on-looking guests threw gold replica coins at the couple.

The pretty, but corpulent bride was concealed beneath yards of white satin and filmy lace embellished with sequins and pearls. The gold coins caught in her dark hair and landed on the long train of her gown as she ascended the staircase. The groom was taller than the average Egyptian, slim and good-looking. He wore a pale blue velveteen tuxedo, ruffled shirt, and patent leather shoes.

Once inside the ballroom the couple was escorted to their *kusha*, a raised dais framed by a curtain of white carnations. They sat on gold painted 'Louie Farouk' thrones under a canopy of burning spotlights while a seemingly endless procession of guests and family came forward to offer congratulations and fill the Bride's satin purse with money.

The guests were seated in groups of eight to ten around tables adorned with fragrant flower arrangements. A sussi wallah resplendent in white billowing breeches, red waistcoat with gold braided trim, and gold sashes, circulated between the tables pouring *khashaf*, a drink made from grenadine and rosewater. As he leaned forward, a long stream of crimson liquid cascaded from the spout of an enormous glass urn decorated in silver filigree. The urn was strapped to his back and as he held the glass at arm's length, not a drop was spilt.

The Garden Ran Down to the Nile

An adjoining room held the food laid out on long tables that groaned under the weight. An enormous ice sculpture in the shape of a swan occupied the center table surrounded by every conceivable starter and savoury; red and black caviar, cracked crabs, prawns, mussels, quails eggs and lobster bisque. There was a whole roasted lamb, a turkey, kebabs and a pyramid of stuffed pigeons. An array of Egyptian mezze; falafel, lentils, ful medames, stuffed vine leaves, peppers and cabbage, courgettes, aubergine and tomato salad, cous-cous, rice and babaghanou. A silver tray was piled high with bread and rolls accompanied by ta'mayya, tehina and tabbouleh. Another table supported a mountain of fruits; pomegranates, guavas, mangoes, oranges and bananas. There were desserts made from dates, apricots, sultanas and pistachios, and large circular plates piled high with colourful sticky cakes and pastries; baklava, konafa and petits fours topped with coconut and rosewater. The guests attacked the feast with gusto. Plates were piled to capacity, heavy with calories and the promise of indigestion.

An Egyptian band played throughout dinner then was joined by a singer who sang in the style of Umm Kulthum. She wore a black ma'alayah and was accompanied by her entourage who opened the evening's entertainment with traditional folk songs. A voluptuous singer, drowning in blue eye shadow and false lashes soon took the spotlight. Circulating round the tables, she persuading enthusiastic guests to sing along with her. She resembled the movie posters seen around town with her tumbling red curls, scarlet lips, and red lacquered nails.

From the opposite end of the room, the sounds of a tabla, rababa, and cigats (finger cymbals) announced the appearance of Hannan—one of Egypt's well known belly dancers. She swirled on to the floor under shimmering spotlights in a series of hip-drops and figure-eight's, making her way to the dais where she proceeded to undulate to the delight of the groom and embarrassment of the bride.

By now the reception was in full swing. The dance floor pulsated with guests. Young men threw off their jackets, loosened their ties, and took to the dance floor. Little girls in white and pink ruffles imitated their older sisters in the art of raqs al-sharqi (dance of the east). At the end of the evening a man swinging a brass brazier from a long chain perfumed the air with incense and led the newlyweds across the room to an enormous five-tiered confectionary decorated with sugar garlands and flowers. As the couple cut the cake, curtains were drawn back releasing a dozen white doves that flew round the room and took refuge on the cornices. The cake was handed out as the guests departed.

Dancing has been a part of the Egyptian culture for centuries, depicted on tomb walls and written on papyrus. In the late 1800s dancing girls performed their unveiled dance in the streets for festivals or special occasions such as a marriage or birth. In private their performances were more lascivious, sometimes wearing very little or almost transparent costumes. The belly dance performed in hotels today is adapted and improvised for the audience. It is pure cabaret that is sometimes choreographed using flamboyant backing dancers, and bears little resemblance to the traditional baladi—although it derives from the same traditional dance.

The cabaret dancer of today accentuates the more earthy sexuality of the dance in her interpretation of the music, which only helps to misconstrue the original dance and its dignity. But visitors love it. They flood into the main hotels waiting until well after midnight to see one of the popular dancers like Dina. The top three dancers that I had seen on many occasions are now legends: Nagwa Fouad, Sohair Zaki, and Fifi Abdou.

When cinema became popular in Egypt in the forties, everyone was able to see the gracefulness and the beauty of this so called woman's dance when performed on screen by icons: Tahiyya Karioca, Naima Akef, and Samia Gamal. To see true raqs al-baladi in its purest form today, you must see it at social gatherings, weddings and within the Egyptian home where it is taught as a cultural and social grace to every little Egyptian girl.

The Evil Eye, also known as the glance of malice, is just as common in Egypt today as it was centuries ago. It is an old belief that the negative emotions of man: envy, jealousy and possessiveness, are sent out through rays of energy from the eye, causing illness or injury. Therefore, it is not a good thing to complement a child without touching him, as the touch counteracts the effect of the complement. The evil-eye could be cured by laying a broomstick on the floor and scissor-stepping seven times over it.

Animals can also be affected by the evil-eye and many donkeys and horses are decorated with charms and adorned with henna tattoos in the shape of a hand (the Hand of Fatima, or Chance). Mary Whately recalls a Coptic lady who sent her a message saying that her only son was ill and: "she wished to know if I thought it would be advisable to bring a monkey and keep it in the house, as some neighbours suggested. The Monkey kept in the house is thought to draw off the evil influence from the child to itself."

The Garden Ran Down to the Nile

Joan Shoucair was a British ex-pat who lived in the penthouse flat at 8 Ahmed Pasha Street, Garden City. She was anxious about another form of superstition. An enormous white owl had taken up residence close by her home and every evening he would sail by on silent wings casting haunting shadows over her rooftop garden. Her husband, Albert Shoucair, a successful Egyptian photographer (*Jewels of the Pharaohs* by Cyril Aldred) had recently died, and she believed the owl was a bad omen; an omen of death. Joan was from a vanished class of Cairo's belle époque whose wealth had been lost under the Nasser regime. Her home was the penthouse floor, very English in style with the usual oriental touches and artefacts that comes from years of living in an eastern country. On the dining room walls hung six beautiful and original watercolours by David Roberts, and in the sitting room on either side of the fireplace, two enormous pen drawings, one of an eagle the other of an Egyptian vulture. Both drawings had the signature of Vivant Denon; artist, scholar, and *bon vivant*, who had travelled to Egypt with Napoleon Bonaparte in the late 1700s and wrote one of the most important works in twenty-four volumes ever published on Egypt, *Description de l'Egypte*. I could only hope that Joan had the drawings insured.

We lived in a flat on Sharia Mahmoud Badri el Din in Mohandessin (Engineers City), a newly built and sparsely inhabited suburb. The building was leased by the British Embassy and was situated west of Zamalek, just opposite the Zamalek football stadium where the street outside became a sea of fans when the two most popular football teams, Ahly and Zamalek, were playing.

A high block wall surrounded the building and our garden where blood red canna loomed like bean stalks shading the blue iris and agapanthus beneath. Terracotta pots lined the steps of the porch that was washed down every day by Samira to keep the dust down. On the few days a year that it rained, everything would be washed clean, the leaves of the plants would glisten and the air in the city became breathable. It was a comical sight to see all the Egyptians coming out side to stand in the rain.

Our flat was two apartments converted to one, and was furnished with Government Issue furniture from John Lewis and Liberty. We had three reception rooms; four bedrooms, and several balconies where I watched the panorama of Egyptian life pass by.

Every Thursday two old hags would drive a herd of fat-tailed sheep down the middle of the road. They would stop outside the flat, sit on the curb and talk—accompanied by animated gestures, while the sheep grazed on invisible vegetation around them.

I returned to Mohandessin twenty-five years later and found it barely recognizable. A blending of cultures, it now had a portentous atmosphere of affluence with its wide divided tree-lined road and prestigious high rise businesses. The area had been built up so much it took some time to recognize the old neighbourhood and find my old flat. The dirt streets were now paved and the flame trees overgrown. When I eventually saw my flat it had become an internet company supplying pharmaceutical instruments. The boab's hut was still there, but boarded up. The garden of red cannas had gone—or died from lack of water, and the once small palm trees had grown to the height of the building. Everything had changed so dramatically it felt as though I was looking through a window at my past life and not being able to take part. I felt a sense loss, exiled from what I had once thought an idyllic life.

Eighteen

Snippets

▲▲▲

Pyramid of Meidum

About three hours' drive south of Cairo between the west bank of the Nile and the Fayyoum, the imposing Pyramid of Meidum rises up from a mountain of collapsed casing stones and countless centuries of accumulated debris and sand. It is an ominous structure that dominates the landscape. Built by the third Dynasty Pharaoh, Huni, and completed by his son, Snefuru, first king of the fourth Dynasty, and father of Khufu—the builder of the great pyramid at Ghiza. Known as the false pyramid because it was built around a stone core, this once classic limestone structure has succumbed to 4,600 years of wind and deterioration; leaving a mountain of three uneven layers or mastabas, that rise to a height of over 300 feet.

Because of its remote location it is not often frequented by tourist. The area was empty on the day we visited in 1979—with the exception of one galabehya clad old man from the local village. He had a face like a walnut and offered to take us inside the pyramid for a small fee.

The Garden Ran Down to the Nile

The shimmering heat of mid-day danced across the desert as we silently made our way over the uneven terrain and up the incline of sand and rubble to the first mastaba; our feet sinking with every step. At the north face we ascended a rickety old ladder that was precariously angled to reach the entrance—a small opening bored into the smooth surface of the pyramid about fifty three feet above the level of sand. The guide lit his lantern, and leaving the sunlight behind, we ducked inside. As our eyes adjusted to the darkness, we made the 234-foot descent down a steep black void no more than five feet in height. The walls were cold, almost damp, and the silence broken only by our footfalls. After some time the gradient levelled off and I assumed we were then in the lowest region of the pyramid. The air was stale and the atmosphere permeated with the smell of bat dung and centuries resurrected. Traversing over a narrow gangplank the guide held the lantern over the black void, revealing below two small chambers into which litter had been thrown. We continued on another thirty feet where the tunnel abruptly stopped. The guide and light disappeared in an upward shaft with a narrow aperture decreasing in size until it reached the small empty burial chamber above. The celebrated Egyptologist Maspero believed that the tomb had been broken into in ancient times and the sarcophagus removed. The air was now so thin and oppressive that I could hardly breathe. The silence resounded in my ears and the dim and flickering glow of the lantern cast eerie shadows across the tomb walls. Some solitary encounters can be visionary, but my encounter with Huni's pyramid was claustrophobic and more than a little frightening, if only in my own imagination.

The Pyramid has changed little since the turn of the eighteenth century when Vivant Denon passed by. Unfortunately it was during the time of the inundation when the Bahr Yussef (Joseph's Canal), a tributary branch of the Nile linking the river to the Fayyoum, was swollen and prevented Denon from visiting. He had to make do with drawing the pyramid as seen through a telescope.

Harrania

Close to the Ghiza Pyramids off the Sakkarah road is the rural village of Harrania where the children of the village do improvisational high-warp weaving. The idea was conceived by the late Ramses Wissa Wassef, a Coptic Egyptian whose theory was that all children have an inborn creative talent and the ability to express themselves.

Wassef was disenchanted with the art education of the industrial age and felt that improvisation should come from the child's own imagination and inspiration. The children were encouraged to observe their own surroundings and the day-to-day occurrences of village life, animals and birds, the desert, and the farmland. They were given a unique opportunity to learn a trade within the village using free expression by means of a loom. Given simple instructions on operating the loom, the children created pictures from their own imaginations. Having no pre-conceived ideas about art, only their natural response to plants, animals, and village life, they quickly expressed themselves. Colourful birds, animals, and people were set against flowing backgrounds of trees, fields and villages.

Plants used for dying the wool are grown on the premises. The children come and go as they please and are paid whether their tapestries are sold or not. When the tapestries are sold, a portion goes to cover the costs of materials and the running of the school and the rest goes to the weaver. The children were very proud of their creations and seemed to enjoy having an audience. Batik and pottery were also taught. The school was run by Ramses Wissa Wassef's wife, Sophie.

Kirdassah

Baedeker in 1914 says little about Kirdassah except that it was a prettily situated village amidst palm groves and a 'sufficient attraction for an excursion, especially on Monday, which is the weekly market-day.' The modern Baedeker says less, only that 'woven carpets in native traditional patterns are made and offered for sale.' Kirdassah at the time I was there had not changed much since those descriptions. Once the old caravan route to Libya supplying goods to desert travellers, it was now a center for weaving textiles.

The small village of Kirdassah was reached by turning right off the Pyramids Road onto the Canal Road where you drove for several miles past mounds of dirt and wild foliage on the left, and the canal on the right, where bulrushes and papyrus thrived in the mud and evaporating water. It was easy to miss the dirt tract turn-off that ran through a small community for a half mile before you came to the main shop that specialized in galabehyas. The rooms were jammed full; every colour, size and manor of decoration from very cheap to relatively expensive, yet half the price of the bazaars in Cairo.

A handful of curio shops spilled out onto reed mats encroaching into the main dirt road—where a clandestine and somewhat illicit collection of stuffed crocodiles and various other animals were on sale. Every so often the village was visited by the Egyptian Environmental Affairs Agency in a bid to alleviate this kind of trade.

The famous rag rugs sold all over the country were also made here. You could wander through the workrooms and watch weavers on old wooden looms as they did in ancient times. My daughter liked to sit with one old man at the loom as he wove. He would let her slide the shuttle carrying the strands of weft through the strands of warp.

Now, you fly down a newly built ring-road to the widened paved Canal Road where dozens of glass fronted shops sell the same factory made galabehyas. The embroidery work is no longer done by hand, but machine stitched using newspaper as backing that you have to pick off before wearing, and few have the deep pockets that once were standard. The charm and authenticity of old Kirdassah has vanished.

Heading back down the Canal Road, towards Pyramids Road, was the famous and well-frequented Andrea Chicken House, an open-air restaurant. You could sit under an arbour of vine leaves and enjoy a spit-roasted chicken dinner with Egyptian salad, ballade bread and wine.

Dozens of chickens rotated on a spit barbeque in full view and there were donkey rides for the children while you ate your meal—

one of best in Cairo. The only drawback was the feral cats that roamed around the tables and walked overhead along the arbour, sometimes with disastrous consequences.

In 2007 I had lunch there. It was six times the size and shaded by mature trees. It was one of the places that had actually improved and still one of the best places to eat in Cairo, but in 2008, I went back to find the canal filled in and Andrea's closed. When enquiring I was told the Government was going to build another main road.

The Delta

If it were not for the inundation of the Nile, Egypt would be a barren country of sand and rock. The silt from the river makes the soil rich and the land alongside fertile. Trees are numerous and easily cultivated and few countries have such a large variety of fruit and vegetables. The wealth and prosperity of Egypt has always depended upon agriculture and since the irrigation works constructed during the reign of Ismail, and the building of the High Dam at Aswan, a considerable increase in the productivity of the country has taken place.

Cairo, Alexandria, and Port Said, sit on the outskirts of the region known as the Delta. From the air the lush and fertile farmland looks out of place next to the great stretches of ochre coloured emptiness. Looking at a map, the paint box green of the flora fans out like a lotus blossom, its canals and waterways searching for the Mediterranean, spilling onto the desert where it stops abruptly. You can actually stand with one foot on the green land and one foot in the desert. The Delta is undoubtedly the largest gift of the Nile and home to approximately 28 million people—primarily farmers.

Many wealthy Egyptians who worked and lived in Cairo had houses and working farms in the Delta where they took refuge from the city on weekends and holidays. Dr. Gouda was a retired gynaecologist, a jolly rotund man with a booming voice and a beaming smile. The little hair he had left was swept over a tonsure of shining head, which he mopped occasionally with a wilted handkerchief. Several of us were invited to his house one Saturday for lunch and an afternoon of tropical inertia beneath the date palms. The drive took two hours from Cairo along the main road that ran parallel to the railway and turned off across the Delta, where order emerged from chaos. Through Tanta towards Kafr el Zaiyat, the lush fertility of the flat landscape is crisscrossed with numerous canals and dotted with brown mud villages where great stretches of sugarcane and cornfields make you forget that 90 per cent of Egypt is desert.

Dr. Gouda's secluded property gave privacy a new dimension. His farm was surrounded by orange groves where an extended family of fellaheen lived and worked within the grounds. Smoke rose from cooking pots and women in black ma'alayahs sat on the ground cradling their children whose kohl-lined eyes blinked against the intrusion of unwavering flies. Chickens, goats, rabbits, ducks, and geese roamed freely and bees from a dozen beehives buzzed among the fruit trees. A little stream rushed gently through the farm where a small man-made pond served as home to minute green frogs that played on the lily pads and hid in the profusion of pink and white water lilies. Iridescent dragonflies and blue damsels hovered and darted over the surface of the water, and a large brown toad kept a watchful eye.

On the other side of the brook were two eagles and four scrawny monkeys that Dr. Gouda had rescued from somewhere and kept in large wire cages under a hypostyle of date palms. Numerous pathways meandered through a garden of roses, bougainvillea, prickly pear, and blood red hibiscus. Lofty banana trees soared upwards heavy with unripe fruit. Covered by a faded orange tarpaulin, couches strewn with throw cushions in bright colours became an enticement for a siesta in the heat of the afternoon.

A two-storey house, Mediterranean in style, stood in the center of the garden. You looked out from the flat terraced roof over a tranquil canal. An enormous weeping-willow trailed its leaves in the gently flowing water while bee-eaters swooped to pick off unsuspecting insects.

Lucie Duff Gordon had a sincere and passionate love of the country and the people. She wrote of the: "True poetical pastoral life of the Bible in the villages where the English have not been."

On another occasion in the Delta, we spent the day at the house of a prominent Egyptian businessman. His large farmhouse had a veranda shaped like the bow of a ship that overhung one of the many canals throughout the area.

At certain times of the year our host employed an entire village to work his orange groves. We visited the village and one of the mud-brick dwellings, and seeing us astride small donkeys our party must have looked strange to the villagers. One of the guests was a corpulent Scandinavian woman of about sixty. She wore men's trousers and smoked a nasty smelling pipe. She had lived in Egypt for over thirty-years and spoke fluent Arabic.

As we arrived on donkey back, the village children ran out to greet us. They stood smiling, their large unblinking eyes questioning. Everyone seemed eager to greet us. Like most villages in the country, mud brick takes the place of lath and plaster. Straw and mud are mixed together and shaped and poured into wood framed moulds and left to dry in the sun. When they're dried they're cemented together with animal dung and more mud. The roofs of the houses are formed with palm branches and millet. On the outer walls children had painted pictures in a blaze of colour depicting everyday life; a large round turkey, a mosque, and a helicopter—that was not so every day. The people were adaptable and ingenious having an uncanny ability at turning almost anything into a home. Within the house, I had expected to see only reed mats and a few crude pieces of roughly hewn furniture, but there was a full sized wooden bedstead complete with mattress and pillows. Pictures hung on the whitewashed walls and a threadbare oriental carpet covering most of the dirt flooring.

The Fayyoum

A day out with the British-Egyptian Society to the Fayyoum and Lake Qarun, the ancient Lake Moeris found me scaling the side of the Hawarah pyramid of Amenemhat III. Built from sun-dried bricks of Nile silt and straw, the pyramid of Amenemhat III is small in comparison to Menkura at Ghiza and the Tura limestone casing has collapsed into a large pile of rubble making the entrance inaccessible.

The site was one of Sir Flinders Petrie's major archaeological discoveries in 1887. Petrie's working conditions were less than comfortable, living bivouac in a small tent and storing important mummies under his bed, as he recalls: "Being limited to a space six and a half feet long, and about as wide as the length . . . Besides bed I have nine boxes in it, stores of all kinds, basin, cooking stove and crockery, tripod stand . . . and some antiques; and in this I have to live, to sleep, to wash, and to receive visitors."

When Petrie broke through the original entrance, all the passageways were clogged with mud and he had to strip off his clothes and slide nearly naked through the narrow passage—making measurements as he went. The burial chamber was reached forty-feet down and Petrie found himself waist deep in salt water amid rotting wood and skulls. It proved to be worth it because the magnificent sarcophagus of Amenemhet III was found.

Amenemhet III was a pharaoh who was very interested in developing the Fayyoum that now skirts the modern canal, Bahr Yussef—Joseph's Canal. Herodotus, according to Murray's Handbook, says that there were twelve courts within the labyrinth, 1500 chambers above ground and 1500 beneath. The underground chambers contained the sepulchres of the kings who built the labyrinth, and also those of sacred crocodiles.

Our assent of the pyramid was easy, taking about ten minutes to reach the summit that has over the years subsided, leaving a substantial plateau from which the view of the surrounding area is magnificent. Standing on the apex a warm breeze gave respite from the blazing sun. The view stretched far across the vast labyrinth complex in all directions. The remnants of the excavations appeared as heaps of anthills. Looking to the right, the canal snakes its way through the Fayyoum, reflecting the sun in silver ripples and blinding you with its brilliance. The lush green farmland defies the desert to come any closer reminding you that the Nile today is just as important to Egypt as it was in Pharaonic times.

Dakhla Oasis

The Dakhla Oasis tourist springs, is the largest oasis after the Fayyoum, and the most populous with over 20,000 inhabitants. We had coffee at a small rest house under the shady fronds of towering Dom palms and tasted the brackish water of one of the natural mineral springs from a community tap over a font in the side of a stonewall. There was a working mill where flour was ground for the making of baladi bread.

Dakhla is famous for its produce and driving through the village you are accosted by a kaleidoscope of colour from the market stalls along the roadside. Fruits of every sort are piled high in brilliant pyramids. The vermillion of apricots, tangerines and oranges, the gold of lemons, grapefruits, bananas, and prickly pear, the green of limes, mangoes, and melons, and the deep burnished brown of dates and olives. The fruit is larger than average and there is sweetness in the juice that comes from the richness of the soil baked under an eternal sun.

Madinat

The village of Madinat lies in the heart of the Fayyoum, once the ancient town of Crocodilopolis it is the commercial and economic center and capital of the Fayyoum. Rustic hand-made baskets of every size were woven by the locals and sold on the streets. A café sat over a canal where three huge waterwheels reclaimed from the countryside creaked and groaned as they turned, spraying the air with a fine mist. The groaning—or singing, comes from the creaking of the wood as the wheels turn. The waterwheels are for the tourists now, but several of these giants are still irrigating the land throughout the countryside.

In 1815 Giovanni Battista Belzoni, a hydraulic engineer as well as an archaeologist, had been engaged by Mohammed Ali to replace the traditional waterwheels with a hydraulic machine to lift the water, but the design failed and the waterwheels, fortunately for us, remained.

Beni Suef

Seventy-three miles south of Cairo lays Beni Suef, the capital of a province that once contained one hundred seventy one villages and 372,412 inhabitants. In the Middle Ages, Beni Suef was famous for its manufacture of flax, which was exported to Tunisia, Morocco and the rest of the Barbary. Around 1843 when John Gadsby wended his way up the Nile, he perceived that cotton, sugar cane, indigo, palm trees, and flax, grew wherever there was irrigation: "In no country in the world is Abundance secured with less labor. The country at present produces sufficient food for 4,000,000 people. The cotton crop is worth nearly £1,000,000 sterling per year."

Amelia B. Edwards found the approach to Beni Suef rather pretty: "The khedive has an Italian-looking villa here, which peeps up white and dazzling from the midst of a thickly wooded park. The town lays a little back from the river. A few coffee-houses and a kind of promenade face the landing-place; and a mosque built to the verge of the bank stands out picturesquely against the bend of the river."

Amelia was moored at Beni Suef for four days when the wind and river was against them. In 1873 the town did not have a first-rate reputation and Amelia and her party experienced a night of adventure when all the guards on board fell fast asleep and Amelia heard a man swimming softly around their boat: "To strike a light and frighten everybody into sudden activity is the work of a moment. The whole boat is instantly in an uproar. Lanterns are lighted on deck; a patrol of sailors is set; Talhamy loads his gun; and the thief slips away in the dark like a fish.

"The guards, of course, slept sweetly through it all. Honest fellows! They were paid a shilling a night to do it and they had nothing on their minds.

"Having lodged a formal complaint next morning against the inhabitants of the town, we received a visit from a sallow personage clad in a long black robe and a voluminous white turban. This was the chief of the guards. He smoked a great many pipes; drank numerous cups of coffee; listened to all we had to say; looked wise; and finally suggested that the number of our guards should be doubled.

"I ventured to object that if they slept unanimously forty would not be of much more use than four. Whereupon he rose, drew himself to his full height, touched his beard and said with a magnificent melodramatic air: 'if they sleep they shall be bastinadoed till they die!'"

Florence Nightingale's boat was moored at Beni Suef for three days due to lack of wind. The party went ashore to buy pots and pans, but she was never allowed to go ashore without her guide, whom she referred to as her Efreet.

In 1826 a certain Mr. Peel established the cotton industry of Egypt, in a factory built by Mohammed Ali, which stood alongside numerous sugar plantations and groves of date palms. By 1903 the cotton boom had brought enormous wealth to the landowners. The Khedive had a villa in the midst of a thickly wooded area, there was a good main road from Beni Suef to the Fayyoum, and Beni Suef itself was a pleasant village that contained a telegraph, a post office, a small bazaar, a steamboat stop, a railway station, and a weekly market.

Peel's great, great granddaughter, Joan Tracey, had been born in Alexandria and lived at the Villa Fashada in Ramleh. Joan's great-grandfather, grandfather, and grandmother; neé Bramell, had also worked at Peel's Cotton Factory. Both sides of Joan's British family can be traced back to Egypt during the early 1800s. Her great, grand aunt, Julia Saunders, had been present when the Suez Canal was opened by the Empress Eugéne of France in 1869. Julia also attended the famous performance of Aida at the Cairo Opera House on the same night as the Empress. Joan's father was a Government

Official in the Irrigation Department in 1908. He was responsible for raising the High Dam, and the construction of the railway between Alexandria and Cairo.

When Joan was eighteen, she came to live with her Grandmother, Constance Bramell in Beni Suef and remembers the house they lived in with its enormous garden of fruit trees; "There were grapefruits, oranges, bananas, mangoes, figs, dates, and grapevines. We had turkeys, chickens, and a dairy cow." She played croquet on the lawn and went to dances at Shepheard's Hotel when the 'Shepheard's Brigade' (so called by the military) was in residence: "On New Year's Eve 1935, my Grandmother and I took the Cairo Express train to Cairo and stayed at Shepheard's Hotel. We attended a ball and later slept in huge Victorian brass beds under fly netting."

Beni Suef is still the provincial capital and a large farming community, but there are more donkey carts than cars and nothing of any particular interest to see. Today it is a ramshackle stopping point for transport to the Red Sea and rarely gets mentioned in the guidebooks.

El Alamein

A long stretch of baking highway winds through sixty-five miles of seemingly unending scrub covered desert dotted with fig groves wilting under the sun-drenched sky. To the north, salt forms a light powdery film across the sand dunes that rise and fall like waves revealing the Mediterranean in iridescent shades of sapphire and aquamarine. Heat radiates off the tarmacadam highway as mile after mile of monotonous landscape races by. Finally in the middle of nowhere the site of one of the bloodiest battles of World War II emerges—El Alamein, where the British Eighth Army, under the command of Field Marshall Montgomery, fought against Rommel's Afrika Corps. It was the turning point of the North African campaign.

In Arabic the name El Alamein means two flags. In the British Military cemetery there are more than 7000 simple white gravestones with the badge of the regiment etched above the names of the young men of the British Empire and Commonwealth who gave their lives at that historic battle. Wild flowers grow between the plots in the immaculately kept cemetery, which is maintained by the War Graves Commission. It creates a picture so serene that it did not seem strange to hear birds singing in the Libyan Desert. A rose garden surrounds the arched entryway where a plaque reads: '1939 – 1945 The land on which this cemetery stands is the gift of the Egyptian people for the perpetual resting place of the sailors, soldiers, and airmen who are honoured here'

An Italian memorial stands west of Alamein and a German memorial on a hill overlooking the Mediterranean. There was a small military museum a few miles up the highway that housed tanks and artillery, profiles of Montgomery and Rommel, and numerous artefacts and dusty photographs of the famous battle. Commemorative services were held at El Alamein each October.

Mahalla el-Koubra

Egypt has always been famous for its cotton industry and the quality of the textiles and towels is world renown. The district of Mahalla el-Koubra lies north of Cairo in the city of Gharbiya. It's a large industrial and agricultural city and in 1979 had 408,000 inhabitants.

The district even had fast-food restaurants; a Pizza Hut and a Kentucky Fried Chicken. Some of the numerous factories and textile mills were open to guided tours. You could see raw cotton being processed through cleaning, spinning, weaving, and printing. There was a gift shop and the famous el Koubra carpet factory where carpets were hand-woven and could be purchased at discounted prices.

Lake Qarun

Lake Qarun is fed from the Nile by way of Joseph's Canal, and teems with fish and wildlife. We ate black coloured bottom fish caught the same day from the lake. It was not gutted before it was cooked so the eating was done with care. A wonderful place for bird watchers, in the shallows, heron, crane and spoonbill seem to walk on water, and ducks, wild geese, and coots drift on the glass-like surface that reflects the clouds in a cerulean sky. Fishermen in small boats cast their nets in the same way as their Pharaonic ancestors, and sitting on the bank looking out across this man-made lake you forget the dirt, the noise and the impatience of the city.

The Petrified Forest

The stretch of desert known as the Petrified Forest at Wadi Digla, offers complete respite and almost deafening silence. It lies behind the Mokattam Hills off the narrow grey line of tarmacadam road that stretches through miles of Libyan Desert.

The terrain gently rises and falls in small hills and valleys where you can still find pieces of petrified tree trunk. Thousands of seashells lay scattered across the landscape and strange rock formations emerged from the desert floor. On close inspection embedded fossils were abundant. It's debatable whether the trees were indigenous or floated in by the water that once covered the area many thousands of years ago. I like to think of a forest standing in the middle of the desert like some vast prodigious oasis.

Khamseen

I awoke with a choking feeling one morning to a dark and oppressive atmosphere that seemed to hang in the room. Opening the shutters I found Mohandessin disappearing in a rolling cloud of sand and dust—announcing that the Khamseen had arrived. The sky was burnished orange and the air un-breathable. Paper and rubbish took flight in whirlwinds of hot, gusty air to gather in some other part of the city. Khamseen means fifty in Arabic, the fifty days of hot winds that blow in from the desert covering everything with a fine powdery layer of sand and dust. During these fifty days the wind blows, not continuously, but intermittently. It sweeps relentlessly across the desert descending on the city without mercy.

My first experience with the Khamseen was two years earlier while travelling across the desert returning to Cairo from Ismailia. The driver was from the Embassy and as we sped through the shimmering heat, we noticed a wall of sand in the distance, blocking out the sun and hurtling towards us with such velocity that it was upon us before we had time to realize what had happened. The whirlwind engulfed the car completely sending us in a frenzy of coughing and panic. We had to stop, as it was impossible to continue through the swirling maelstrom of blinding grit. There was nowhere to turn for respite, nowhere to shelter from the slapping, stinging sand that penetrated cracks and crevasses, blinding eyes, and clogging nostrils. I tied a scarf around my nose and mouth enabling me to breath and sent a silent prayer to Allah. Minutes later the storm had vanished leaving us with grit in our mouths, red-ringed eyes, and sand in every extremity.

Dancing Horses

The desert is unpredictable and volatile. It changes shape and colour with every hour of the day. The surface undulates with little mounds and wadis, and nothing grows except patches of scrub around which the glitter of mica sparkles in the sunlight. The surface of the sand can be hard as rock, or soft as sugar, but always capricious. And so it was on the evening we attended an Egyptian tent party held on the edge of the desert.

The sun was setting behind the pyramids of Ghiza in a golden penumbra when we entered the large Bedouin tent on the outskirts of Cairo. Inside, the tent was hung with colourful appliqué tapestries and bright fairy lights that criss-crossed overhead, illuminating the interior. At one end of the tent was a table laden with traditional food behind which waiters in white and gold galabehyas stood in attendance. We sat on poufs and leather ottomans placed on the ground around long tables and watched the entertainment. A group of musicians, a magician who conjured doves from a silver box, a provocative belly dancer whose cantilevered bosoms spilled over her green-fringed costume, a Nubian folklore troupe who performed the traditional raqs al-assaya (combat stick dance) and six graceful girls in purple harem pants that danced a faultless ballet under flaming shamadans (candelabras) balanced nimbly on their heads.

Illuminated by blazing torchlight, the finale was held in the open air under the shadow of the Pyramids and a canopy of stars that seemed to touch the horizon. Three Arabian stallions were ridden into the improvised arena to the sound of drums and musical instruments. The saddles and bridles were adorned with colourful tassels, their thick manes and tails brushed to a high sheen, their black bodies glistening. The Bedouin riders looked as though they had ridden straight out of the Arabian Nights, handsome and dignified in their ceremonial dress. The horses tossed their heads, flicked their tails, and with dancing hooves, struck the sand to the rhythm of the drums. Hot air from their flared nostrils vaporized into puffs of steam as it hit the cool night air.

Epilogue

▲ ▲ ▲

*'One wonders that people come back from Egypt and
live lives as they did before'*
                    Florence Nightingale

A warm breeze blew around my face as I stepped from the house. The sun spilled its golden light onto the pavement through which a network of cracks had worked. It was mid-morning on a warm September day and I was leaving Egypt. Mohammed had carried the luggage to the car and now he stood looking at me, his face lost in shadow. I shook his gaunt hand. His valedictions were in Arabic. As we drove away I watched him standing straight and silent in the middle of the road, his long bony fingers together as if in prayer and then raising his hands above his head, in the wavering heat, disappeared in a swirling cloud of ochre coloured dust and like a vanishing jinni he was gone.

As we drove to the airport I tried to take in everything around the city, to remember the past four years and tuck every experience neatly away. I thought of the desert with its undulating shifting sands and its windswept dunes. I envisaged the brown and weathered faces of the old men in the fields and the scent of jasmine and honeysuckle in the warmth of the evening, the palm trees bent heavy with dates, the crimson red flame trees, the delicate blue jacaranda and the blanket of stars that covered the pyramids at night twinkling like sequins upon a velvet background.

I was acutely aware of everything around me, every variation of colour. The black outlines of the rooftops, the shouts of the people, the noise and the fumes of the traffic. Everyone had smiled and said how lucky I was to be going home. They didn't realize that this was my home, that I was rooted too deeply in this antique land, that Egypt had crept into my heart and it had made its home there.

It was not with gladness that I boarded the plane but with an ardent sadness as I looked down over the land, already longing for a country that I had not yet had time to lament. Egypt was the only place I had felt totally content. Could I ever be completely happy anywhere else?

The plane flew out over the vast expanse of desert that had known centuries of Pharaohs, then doubled back over the landscape so familiar to me. The sun was radiating off the desert and the ascending air currents carried small particles of dust and sand up into the atmosphere turning the sky to warm topaz. The plane banked over the desert revealing the golden complex of Sakkarah scarred with decades of excavation. Beyond was the Ghiza plateau with its monumental pyramids sharply defined in violet shadow. The ubiquitous sphinx still guarding its domain was just distinguishable.

What can one say about a country whose roots are steeped so deeply in history, a civilization built by poets and scholars, by kings and conquerors, the origin of great religions? And what had Egypt taught me? Patience, compromise, independence, humility?

As the plane climbed over the city the sunlight glistened off the domes of the mosques. The minarets look like knitting needles and the dense sprawl of grey flat-roofed buildings contrasted the brilliant emerald gardens of palatial residences. As my attention turned to the Islands of Rhoda and Gezira surrounded by the river, I remembered the proverb that 'who-so-ever will taste the waters of the Nile will one day return'. I tried to distinguish my flat or even Mohandessin, but the landscape was becoming smaller and then Egypt was gone, dispelled under a blanket of cloud and distance, yet Egypt's spell would be everlasting.

Glossary

Al-Haj	pilgrimage
Arabesque	meshrabeya design
Archimedean screw	ancient device for lifting water
Bab	gate/door in the city walls
Bairam	feast following Ramadan
Baklava	sticky desert
Baksheesh	share the wealth
Baladi	country
Bedouin	Nomadic desert people
Berseem	Egyptian clover
Bey	Lord: Ottoman title
Boukra	tomorrow
Bowab	caretaker
Calèche	horse drawn carriage
Canoptic jar	containers for viscera
Chibouque	water pipe
Cigats	finger cymbals
Copt	Egyptian Christian
Corniche	Seafront road
Dahabeyah	house boat
Daraboka	drum
Dragoman	guide & translator
Effendi	Turkish title of respect
Fellaheen	Egyptian farmers
Felucca	Egyptian sailboat
Ful	red beans
Galabehya	traditional long kaftan

The Garden Ran Down to the Nile

Gamoosa	water buffalo
Gezira	Island
Gomeyah	government grocery store
Hadj	pilgrimage to Mecca
Howajji	Christian
Id al-fitr	breaking the fast
Inshallah	God willing
Kasr	castle
Khamseen	literally fifty (fifty days of wind)
Khashaf	seller of grenadine & rosewater
Khedive	Viceroy of Egypt
Kiosk	small moveable shop
Kirbeh	brass or earthenware vessel
Kom	mound of earth covering ancient site
Lemoon	lemonade
Ma'alesh	never mind
Madrassa	school
Makwagi	man who irons
Ma'alayah	black shawl worn by women
Mastaba	bench
Meshrabeya	lattice-work screening
Midan	open space or square
Mihrat	wooden plough
Minaret	tower where call to prayer is made
Mish-mish	apricots
Mit	village
Mosque	place of prayer facing Mecca
Moulid	festival or birthday celebration of a Saint
Mousky	bazaar
Muezzin	official in a mosque
Pasha	Turkish title

The Garden Ran Down to the Nile

Qasr	palace or mansion
Rababa	a two stringed musical instrument
Ramadam	Moslem holy month
Raqs Assaya	combat stick dance
Raqs Sharki	dance of the East
Reis	captain
Sakieh	water lifting device turned by an animal
Shadoof	ancient water lifting device
Shamadan	chandelier worn on head by dancers
Sharia	street
Shisha	water pipe
Sherbuli	seller of lemonade or pomegranate juice
Suffragi	waiter
Sultan	title ruler or king
Suraya	palace
Sussi wallah	liquorice drink seller
Tabla	Egyptian drum
Tarboosh	fez
Tel	land or ancient site
Ushebti	small Egyptian deity
Viscera	lungs, liver, stomach and intestines
Wadi	dried up watercourse
Yashmak	face veil worn by women
Zabayeen	Coptic tribe
Zabib	dark spot on forehead from prayer
Zagharit	cry of joy
Zeer	earthenware jar

Bibliography & Sources

Adams, William Henry Davenport: *The Land of the Nile* (London, T. Nelson & Sons, 1871).
Aldridge, James, *Cairo: Biography of a City* (London, Macmillan, 1969).
Allen, Charles: *A Glimpse of the Burning Plain* (London, Michael Joseph, 1986).
Allin, Michael: *Zarafa* (London, Headline Book Publishing, 1998).
Bacon, Lee: *Our Houseboat on the Nile* (Boston & New York, Houghton, Mifflin & Co., 1902).
Baedeker, Karl: *Egypt & the Sudan; seventh edition* (Leipzig, K.B. Publishing, 1914).
Baedeker, Karl: *Lower Egypt; second edition* (Leipzig, K.B. Publishing, 1885).
Bevan, Samuel: *Sand and Canvas* (London, Richard Barrett, 1849).
Bird, Michael: *Samuel Shepheard of Cairo* (London, Michael Joseph, 1957).
Blanch, Lesley: *The Wilder Shores of Love* (London, John Murray, 1954).
Blottière, Alain: *Vintage Egypt* (France, Flammarion, 2003).
Boyle, Clara: *Boyle of Cairo* (Kendal, Titus Wilson & Son Ltd., 1965).
Brendon, Piers: *Thomas Cook: 150 Years of Popular Tourism* (London, Secker & Warburg, 1991).
Burton, Sir Richard F.: *Pilgrimage to Al Madinah & Mecca* (London, G. Bell & Sons, Ltd., 1913).

Butler, Edith Louisa: *Things Seen in Egypt* (London, Seeley, Service & Co., 1912).

Butler, Elizabeth Southerden: *From Sketchbook and Diary* (London, Burns & Oats, 1909).

Caillard, Mable: *A Lifetime in Egypt: 1876-1935* (London, Grant Richards, 1935).

Carman, B. & J. McPherson: *Bimbashi McPherson: A Life in Egypt* (London, Barry Carman & John McPherson, 1983).

Cecil, Lord Edward: *The Leisure of an Egyptian Official* (London, Hodder & Stoughton, 1921).

Cooper, Artemis: *Cairo: In the War 1939-1945* (London, Hamish Hamilton. 1989).

Cromer, Evelyn Baring, The Earl of: *Modern Egypt* (London, Macmillan, 1908).

Din, Mursi Saad el & Cromer, John: *Under Egypt's Spell* (London, Bellew Publishing, 1991).

Edwards, Amelia Blandford: *A Thousand Miles up the Nile* (American Publishers Corp., 1888).

Egyptian State Railways, Written under the supervision: *Egypt and How To See It; 1910 - 1911* (Cairo, Ballantyne & Co. Ltd., 1910).

Fagan, Brian M.: *The Rape of the Nile* (London, MacDonald & Jane's, 1977).

Flaubert, Gustave: *Flaubert in Egypt: A Sensibility on Tour* (New York, Penguin, 1972).

Frank, Katherine: *Lucie Duff-Gordon: A Passage to Egypt* (London, Hamish Hamilton, 1994).

Gadsby, John: *My Wanderings: being travels in the East in 1846-47, 1850-51, 1852-53* (London, Gadsby, 1860).

Guerville, Amédée Baillot de: *New Egypt* (London, William Heinermann, 1906).
Hale, Rev. E.E. & Susan: *A Family Flight Over Egypt* (Boston, D. Lothrop & Co., 1812).
Howarth, Davie & Stephen: *The Story of P&O: the Peninsular & Oriental Steam Navigation Company* (London, Weidenfield & Nicolson, 1986).
Iden, Rev. Thomas Medary: *Upper Room Letters from Many Lands* (Michigan, George Wahr Publishing, 1925).
Irby, James & Charles Leonard Mangles: *Travels in Egypt and Nubia, Syria & Asia Minor:* (Reprinted London, Darf Publishers Ltd., 1985).
Jesson, B.M.W.: *The Glamour of Egypt* (London, Heath Cranton Ltd., 1904).
Johnson, Shirley: *Egyptian Palaces* (American University in Cairo Press, 2006).
Kelly, Robert Talbot: *Egypt Painted & Described* (London, Adam & Charles Black, 1904).
Kinglake, Alexander William: *Eothen* (London, J.M. Dent & Sons Ltd., 1908).
Lane, Edward William: *Manners & Customs of the Modern Egyptians* (London & N.Y. & Melbourne, Ward, Lock & Co., 1890).
Lauer, John Philippe: *Saqqara: Royal Cemetery of Memphis* (London, Thanes & Hudson, 1976).
MacMillan: *Women of the Raj* (New York, Thames & Hudson, 1988).
Manning, Rev. Samuel: *Land of the Pharaohs: Egypt & Sinai* (Manchester, The Religious Tract Society, 1891).
Mayes, Stanley: *The Great Belzoni* (New York, Walker & Company, 1961).
Marlowe, John: *Spoiling the Egyptians* (Kent, André Deutsch, 1974).

Murray, John: *Murray's Handbook for Egypt* (London, John Murray, 7th edition, 1888).

Myntti, Cynthia: *Paris Along the Nile* (Egypt, The American University Press, 2000).

Nelson, Nina: *Shepheard's Hotel* (London, Barrie & Radcliff, 1960).

Nelson, Nina: *The Mena House Oberoi* (Cairo, The Palm Press, 1997).

Nightingale, Florence: *Letters from Egypt: A Journey on the Nile 1849-1850* (London, Barrie & Jenkins, 1987).

Oliver, Mildred Alice: *Letters from Egypt* (Printed for private circulation at the Euston Press, 1933).

Poole, Sophia Lane: *The Englishwoman in Egypt: Letters from Cairo* (London, Charles Knight & Co., 1844).

Prime, William Cowper: *Boat Life in Egypt & Nubia* (New York, Harper & Bros., 1865).

Quibell, Annie Abernethe: *A Wayfarer in Egypt* (London, Methuen & Co. Ltd., 1925).

Quibell, Mrs Annie: *Tombs of Sakkarra* (Cairo, Church Missionary Society, 1925).

Rafaat, Samir W.: *Cairo, the Glory Years* (Harpocrates Publishing, 2003).

Rameses (Major C.S. Jarvis): *Oriental Spotlight* (London, John Murray, 1937).

Reynolds-Ball, Eustace: *Cairo of Today* (London, Adam & Charles Black, 4th edition, 1905).

Reynolds-Ball, Eustace: *The City of the Caliphs* (London, T. Fisher Unwin, 1898).

Ritchie, J. Ewing: *The Cities of the Dawn* (New York, T. Fisher Unwin, 1897).

Rowlett, Mary: *A Family in Egypt* (London, Robert Hale Ltd., 1956).

Sabini, John: *Armies in the Sand: the Struggle for Mecca & Medina* (London, Thames & Hudson, 1921).

Sladen, Douglas: *Egypt and the English* (London, Hurst & Blackett Ltd., 1908).

Sladen, Douglas: *Oriental Cairo: The City of the "Arabian Nights"* (London, Hurst & Blackett Ltd.).

Steevens, George Warrington: *Egypt in 1898* (Edinburgh & London, Wm. Blackwood & Sons, 1898).

Thackeray, William Makepeace: *Cornhill to Grand Cairo* (Heathfield, Cockburn Press Ltd., 1991).

Twain, Mark: *The Innocents Abroad* (London, Chatto & Windus, 1894).

Van Dyke, John C.: *In Egypt: Studies & Sketches Along the Nile* (London, Charles Scribner's Sons, 1931).

Warner, Charles Dudley: *My Winter on the Nile* (Connecticut, American Publishing Co., 1876).

Whately, Mary Louise: *Letters from Egypt: To Plain Folks at Home* (London, Seeley, Jackson & Halliday, 1879).

Wilkinson, Sir John Gardner: *Handbook for Travellers in Egypt* (London, John Murray, 1847).

Winstone, H.V.F.: *Howard Carter* (London, Constable & Co. Ltd., 1991).

Other Sources:
The Illustrated London News (19th Century)
The Graphic (19th Century).

Note: All spellings and punctuation in the anthology part of the book is as it stands.

Acknowledgments

I would like to thank Sir Derek Plumbley who took time out of his busy schedule as British Ambassador to answer my many questions and give me a reminiscent tour around the Residence. Michael and Levinia Davenport, who at the time were living at 20 Zanki Street and also allowed me to reminisce throughout the house and gardens. To Wafik and William Doss of the Windsor Hotel for their hospitality, and to Joan Tracey who shared her impressionable childhood memories and her family's history of the cotton industry in Egypt.

I cannot leave out the seemingly inexhaustible stream of 19th and 20th century authors, artists, scholars, hoteliers, and architects who have inspired generations through their paintings, grand hotels, and the literary accounts they felt compelled to leave behind.

Most of all to the Egyptian people themselves whose warmth and friendliness has made this book possible.

www.ingramcontent.com/pod-product-compliance
Lightning Source LLC
Chambersburg PA
CBHW060148050426
42446CB00013B/2727